BLOOD

AT THE

ROOT

BLOOD
AT THE
ROOT

A RACIAL CLEANSING
IN AMERICA

PATRICK PHILLIPS

W. W. NORTON & COMPANY

Independent Publishers Since 1923

New York • London

For information about permission to reproduce selections from this book,
write to Permissions, W. W. Norton & Company, Inc.,
500 Fifth Avenue, New York, NY 10110

For information about special discounts for bulk purchases, please contact
W. W. Norton Special Sales at specialsales@wwnorton.com or 800-233-4830

Manufacturing by Quad Graphics, Fairfield
Book design by Chris Welch
Production manager: Louise Mattarelliano

Library of Congress Cataloging-in-Publication Data

Names: Phillips, Patrick, 1970– author.
Title: Blood at the root : a racial cleansing in America / Patrick Phillips.
Description: First edition. | New York ; London : W.W. Norton & Company,
[2016] | Includes bibliographical references and index.
Identifiers: LCCN 2016018237 | ISBN 9780393293012 (hardcover)
Subjects: LCSH: Forsyth County (Ga.)—Race relations—History.
Classification: LCC F292.F67 P47 2016 | DDC 305.8009758/265—dc23 LC
record available at https://lccn.loc.gov/2016018237

W. W. Norton & Company, Inc.
500 Fifth Avenue, New York, N.Y. 10110
www.wwnorton.com

W. W. Norton & Company Ltd.
15 Carlisle Street, London W1D 3BS

1 2 3 4 5 6 7 8 9 0

Southern trees bear strange fruit,

Blood on the leaves and blood at the root.

—*Lewis Allan, 1937*

CONTENTS

LAW OF THE LAND

All night, as Mae Crow drifted in and out of consciousness, searchers called through the pines, the sound of her name rising and fading into the drone of the tree frogs. There, in the woods along the Chattahoochee River, in the Appalachian foothills north of Atlanta, she'd been beaten and left to die, and now lay too bloodied and breathless to answer. Near dawn, as the first rays of sunlight dappled the gulley, a farmer who'd known Mae all her life came stamping down a narrow footpath. He stopped in his tracks, turned, and hollered for the others to come.

By the next day—September 10th, 1912—the Forsyth County sheriff had arrested three young black suspects. And while it would take two months and three separate deployments of the Georgia National Guard before Ernest Knox, sixteen, and Oscar Daniel, eighteen, were formally tried, convicted, and sentenced to hang, for the third prisoner, a 24-year-old man named Rob Edwards, death came quickly. When a rumor spread that "Big Rob" had confessed to the crime, a group of white farmers stormed the county jail and, according to one witness, shot Edwards as he cowered in his cell, then bashed in his skull with crowbars. Others say Edwards emerged alive, pleading for mercy, and died while being dragged from the back of a wagon, a noose cinched tight around his neck. As spectators streamed toward the town square, someone lobbed a rope over the yardarm of a telephone pole and hoisted Edwards's limp body skyward. People took turns with pistols and shotguns, and each time a load of buckshot spun the mutilated corpse, the crowd of hundreds roared.

There was nothing unusual about the lynching of a black man in Georgia in 1912, and the next morning the sight of Edwards's body, laid out on the courthouse lawn, seemed to satisfy those most hungry for vengeance. But a few weeks later, newspapers reported that Mae Crow, known as one of the most beautiful girls in all of Forsyth, had weakened and died from her injuries at the age of eighteen. On the day of her funeral, groups of white men gathered at crossroads all over the county. They talked quietly on the porches of country stores and huddled in the dusty thresholds of barns. At the graveside they held their hats over their hearts, eyes blazing as they watched Mae's mother, Azzie, weep over the casket. They were quiet and respectful all afternoon, according to one schoolmate of Mae's. But when darkness fell, she said, "all hell broke loose" in Forsyth County.

That was the night bands of white men set out on horseback, riding toward the little clusters of cabins that dotted the woodlands and pastures along the river. Using posted notices, scrawled letters, rifles, torches, and sticks of dynamite, they delivered a message to their black neighbors—including many they had known and worked with all their lives. The black people of Forsyth could either load up and get across the county line before the next sundown, or stay and die like Rob Edwards.

By the end of October, the night riders had forced out all but a handful of the 1,098 members of the African American community—who left in their wake abandoned homes and schools, stores and livestock, and harvest-ready crops standing in the fields. Overnight, their churches stood empty, the rooms where they used to sing "River of Jordan" and "Go Down Moses" now suddenly, eerily quiet.

The purge was so successful that within weeks there was no one left for the mobs to terrorize, and whites who had either taken part in the raids or simply stood aside as they passed now settled back into the rhythms of farm life. They shooed stray livestock into their own pens, milked their neighbors' lowing cows and slopped their starving hogs, and at family tables they bowed their heads and said grace over the last of the meat raised by black hands. Eventually they picked the leaning corn rather than watch it all go to waste. And when, years later, the last remaining "Negro cabins" collapsed, they salvaged the boards and tore down the rotten fence posts that had once marked a border between black and white land.

Generation after generation, Forsyth County remained "all white," even as the Great War, the Spanish influenza, World War II, and the civil rights movement came and went, and as kudzu crept over the remnants of black Forsyth. The people of the county, many descended from the lynchers and night riders, shook their heads as the South changed around them. They read about the clashes in Montgomery, and Savannah, and Selma, and felt proud of their county's old-fashioned ways, its unspoiled beauty, and a peacefulness that they saw as a direct result of having "run the niggers out." But now and again throughout the century, whenever someone intentionally or unwittingly violated the racial ban, white men could be counted on to rise up like they always had and drive the intruders away. Years might pass between such episodes, but each time it happened, Georgians were reminded that while the racial cleansing of 1912 seemed like ancient history, in truth, it had never really ended. In truth, many in Forsyth believed that "racial purity" was their inheritance and birthright. And like their fathers' fathers' fathers, they saw even a single black face as a threat to their entire way of life.

———

I KNOW BECAUSE I was raised in Forsyth, just a few miles from Pleasant Grove Church, where Mae Crow's casket was lowered into the ground. My family moved there in 1977, when I was in the second grade, and I spent my boyhood and teenage years living inside the bubble of Georgia's notorious "white county." At first, I was too young to understand that Forsyth was different from the rest of America. But as I grew older, I realized that many people there lived as if much of the twentieth century never happened—as if there had been no Montgomery Bus Boycott, no *Brown v. Board of Education*, no Civil Rights Act of 1964. Instead, whites in Forsyth carried on as if the racial integration of the South somehow did not apply to them. Nearly everyone I knew, adults and children, referred to black people as "niggers," and for the entire time I lived there in the 1970s and '80s, "whites only" was still the law of the land. Only in hindsight, and from a great distance, did I come to see that I'd grown up not in the America most white people imagine, but something closer to the fearful, isolated world of apartheid South Africa.

In 1987, to mark the seventy-fifth anniversary of the expulsions, a group of activists organized a peace march to protest the ongoing segregation of the county. The Brotherhood Marchers, as they were called, boarded a chartered bus at the King Center for Nonviolent Social Change, in Atlanta, then drove up Highway 400 toward Forsyth. When they reached the outskirts of Cumming, the county seat, blacks and whites climbed down off the bus, lined up on a two-lane country road, and began the first civil rights demonstration anyone in Forsyth County had ever seen. Almost immediately they were attacked by hundreds of locals who had gathered in a nearby pasture, then flooded toward the road, waving Confederate flags and carrying signs that said, "FORSYTH STAYS WHITE!" Men, women, and children joined in a chant of "Go home, niggers! Go home, niggers!" and pelted the peace marchers with rocks, bottles, bricks, and whatever else they could find in the weeds beside the road.

When he discovered that many of the "counterprotesters" had come heavily armed, county sheriff Wesley Walraven warned the Brotherhood Marchers that he could no longer guarantee anyone's safety and urged them to abandon the demonstration. The main group of activists reluctantly climbed back onto the bus, and as they rolled down the on-ramp and headed back to Atlanta, local whites cheered in triumph. Even march organizers like Hosea Williams, among the most hardened veterans of the civil rights movement, were shocked by the scene. Williams had led the first Selma march in 1965, and had survived the attacks of billy-club-wielding Alabama state troopers. Yet there he was, decades later, facing another mob of violent white supremacists. Twenty-seven years had passed since "Bloody Sunday" on the Edmund Pettus Bridge, but Williams knew what he was looking at in 1987: segregation was alive and well in Forsyth County, Georgia.

My mother, father, and sister were among a handful of Forsyth residents who'd marched in solidarity with the protesters that day, and when the buses left, they found themselves face-to-face with hundreds of men who, in the blink of an eye, had turned from a crowd of good ol' boys and rednecks into a violent mob. Unlike nearly everyone else on the march, my family lived in Forsyth, and when Sheriff Walraven recognized their situation, he hurried my parents and my sister into the back of a police cruiser, where they hunkered down below the windows as men swarmed around the car, screaming, "White niggers!"

I was sixteen that year and had arrived late to meet my parents for the march. When I finally got to the Cumming square and began searching for them, I found myself shoulder to shoulder with hundreds of other young men walking toward the county courthouse. Only when one of them held up a piece of rope tied into a thick noose did I realize that I was not at a peace rally but had somehow stumbled into the heart of the Ku Klux Klan's victory celebration. As I ducked my head and struggled to make my way out of the crowd, I heard the buzz of a microphone switching on. "Raise your hands if you love White Power!" a shrill voice screamed into the P.A., as the people of my hometown surged all around me and howled in unison: "White Power!"

That night, news stations all over the country showed footage of hoarse-throated men yelling, "Go home, niggers!"—followed by shots of Jesse Jackson, Gary Hart, and Coretta Scott King standing at podiums, condemning the violence and bigotry. How, they asked, nearly two decades after the assassination of Martin Luther King Jr. and only forty miles from his birthplace, could the fires of racial hatred still be burning so fiercely in the north Georgia mountains? The next day's *New York Times* featured the story on page 1, with a quote from Frank Shirley—head of the Forsyth County Defense League—that made it sound as if, in Forsyth County, Georgia, no time had passed at all since 1912. "We white people won," he told reporters, "and the niggers are on the run."

Blood at the Root is an attempt to understand how the people of my home place arrived at that moment, and to trace the origins of the "whites only" world they fought so desperately to preserve. To do that, we will need to go all the way back to the beginning of the racial cleansing, in the violent months of September and October 1912. That was the autumn when white men first loaded their saddlebags with shotgun shells, coils of rope, cans of kerosene, and sticks of dynamite—and used them to send the black people of Forsyth County running for their lives.

I FIRST HEARD the story in the back seat of a yellow school bus as it lumbered past the cow pastures and chicken houses out on Browns Bridge Road. My parents bought land there in the mid-1970s, hop-

Cumming, Georgia, January 17th, 1987

ing to escape Atlanta's vast suburban sprawl and to rediscover some of the joys of small-town life they had known growing up in Wylam, Alabama, just west of Birmingham. The first "lake people" had come north after the damming of the Chattahoochee River formed Lake Lanier in the 1950s, and by the early '70s young professionals like my parents were just beginning to transform the county into a bedroom community of Atlanta.

When we moved in the summer of 1977, I was a typical suburban kid. But as soon as I started school in September, I realized that to everyone at Cumming Elementary, I was a city slicker from Atlanta. I'd grown up playing soccer instead of football. I could ride a bike but not a motorcycle. And one day when I pointed excitedly at a herd of muddy Holsteins, the farm boys all burst out laughing, then just shook their heads in pity.

I had entered a world where nobody liked outsiders. Everyone on the bus seemed to be sitting next to a cousin, or a nephew, or an aunt, and I noticed that a lot of them had the same last names as the roads they lived on. The Pirkles got off at Pirkle's Ferry, the Cains at Cain's Cove. And in the mornings, a boy named John Bramblett was always standing with his lunch box next to a sign that said "Doctor Bramblett Road." Their families had lived in Forsyth for so long that now you could navigate by them like landmarks—all those clusters of Stricklands and Castleberrys and Martins. I still remember my second-grade teacher, Mrs. Holtzclaw, who lived out on Holtzclaw Road, saying at the end of my first day, "G'won now'n' fetch yer satchel, child." It was as if, having moved forty miles north of Atlanta, my parents had transported us a century back in time.

As soon as kids heard where I was from, their questions were relentless: Did we live in a skyscraper in Atlanta? Had I ever been to a Falcons game? Did I see a bunch of niggers there? Had the niggers ever tried to kill us?

I'd heard kids call black people "niggers" in my old neighborhood, but my father didn't allow it, and I'd seen many times how that one word could turn him fierce. I also remembered Rose, the black woman who'd cleaned house for my mother, and I could faintly recall skinning my knee once when no one else was home. Wasn't it Rose who laid a hand on my back and said, "Alright, it's gonna be alright," pressing my face into the cool white cotton of her apron? And I remembered how a dozen women like Rose used to gather on the corner by our house, then walk down the hill and out of sight—back to their own kitchens and their own little boys, in places I knew nothing about, except that they were very far away.

Sitting on the school bus in Forsyth, I understood that for the kids around me, the color line was drawn not between rich and poor, not between white employers and black servants, but between all that was good and cherished and beloved and everything they thought evil, and dirty, and despised. It was one "nigger joke" after another, and at first I was too afraid to do anything but smile when they smiled and laugh when they laughed. But eventually I got up the nerve to ask my friend Paul why everyone in the county seemed to hate black people so much, especially since there were none of them around.

Paul looked at me in disbelief.

"You don' know nuthin', do you, Pat?" he said, slumping down beside me in the bus seat. "You ain't never heard 'bout the KKK?"

I started to say I had, that I had seen them at a parade once, and that—

Paul just shook his head.

"Long, long, *long* time ago, see, they's this girl got raped and killed over yonder," he told me, glancing out the window. "And when they found her in the woods, y'know what they done?"

When I said nothing, Paul spat in the floor, then broke into a wide grin. "White folks run all the niggers clean out of Forsyth County."

FOR TWENTY YEARS, that was all I knew: a myth, a legend—or at least the faintest outlines of one. And I admit that long after that day on the bus, when I went to college in the North, I'd sometimes tell the story just to shock people. It was a kind of brag, about how I'd grown up in *Deliverance* country, in an honest-to-God "white county" whose borders were patrolled by gun-toting, rock-throwing rednecks with nooses slung over their shoulders. My classmates were horrified but fascinated, since the story fit every stereotype they'd ever heard about the South and confirmed their sense of being enlightened and evolved compared to all the Jethros and Duke Boys down in Georgia. Yet even after repeating it for years, after making the tale a staple of my act, I knew little more than I had as a kid, and nothing at all about the real mystery at the heart of Forsyth: those nameless, faceless, vanished people who'd once lived in the place that I called home.

By 2003 I was far from my childhood in Georgia and spending most of my time in the library, doing research on the bubonic plague outbreaks of seventeenth-century London. In those days, archives all over the world were digitizing their collections, and it was still astonishing to me that you could summon up old manuscripts and documents with just a few clicks. The more I searched the historical records, the more I realized that the Internet was becoming a kind of Hubble telescope, aimed back into the past. If you looked through it long enough, and with care, once faint and distant events started to emerge like clear, bright stars.

One night I decided to see what the telescope might reveal about the founding myth of my own home place: that old ghost story about a murdered girl and a rampage by white-sheeted night riders. I had always wondered if the whole thing was just a racist fantasy, but when I typed "Forsyth" and "1912" into a database of old newspapers, a list of results came up, with headlines that, sure enough, told of an eighteen-year-old woman named Mae Crow who was raped and killed, allegedly by three black men. "Girl Murdered by Negro at Cumming," one front page read. "Confessed His Deed . . . Will Swing for Their Crime," said another. I clicked a link that led to an article in the *Atlanta Constitution*, which slowly knit itself into an image. When it filled the screen, I stared in wonder.

I'd thought of the story of Mae Crow's murder as a kind of tall tale all my life and had even questioned whether African Americans ever *really* lived in Forsyth. But now I was suddenly confronted with the truth—or at least something closer to it than I ever thought I'd get: three white soldiers in front of a train car, standing guard over six black prisoners. These were the first faces of black Forsyth I had

Atlanta Constitution, *October 4th, 1912*

ever seen, and while there was no way to know if they were really guilty of the "revolting assault," when I zoomed in and panned across the photograph, I could hardly believe my eyes. Young, fearful, as alive as you and I, the prisoners stared back at me from the very twilight of that old world, and at the dawning of the all-white place I knew. As they peered across the century, frozen there beside the train tracks, I couldn't shake the feeling that the image came to me bearing not just a secret but an obligation.

As I read more about the accused, I realized that the picture raised more questions than it answered. If two of those faces belonged to the "Knox and Daniel" who were doomed to "swing for their crime," which two? And if they were the ones who stood accused of raping and killing Mae Crow, who were the others? That teenager in the middle wearing a porkpie hat, his limbs growing so fast that his white shirt was already a size too small? What about the young boy on the right in overalls, resting an elbow on the thigh of an older, visibly worried man? And who was the lone woman, petite and fine-boned, who seems to be—maybe I am imagining this—almost smiling? Was it really true, as the headlines claimed, that she had helped "fasten the noose" around the neck of her own brother? And who was that big man in front: legs spread, arms gripping his knees, as if to shield the group?

This book began with my first glimpse of that photograph, and my realization that while the stories I'd heard were riddled with lies and distorted by bigotry, at their heart lay a terrible, almost unbearable reality. These were real people being led to real deaths, at the start of a season of violence that would send a ripple of fear out across the twentieth century. In the glow of that computer screen, I also began to see how the tale, stripped of names and dates and places, made the expulsion of the county's black community seem like only a legend—like something too far back in the mists of time to ever truly understand—rather than a deliberate and sustained campaign of terror.

Having lived my entire life in the wake of Forsyth's racial cleansing, I wanted to begin reversing its communal act of erasure by learning as much as I could about the lost people and places of black Forsyth. I was determined to document more than just that the expulsions occurred: I wanted to know where, when, how, and to whom.

It was then I set myself the task of finding out what really happened—not because the truth is an adequate remedy for the past, and not because it can undo what was done. Instead, I wanted to honor the dead by leaving a fuller account of what they endured and all that they and their descendants lost.

BLOOD

AT THE

ROOT

1

THE SCREAM

On Thursday, September 5th, 1912, Ellen Grice let out a terrifying scream. Some say this occurred at the house of her parents, Joseph and Luna Brooks, others that Grice was at her own home when her husband, a young farmer named John Grice, came in "about midnight and found his wife, and at once sounded an alarm." A century later, there is no way to know exactly what led to her cry for help, who first heard it, or what transpired in the minutes after. But soon newspapers all over the South were telling readers what Ellen Grice said then: that she had been "awakened by the presence of a negro man in her bed."

When they heard Grice's story of a black rapist forcing his way through an open window, the white men of Forsyth County didn't waste time asking a lot of questions. By the next morning, the news had spread from house to house, country store to country store, and all of white Forsyth was in an uproar. When word reached the county seat of Cumming, a team of bloodhounds was assembled and a posse of white men were deputized on the spot. As they saddled their horses and rode off in search of Grice's attacker, they were led by a man who would play a central role in the bloody "race troubles" to come: Sheriff William Reid.

Bill Reid turned fifty in 1912 and was in the middle of his second term as sheriff of Forsyth. The job had brought a major improvement in his family's fortunes, and a portrait taken around the time of his election shows just how quickly Reid transformed himself into one of Cumming's leading citizens. As they pose in a photographer's studio, Reid's young sons wear double-breasted suits and silk ties; his wife, Martha, is dressed in fashionable satin; and Reid himself—with his dapper tie pin and pomaded hair, his coat thrown open to reveal a gold watch chain—looks like anything but a hayseed just in from the fields.

But that's precisely what he'd been when he took office in 1906, having grown up on his father's farm, where the Reids raised corn and hogs and struggled through the lean years, like everyone else working the tough red clay of the Georgia foothills. Having quickly made a name for himself in town, Reid wore his badge and revolver with a certain amount of swagger and was in no hurry to return to the family farm. And while contemporary newspaper accounts make it clear that he was the face of the law in Forsyth, Reid's name also appears on an obscure but no less significant document from those days: a yellowed sheet of onionskin that a secretary fed into the platen of her Underwood in the 1920s. Across the top, she typed, "KNIGHTS OF THE SAWNEE KLAVERN OF THE KU KLUX KLAN." Below, among the names of a hundred charter members, is Forsyth County Sheriff William W. Reid.

REID'S CHIEF RIVAL in the 1912 election had been his own deputy, Mitchell Gay Lummus. A leaner, younger man at thirty-four, he was the grandson of a Confederate war hero named Andrew Jackson Lummus. The farm in Vickery's Creek where Lummus grew up was surrounded not only by white neighbors but also by a number of well-established black farmers, including Jasper Gober, Archibald Nuckolls, and Isaac Allen. By the summer of 1912, Lum-

*Sheriff Bill Reid c. 1908, with wife, Martha, and sons
William and Robert*

mus, too, had set his sights on the job of county sheriff. He was
undoubtedly looking to move up in the world, like Reid, but Lummus also needed the money. His wife, Savannah, had died of meningitis in 1909, and he'd had no choice but to hire a live-in nanny
to help raise his three young and suddenly motherless girls: Lillie,
eleven, Jewell, eight, and Grace, three. A hopeful Lummus declared
his candidacy in May of 1912, but lost to Reid that July.

And so it was the stout and garrulous Bill Reid, not tall, quiet

Gay Lummus, who sat in the sheriff's office in the early hours of Friday, September 6th, listening to the tale of Ellen Grice's "outrage" at the hands of a black rapist. By midmorning, Reid and his posse had ridden eight miles south of Cumming and arrived at a cluster of tenant farms near Ellen Grice's house. When a group of young boys tore down the road, yelling that the sheriff was coming with a pack of bloodhounds, the black field hands and sharecroppers of Big Creek knew enough to get out of sight. Lummus was second-in-command, and so it fell to him to dismount and pound on doors, demanding that one family after another come out into the yard and speak with the sheriff.

By sunrise on Saturday, September 7th, Reid and Lummus had arrested and jailed a teenager named Toney Howell, along with four other men held as accomplices: Isaiah Pirkle, Joe Rogers, Fate Chester, and Johnny Bates. Howell was the nephew of two of Cumming's most respected black residents, Morgan and Harriet Strickland, and was staying on the farm they owned in Big Creek, to provide some much-needed help during the fall harvest. What the other prisoners had in common was that they were unmarried, illiterate black men who happened to live near the scene of the "dastardly assault." The *Macon Telegraph* hinted at the arbitrary nature of their arrests when a reporter wrote that the posse had ridden out to Big Creek and "rounded up suspects."

Toney Howell also stood out for having been raised not in Forsyth but in neighboring Milton County. Much like Emmett Till in Money, Mississippi, forty-three years later, this made him conspicuous as the stranger in the group, and one of the few black faces in Big Creek unknown to Reid and Lummus. The *Atlanta Georgian* would later admit that the evidence against Howell was entirely circumstantial, and in 1912 the very definitions of words like "assault" and "rape" were kept deliberately vague and used to describe almost any incident involving black men and white women.

Sheriff Bill Reid and Deputy Gay Lummus, c. 1912

This means that once Toney Howell stood accused of having entered Ellen Grice's bedroom, he was widely regarded as being guilty of some kind of sexual "assault," whether or not he had actually been there, and whether or not he had ever touched Grice. "If a lynching takes place," said one journalist, "Toney Howell will probably be the victim." In the Jim Crow South, this was the kind of reporting that functioned not just as a prediction but as a directive to potential lynchers.

By lunchtime that Saturday, the town of Cumming was bustling with families from outlying sections, making their weekly trip to market. With Howell and four other black men locked in the Forsyth County Jail, talk of Ellen Grice was on everyone's lips. But "no excitement prevailed," according to the *Georgian,* until Grice's father, Joseph Brooks, arrived in town, bringing word that his daughter was in "critical condition" from the alleged attack out in

Big Creek. This news had an electrifying effect on the crowd, and soon a group of whites gathered around the little brick jailhouse on Maple Street and demanded that the prisoners be brought out. As more and more people arrived at the square, the town buzzed with what one reporter called "a determined spirit of speedy vengeance."

PICKING HIS WAY through that crowd, the Reverend Grant Smith must have looked like any other "hired man" in Forsyth. At forty-eight, he was part of the county's poor black underclass, a group that, though they represented 10 percent of the total population, were almost totally disenfranchised by the Jim Crow laws of Georgia. While emancipated slaves had been guaranteed the right to vote by the Fifteenth Amendment in 1870, the Georgia legislature countered by adopting the nation's first cumulative poll tax in 1877, then established one of the first "white primary" systems in 1898. The result—in a place where the vast majority of African Americans could not afford the poll tax, and where Democratic primary winners were, almost without fail, elected to office—was that men like Grant Smith had no chance of representation in the local government and virtually no power to resist the will of the white majority.

Smith earned his living picking corn and cotton in the rolling, terraced fields of the county, and it's likely that on the morning of the "excitement" he was helping bring an employer's harvested crops to market. But to black churchgoers, he was also well known as a preacher, and as the son of Reverend Silas Smith, one of the area's leading clergymen, whose ornate signature had graced the bottom of "colored" marriage certificates during Reconstruction. Silas and Joanna Smith's oldest son, Grant had been conceived in the chaotic war year of 1863 and was part of the very last generation of African Americans born into slavery. Though he was too young to remember it, Grant Smith was the only one of his nine siblings who began life as the legal property of a white man.

But having been born on the eve of emancipation also meant that Smith's earliest memories included going to one of the freedmen's schools that sprang up all over Georgia after the Civil War, when northern aid societies and the federal government succeeded in establishing a right to education for Georgia's former slaves. As a result, unlike his younger brothers and sisters, who came of age after the end of congressional Reconstruction—and after the colored school system was dismantled in north Georgia—Smith could read and write. There was no outward sign of it as he shouldered his way past farmers, tradesmen, and merchants hawking their wares on the Cumming square, but during that brief window of hope in the early 1870s, Grant Smith had become something white Georgians feared almost as much as a black rapist: an outspoken, educated black man.

WHEN HE LEARNED that Morgan Strickland's nephew Toney had been accused of rape, and heard white men all around him whipping themselves up into a lynch mob, at some point Reverend Smith turned to someone in the crowd and said exactly what he thought. It was a shame, he said, that so much trouble was being caused on account of a "sorry white woman."

The words were barely out of Smith's mouth before white men all around him froze mid-sentence, stared at each other in disbelief, then tightened their fists around the buggy whips and leather crops with which they'd driven into town. Unable to reach the prisoners inside the jail, and outraged by the alleged attack on Grice, they now saw a target much closer to hand: the book-smart, headstrong, "uppity" black preacher, who had dared to question a white woman's worth. "News of what he had said spread," according to one witness, and "like a flash . . . the infuriated mob was upon him."

The first crack of leather brought people from every direction, eager to push their way into the ring of men surrounding

Smith, who was now being whipped, kicked, and punched by every fist that could reach him. Estimates put the size of the mob at three hundred, and those on the outskirts could barely hear Smith's grunts and cries over the cheering and shouting. When one group of sweat-soaked men tired, they gave way to others, who moved in and took their turn. Witnesses said the preacher was beaten "nearly to death" and that others started gathering scraps of wood for a bonfire, on which they planned to burn Grant Smith alive.

Before they could, Sheriff Reid and Deputy Lummus muscled their way through the crowd and somehow managed to wrest Smith away. They carried him to the courthouse, where he was at first locked inside a huge basement vault—not so much to keep him in as to keep potential lynchers out. After hearing Smith's moans, Reid finally agreed to move "the prisoner" upstairs, where a doctor was summoned to treat and dress his wounds.

It was around this time—as the bloody, half-naked body of the preacher was carried past his office door, and as a crowd of hundreds bellowed for Smith to be handed over—that Mayor Charlie Harris realized he needed help. If he wanted to save Grant Smith and the five black men in the Cumming jail from a lynch party that was growing larger and more determined by the minute, Harris knew he would need more than a skinny deputy like Gay Lummus and a glad-handing, good ol' boy sheriff like Bill Reid. Rising from his chair, Cumming's mayor tapped the little brass lever of a telephone on his desk and told the operator to commandeer all outside lines for an urgent call to Governor Joseph Mackey Brown, in Atlanta. As Harris pressed the receiver to his ear and waited, Sheriff Reid stood nearby, scanning the faces in the mob—and finding among them, no doubt, a great many men who would soon join him in the Sawnee Klavern of the Ku Klux Klan.

AT THIRTY-NINE, MAYOR Charlie Harris was in the midst of his own climb up the social ladder. Like Reid, he was the son of a dirt farmer, but Harris had gone from plowing his father's fields as a teenager to enrolling at North Georgia Agricultural College in the mid-1890s. After college, Harris distinguished himself as a law student at the University of Georgia. And he seems to have made some valuable friends there, for in March of 1908 his name was added to a corporate charter issued by the state of Georgia, granting Harris and his partners the right to build a new railroad—the Atlanta Northeastern, which was to run due north from the state capitol and terminate in the little town of Cumming.

The plan could hardly have been more ambitious or potentially lucrative, given that the hill country of Forsyth had proved remarkably resistant to development after the Civil War, even as nearby cities like Gainesville grew, helped by their location along the Chattahoochee River. Cumming, by contrast, was too far west to use the river for transport and had been bypassed by both the Southern Railway, which followed the river valley, and by the Atlanta, Knoxville & Northern, which passed through Canton, to the west.

County leaders had been courting railroad entrepreneurs since the earliest days of the Gilded Age, and in 1871 a group of citizens had convened a "mass meeting" and appointed a committee to try to persuade the Southern Railway to open a station in Cumming. But while locals predicted the "stupendous results in adding to our county wealth and population," the board of the railroad remained unconvinced. In 1872, that same committee made a public pledge to "tender right of way to the first company that will build a road through the county," and twenty years later, in 1891, Forsyth was still struggling to convince the Richmond and Danville Railroad that Cumming was the ideal terminus for a new branch. Local businessmen had grown so desperate that they offered "to donate to the company the sum of $20,000." The recurrence of such pledges across a fifty-year span attests to the aching desire many residents felt for a rail link, and their frustration as one company after another bypassed Forsyth.

All of this means that when he hung out his shingle on the Cumming square, Charles L. Harris, Esq., arrived with a rare combination of talents. He was an ambitious young lawyer and entrepreneur, yet had the common touch of a local farm boy made good. And during his time in law school he had made connections with powerful men in Atlanta, who could finally put Cumming on the transportation map of the South.

Plans for the Atlanta Northeastern received final approval in 1908, and a stock sale raised $50,000, to be used for preliminary land purchases and the construction of power plants along the route. Once completed, a rail station promised to transform Forsyth's agrarian economy, bringing it once and for all out of the dark days of Reconstruction. "The line which is to be built from Atlanta to Cumming," said the *Constitution,* "will prove one of the greatest developers of a great section. ... When that time comes millions of dollars will be added to the taxable values of Georgia, and hundreds of thousands of people to north Georgia."

Unmentioned in such sunny predictions was the fact that, despite its proximity to the state capitol, Forsyth was still something of a backwater. It could boast of a handful of wealthy planters and progressive leaders but was home to a much larger population of poor, illiterate whites, who were more worried than excited by talk of rail passengers arriving from Atlanta. Though such a line would bring business opportunities to rich and powerful men in town, it would also put Forsyth in contact with all the competition and the dizzying diversity of the city. To many of the county's wary hill people, such radical change was something to be fended off, not welcomed.

But in the summer of 1912, Charlie Harris had a vision of a

Charlie Harris, 1912

future in which gleaming locomotives would roll into Cumming Station—bringing wealth, technology, and all the benefits of the new century right into the heart of Forsyth County. As Harris and his partners spread out their crisp maps and pictured the towering bridges and breathtaking tunnels of the Atlanta Northeastern, it must have seemed like a sure thing. It must have seemed like nothing in the world could stop them.

ON THE SAME MORNING that Grant Smith was horsewhipped on the Cumming square, the black congregations of the county were gathering at the Colored Methodist Campground, just outside of town, preparing for their annual picnic and barbecue. The event brought together hundreds of parishioners from the African American community's many small rural churches—Mt. Fair, Shiloh Baptist, Stoney Point, Backband Church, and Shakerag Church were all there—and was traditionally held just as the harvest began in September. It was a time when even the poorest in the community could partake in one of the great pleasures of farm life: the heaps of roasted corn, black-eyed peas, butter beans, and biscuits, and the whole hogs that had been roasting on spits all night.

But this year, as the first families arrived, they learned that five young men had been arrested out in Big Creek. Word spread that Morgan and Harriet Strickland's nephew Toney had been accused of rape, and when someone coming from the square reported that whites there were threatening to lynch Grant Smith, many in the crowd could stand by no longer. A group of men who had planned to spend the day tending the barbecue pits instead started walking toward town, knowing that Reverend Smith was not much safer in the custody of Bill Reid than he had been in the hands of the mob.

In 1912, the African American community of Forsyth County was largely made up of illiterate sharecroppers and field hands. But there was a smaller group of educated blacks with close ties to prominent whites, and many of them were leaders of the black churches. Among the crowd at that Saturday picnic were men like Joseph Kellogg, who had helped found the Colored Methodist Campground in 1897, and whose two-hundred-acre farm near Sawnee Mountain was the largest black-owned property in the county.

Another attendee was Levi Greenlee Jr., whose recently deceased father, Levi Sr., had been the pastor at Shiloh Baptist for many years, and left to his children more than 120 acres inside the Cumming city limits. Greenlee was so well liked that in the 1890s he was invited to join the Hightower Association, a gathering of white clergymen from around north Georgia, and was inducted as the group's first and only black member.

In surviving church minutes from Shiloh, we can still hear Reverend Greenlee's voice on a typical Sunday, thanking those in attendance "for their donations of $6.36." When Greenlee accepted

Joseph Kellogg, date unknown

the collection plates and looked out over the congregation, he saw the benches filled not only with familiar black faces but also a number of white visitors. Greenlee thanked everyone for their generosity, "and especially our white friends . . . for their 10 and 25 cent pieces." This means that as Levi Greenlee Jr. and other men from the church picnic walked anxiously toward town, they had reason to hope that, scattered among a sea of enraged faces outside the county courthouse, they might find at least a few sympathetic white allies.

AT THAT SAME MOMENT, hundreds of whites from outlying areas were loading their rifles and shotguns and heading toward Cumming, drawn by a rumor that spread like wildfire: an army of black men had been spotted leaving the Colored Campground, people said, infuriated by the attack on Grant Smith. Black rebels, the story went, had filled a wagon with explosives and were planning to "dynamite the town . . . without sparing women and children."

One witness reported that whites "on horseback, in buggies, in automobiles and afoot . . . streamed into town and loitered about the courthouse," as the square became "a mecca for armed men . . . [where] the protruding coat above the hip told that they were armed for war." For anyone who arrived unprepared, enterprising gun dealers had set up tables on the courthouse lawn and spread out their inventory of rifles, shotguns, pistols, and wooden crates filled with ammunition.

If the tale of Ellen Grice's rape represented one of the most vivid fantasies of southern whites, this new rumor was fueled by another: the vision of crazed black men rising up and taking vengeance on their former masters. That fear had recently been stoked by reports of a full-scale "race war" in the north Georgia mountains. Only a month before, in July 1912, headlines all over the state had warned that a "pitched battle between the races" had broken out in the little town of Plainville, sixty miles west of Cumming.

The Plainville incident began innocently enough, with a black girl and a white boy picking peaches in the same orchard. At some point the boy, Ivey Miller, was struck by a rock he said was thrown by the girl, Minnie Heard. But when Heard's father went to town the next day, hoping to explain the misunderstanding and make peace with the Millers, he was set upon and beaten by whites, who warned him never to come back. According to the *Macon Telegraph*, Minnie Heard's father stayed away, but her uncle had the audacity to appear in Plainville the following morning. As soon as they saw him, whites accused Heard's uncle and three other black men of "forming a plot to burn the town." They were lined up against a wall and whipped, until one of the black men saw his chance to escape and took off, firing a pistol over his shoulder as he and the other men ran, pursued by whites who returned fire. As the Southern Railway's afternoon train arrived from Chattanooga, first-class passengers glanced out the windows of a dining car and saw one of their oldest and deepest fears sprung to life: a raging gun battle between whites and armed black men.

Hiding in the woods, wounded and bleeding, the four black men took stock of their situation and quickly came to a desperate conclusion. Having dared to defend themselves against a mob, they now faced the prospect of either being lynched once they were captured or legally hung when they were tried by an all-white jury that was likely to include friends and relatives of the men they had shot. As they peered through the leaves and saw a posse approaching, they decided it was better to be killed in a gunfight than surrender to the kind of white men who regularly tortured, shot, castrated, and burned African Americans alive—often for far less than what these men had already done.

After making it to the cabin of a local black family, the men barricaded themselves inside, took up positions at the windows, and stared out at the gathering mob. Some accounts say the gunfight lasted all night, others that it was over in an hour. By the time the smoke cleared, three prominent whites had been wounded, including the sheriff of Gordon County. Ten black men and two black women were also shot, though their names went unrecorded, and there is no report as to whether they lived or died. The *Macon Telegraph* said "the battle was maintained until the negroes ran out of ammunition, [then] they were beaten into insensibility by whites who crowded into the cabin . . . [and] a lynching was only prevented by officers who pulled their revolvers and stood guard." Newspapers as far away as San Francisco and New York portrayed the event not as a case of black men defending themselves against lynchers but as an "ambush" of white law officers by "a band of negroes."

————

IN SEPTEMBER OF 1912, the Plainville "race war" was still fresh in the minds of the white citizens of Forsyth. As they spun the cylinders of Colt revolvers, oiled the bolts of old Winchesters, and thumbed shells into the barrels of shotguns broken over their knees, the lesson must have seemed crystal clear: whites in Plainville had allowed their own sheriff to be gunned down, and only the brave deeds of a posse had stopped a black insurrection. Milling around the impromptu gun market that had sprung up outside the courthouse, whites became convinced that they were now the ones in terrible danger. Everyone had heard that a black army was rolling down Tolbert Street, trailing behind it a wagonload of dynamite. The town of Cumming, whites believed, would soon be under siege. And as the sun climbed high over the square, they prepared to defend it with every weapon they could find.

2

RIOT, ROUT, TUMULT

Cumming mayor Charlie Harris was among the most moderate voices in the white community, but even he was so anxious after the Plainville "race war" that he gave his wife shooting lessons, in case she needed to defend the house while he was away. Harris's eight-year-old daughter, Isabella, remembered an urgent telephone call her father made on the morning Grant Smith was horsewhipped, telling his wife, Deasie, that it was time to load the rifle.

> In the face of [the] excitement and terror . . . the men downtown heard that a crowd of negroes was assembling near Sawnee Mountain. Their intention presumably was to invade the town, commit robbery, perhaps murder, and intimidate citizens. Father had trained Mother how to shoot . . . and told her to take the gun, loaded but not cocked, to the front porch and have the children around her. If she saw a group of men coming up the grove, she was to fire the gun into the air to frighten them. . . .
>
> [But] while we were sitting there the telephone rang again [and] Leon, my oldest brother, went in to answer it. He came

back with the information that no danger threatened us or anybody else. The rumor had started when two colored boys were seen near Sawnee . . . hunting squirrels.

Although Isabella's mother got that second call before she fired a shot, all over the county whites like her were on edge, watching the horizon with guns at the ready. Such was the level of hysteria, even among upper-class whites like Deasie Harris, that two boys out hunting squirrels—presumably because their families were poor and hungry—could be mistaken for a bloodthirsty black invasion force, intent on "robbery [and] perhaps murder."

AS THEY WALKED from the Colored Methodist Campground, the men from the church picnic must have sensed that kind of fear and hysteria rising to a fever pitch all around them. Whatever urgency and determination they'd felt as they set out, when the group rounded a corner and finally arrived downtown, they were stopped in their tracks by the scene on the square. One witness reported that "fully 500 white men came into Cumming from surrounding areas" and "many arms and munitions were [being] sold to citizens preparing to protect their homes." Another observer said that "old rifles, shotguns ancient and modern, and every variety of pistol possible [was] being loaded and held in readiness."

Everywhere the men looked, whites were strapping holsters to their belts, stuffing their coat pockets with bullets and shotgun shells, and readying themselves for battle. Facing impossible odds against such a force, they abandoned all hope of saving Reverend Smith, Toney Howell, and the other prisoners in the Cumming jail. Instead they retreated, hoping to at least warn families at the Colored Methodist Campground to stay out of town. "The negroes fled," according to one reporter, but before they could slip away, they were spotted by a crowd of whites, who gave chase all the way back to the church barbecue. "A hundred or more white men went to the scene and ordered the negroes to disperse," said another witness. "They accepted the warning . . . and all negroes venturing into town were run out immediately."

Having repelled the men from the picnic, and having warned blacks that the town of Cumming was off-limits, the mob now turned its attention back to Grant Smith. The blood-soaked preacher may have slipped from their grasp that morning, but they knew he was still tantalizingly close, somewhere deep inside the Forsyth County Courthouse. According to Charlie Harris's daughter Isabella, the men refused to disperse even after repeated warnings from Sheriff Reid and Deputy Lummus, and so finally Mayor Harris put down his pen, rose from his desk, and went out to speak with them himself.

"After this mob had come together," Isabella Harris recalled, "my father addressed them from the courthouse steps." When they quieted down, the Cumming mayor tried to reason with the crowd and to reassure them that legal justice would soon be done, so there was no need for anyone to go outside the law. "Father begged them," Isabella said, "to go home, eat their dinners, and get cooled off, change their minds, and not disgrace Forsyth County further."

Harris clearly hoped to appeal to the men's better natures, but as he turned back toward the courthouse door, one farmer yelled out over the rest, "We don't want no dinner, Colonel . . . We wants *nigger* for dinner!"

A roar of approval rose from the crowd, and all Harris could do was shake his head and retreat back inside. With the mob growing louder and bolder, he picked up the telephone and asked the operator to place yet another urgent call to Atlanta. This time Harris told Governor Brown that without protection from the state militia, Grant Smith and the other prisoners were unlikely to survive the night.

Georgia governor Joseph Mackey Brown in 1912

The man on the receiving end of Harris's call was Joseph Mackey Brown, who had been elected governor of Georgia in 1908. The son of Joseph E. Brown, Georgia's governor during the Civil War, Joseph Mackey Brown had been raised in Canton, the seat of Cherokee County, which borders Forsyth, and he still owned a piece of farmland in the foothills. So while "Little Joe" Brown was part of a powerful political dynasty and traveled in the most rarefied circles of Atlanta society, the poor whites of the up-country were deeply familiar to him. He needed no explanation for the tension in Harris's voice when the mayor said that a serious case of "lynching fever" had broken out in Forsyth.

Brown knew what a mob of angry white men was capable of, not only from his upbringing in Canton but also from the reports that passed over his desk week after week. Even a brief sample from contemporary newspapers gives a sense of just how often during Brown's administration Georgia officials confronted the outbreaks of racial terrorism known as "lawlessness":

> February 1, 1910: "Night Riders are said to have killed one negro in Columbia county, and to have burned several homes and churches. To try to bring real facts to the surface would be at the risk of life."

> December 15, 1910: "Terror exists among the negroes . . . of Pike County, due to the whippings of negroes by Night Riders. . . . One of the largest planters in Georgia has appealed to the Governor for troops."

> January 20, 1911: "Owing to the posting of anonymous placards, threatening them with unforeseen dangers, and lynchings, the Negroes of Turner County have left by the hundreds, and are still leaving. This condition of affairs will have serious results at this time of the year for the planters who employ Negroes to work their lands."

Early in the new century, politicians realized that this rising tide of mob violence posed a serious threat not just to law and order but to the agrarian economy and larger business interests of the state. On August 16th, 1912—less than a month before Grant Smith was attacked—the Georgia legislature had passed an act giving the governor unprecedented new powers to intervene in exactly the kind of crisis that was spinning out of control on the Cumming square. Whenever the governor has reasonable cause, the new law said, "to apprehend the outbreak of any riot, rout, tumult, insurrection, mob, unlawful assembly, or combination," he was to order out troops, who would answer not to town and county leaders but to the governor himself.

Critics railed against the measure for weakening local control and "repealing the powers of the mayor and county officials." But that was precisely the point: to take control away from small-town sheriffs, who often either joined lynch mobs or conspired with their leaders. The new law was meant to protect suspects and—more important to the authors of the bill—to safeguard the supply of cheap black labor that Georgia planters and industrialists had depended on since emancipation.

Once Harris convinced the governor that the mob in Cumming was too large for Reid and his deputies to control, Brown put his new powers to the test for the first time. He called Major I. T. Catron of the Georgia National Guard and ordered two elite companies of the state militia—the Marietta Rifles and the Candler Horse Guards—to muster their men, commandeer cars from private citizens, and head directly to Cumming.

When word spread that the governor was sending troops from Marietta and Gainesville, the men at the front of the mob threw themselves against the locked doors of the courthouse, making one last effort to get their hands on Grant Smith before the militiamen arrived. According to the *Atlanta Georgian*, "a number of the more rabid in the mob [tried] to force an entrance . . . and get the negro held there. However, the deputies, headed by M. G. Lummus, held [them] back."

AT SOME POINT during that shoving match, someone in the crowd noticed a dust cloud rising in the distance, and others strained to hear a low droning sound, rising in pitch as it came closer. As more and more people turned to look, a long line of "high-powered automobiles" came into view, barreling down Dahlonega Street and headed straight for the crowd outside the courthouse.

When the convoy of Model T's, Internationals, McIntyres, and Acme Roadsters ground to a halt, most people on the square simply gawked in disbelief. In a place where nearly everyone still traveled by horse and buggy, in mule carts, in wagons, or on foot, this was enough to strike even the most bloodthirsty lynchers momentarily speechless. The cavalry had arrived, just as Governor Brown and Mayor Harris had promised, but they hadn't come on horseback. They rode into town in a gleaming, ticking row of beautiful machines, the likes of which nobody in Forsyth had ever seen.

Fifty-two soldiers of the Candler Horse Guards and the Marietta Rifles spilled out into the street, formed up ranks, clicked the heels of their knee-high black boots, then stood at attention in caped uniforms, shouldering their fifty-two identical Springfield carbines. To the mob of sunburned, overall-clad farmers who had spent the afternoon trying to batter down the courthouse door, the meaning of the spectacle must have been unmistakable. Cumming had been invaded all right, but not by black rebels, and not by crazed black rapists. Instead, a professional army representing the governor and the moneyed interests of the state had come to put everyone in Forsyth, black and white, back in their rightful places.

It was widely reported that although Governor Brown hesitated to intervene in local matters, once he did deploy troops, they would be authorized to take any and all steps necessary. "When soldiers are called upon by the civil authorities," Brown said, "it is to be assumed that it is soldiers with soldiers' weapons that are needed." In a speech before the Georgia legislature, he reiterated that he would use the new law to preserve order, even at the cost of civilian

The Marietta Rifles, "Riot Duty Company," c. 1908

lives. "The suppression of anarchy is the right and duty of all," the governor declared, "and there come times when they must shoot it to death just as they shoot down foreign invaders."

Facing fifty-two "soldiers with soldiers' weapons" who were authorized to fire at will, the rioters in Cumming quickly realized that defying the governor's army, as they had defied Mayor Harris all morning, might well end with a bullet to the head. And so, as the sun sank low over Sawnee Mountain, most of the crowd complied with orders to disperse and finally went home to eat their cold suppers, as Harris had been asking them to do since midday. The last, most stubborn members of the mob looked on in disgust as troops formed a "hollow square" around Grant Smith and escorted the preacher down the courthouse steps and across Maple Street, where he joined the five Grice suspects in the Forsyth County Jail.

As the roar of the mob gave way to the sound of sentries marching up and down the empty streets, the prisoners must have realized that—as unfortunate as they were to have been arrested in the first place—they could now count themselves lucky to be alive. After listening to the curses and threats of the lynchers all afternoon, they must have experienced no moment quite so heart-stopping as when, just after dark, Deputy Lummus appeared in front of their cells with a lantern, swung the heavy iron doors open one by one, and ordered the men to step outside.

Only then did it become clear that the militia's orders were not just to prevent a lynching but to escort the prisoners safely out of the county. A witness described how "the soldiers formed a double column at the jail and marched the six negroes out between them to waiting autos." At the end of one of the most dramatic days in Cumming's history, the last of the would-be lynchers "followed the soldiers to the jail and watched the prisoners" as they passed through a gauntlet of militiamen. "Jeers, muttering, swearing, and hissing were heard" as the black men shuffled awkwardly in their chains. When they made it to a waiting car, they rode out of the county in silence, crouched in the floorboards all the way to the northern outskirts of Atlanta, where they were locked inside the Marietta jail.

Dawn found the Cumming square deserted but for a detachment of thirteen soldiers who had patrolled the streets all night, and the whole place eerily quiet. After breakfast, church bells rang all over the county, and men who the day before had begged Charlie Harris to give them "nigger for dinner" now sat in starched white shirts, hair combed neatly, prayer books and hymnals open in their laps. The last of the Candler Horse Guards returned to Gainesville around noon, and editors in Atlanta were quick to congratulate the governor on having stopped a lynching and prevented the outbreak of another "race war" in the Georgia hills. "Serious Race Riot Averted," declared the *Atlanta Constitution*. "No more trouble in Cumming."

Joseph Brooks and John Grice, the father and husband of Ellen Grice, came to town that Sunday afternoon for a special closed-door meeting with Mayor Harris and Blue Ridge Circuit Judge Newton A. Morris. There is no record of how long they talked or what was discussed, but the meeting raises some provocative questions. One possibility is that Brooks and his son-in-law wanted assurances that there would be a speedy trial, and that Ellen Grice's accused attackers, having escaped a lynch mob, would still be brought to justice.

But it's also possible that there were details about Grice's encounter with Toney Howell that her family wanted to keep out of the public eye. In 1912, few people dared to even speak of consensual liaisons between white women and black men, but that doesn't mean everyone was blind to them. As early as 1892 the anti-lynching crusader Ida B. Wells had denounced what she called "the old threadbare lie that Negro men rape white women." Instead, Wells said, it was often white women who were filled with longing for young black men, and in many cases they claimed to have been raped only after being discovered in bed with black lovers. "There are many white women in the South," Wells wrote, "who would marry colored men if such an act would not place them at once beyond the pale of society and within the clutches of the law."

Such statements were still dangerous and highly transgressive in 1912, but privately many black people in Forsyth must have wondered whether Ellen Grice's story was just one more version of the "old threadbare lie." If Grice really had been found with "a negro man in her bed," wasn't it possible that she had invited him in? Whatever John Grice and Joseph Brooks discussed with Cumming officials, all the papers said was that the topic of their meeting "has not been made public."

With the mobs dispersed, the prisoners safely housed in the Marietta jail, and Ellen Grice's relatives reassured, Mayor Charlie Harris must have been eager to put the whole affair behind him, so he could get back to the business of planning Cumming's future— as terminus of the Atlanta Northeastern Railroad Company. Harris was said to be "incensed" by reports that some black families were abandoning their homes in the wake of the attack on Grant Smith, and in an interview with the *Georgian* the young mayor tried to counteract all the negative attention. "The town is perfectly quiet today," he told reporters, "and the fears of the negroes have been quieted."

Harris was keenly aware of the financial and political risk if people in Atlanta came to associate Cumming with lynchings and mob rule. As he headed home for supper on Sunday evening, he must have hoped that the arrest of Toney Howell would appease the most violent whites in the county, and that when Howell and the other prisoners came back to Forsyth, they would be judged not by a barbaric lynch mob but in the courts of the Blue Ridge Circuit. Harris was no doubt sincere when he said he believed Forsyth's "race troubles" were nearly over, and pleased to think of himself as exactly the kind of law-and-order man favored by Governor Brown.

WHAT HARRIS DIDN'T know was that at that very moment, eight miles east of Cumming, in a little farming village called Oscarville, a woman named Azzie Crow was just beginning to worry. Like nearly everyone in Forsyth, Azzie had gone to church that morning, then spent the afternoon visiting her sister Nancy, whose children were the same age as Azzie's two youngest girls, Bonnie and Esta, and her twin boys, Obie and Ovie. Before leaving church, Azzie had asked her eighteen-year-old daughter, Mae, to come by her aunt Nancy's house that afternoon, because Azzie would need help walking the little ones home.

But now suppertime had come and gone, the sun was low behind the treetops, and there was still no sign of Mae. Azzie finally walked the children home by herself, and along the way she stopped at the farm of George Jordan, whose daughter Alice said she'd seen Mae that afternoon. The two girls had stood chatting at the fork where Durand Road branches east off Waldrip, Jordan recalled, before Mae waved good-bye and hurried off in the direction of her aunt's place.

As the hours passed and their worry grew, Bud Crow finally lit a lantern and walked up and down Durand calling to his daughter, until a neighbor heard and came out to help. Soon search parties were formed, and little groups fanned out over the pine forests, orchards, and cornfields of Oscarville. The last light faded, the lightning bugs came out, and distant voices could be heard in every direction, shouting Mae's name as they searched and re-searched the two miles between Aunt Nancy's place and the Crow household. Men tromped through the woods and along the river's edge until dawn, when yet another group came back with their dogs and lanterns and walking sticks, and reported that there was still no trace of Bud Crow's oldest daughter.

It was only in the next day's papers that firsthand accounts began to appear, written by journalists who'd raced north when they heard that a beautiful white girl had gone missing—in the same north Georgia county where Ellen Grice was said to have survived a rape attempt just days before. "When daylight came" on Monday morning, one reporter wrote, "the search [was] renewed with increased vigor, the party dividing and going into all the remote and secluded spots." It was then, he said, that "several of the searchers were trudging . . . alongside an old abandoned path just one mile from the Crow home, when they stumbled onto the prostrate form of the missing girl."

After a night of searching and praying to hear Mae's voice call back through the woods, or to find that she'd gone to visit a friend without telling anyone or had suffered some mishap that would explain everything, the men had stumbled upon Azzie Crow's worst nightmare. According to witnesses, Mae had severe head wounds, "her throat was badly gashed, and she lay in a big pool of blood." A reporter said that "she had evidently been there for many hours" but was "still alive [and] breathing faintly, and as quickly as possible she was placed in a conveyance and carried to her home, [where] Dr. John Hockenhull and G. P. Brice . . . began a battle to save the girl's life."

News of the attack spread quickly, and by the time word reached Cumming, whites were "seething with bitterness." A reporter for the *Georgian* noted that "the inflamed state of the public mind had not had time to quiet down" since the Grice assault, when hundreds of local men were driven away from their own town square at the point of a bayonet. Now, as people listened to accounts of Mae Crow's gruesome injuries, many concluded that the black rapists of the county, emboldened by the protection of government troops, had once again attacked a white girl.

This time, though, the Candler Horse Guards and the Marietta Rifles were nowhere in sight, having been ordered back to their bases in Gainesville and Atlanta. That left this new wave of "race trouble" in the hands of the county sheriff and hundreds of outraged local whites. The governor, the mayor, and the adjutant general could talk all they wanted about due process and the "rule of law." But to many people in Forsyth County, the time for a reckoning had arrived.

3

THE MISSING GIRL

L ike most farmers' children, Bud and Azzie Crow's oldest
daughter went to school only a few months each year, during the lay-by time between planting and harvest. Even then,
she often missed a quarter of the school session, no doubt when she
was needed to help her mother manage a household that included
eight other children. The last written trace of Mae's life before the

Mae Crow, circa 1912

LOCATION.				NAME.	RELATION.	PERSONAL DESCRIPTION.						
Street, avenue, road, etc.	House number (in cities or towns).	Number of dwelling house in order of visitation.	Number of family in order of visitation.	of each person whose place of abode on April 15, 1910, was in this family. Enter surname first, then the given name and middle initial, if any. Include every person living on April 15, 1910. Omit children born since April 15, 1910.	Relationship of this person to the head of the family.	Sex.	Color or race.	Age at last birthday.	Whether single, married, widowed, or divorced.	Number of years of present marriage.	Mother of how many children. Number born.	Number now living.
	1	2		3	4	5	6	7	8	9	10	11
				Fletcher	Son	M	W	2	S			
				Crow			W	40		20		
				Azza	Wife	F	W	37	M	20	8	8
				Major	Son	M	W	18	S			
				May	Daughter	F	W					
				Lee	Son	M	W	15	S			
				Lee	Son	M	W	11	S			
				Rinda	Daughter	F	W	9	S			
				Olie	Son	M	W	6	S			
				Ova	Son	M	W	4	S			
				Bonnie	Daughter	F	W	1	S			

Crow household in the census of 1910

attack comes from 1910, when a man named Ed Johnson stood in the shadows of a front porch, chatting with Azzie Crow. As they talked, he opened a big black census ledger and dabbed the nib of a fountain pen to his tongue.

Journalists would soon refer to Mae's father as "one of the most prominent planters in this section," a description that might call to mind a plantation owner in a white suit and string tie. In reality, though, Leonidas "Bud" Crow never owned property in the county. He rented the fields he worked and the house in which his family lived. But such had not always been the case for the Crows. In 1861, when Mae's grandfather Isaac walked to Dawsonville and enlisted in the Confederate army, his family owned two hundred acres in and around Oscarville, worth more than $1,000. Yet by the end of his life, after Isaac Crow had fought in some of the bloodiest battles of the Civil War—surviving Manassas, Chancellorsville, and Gettysburg—he was all but destitute.

Isaac Crow, who had gone to war as a property-owning yeoman farmer, came back to a very different life. In 1904, his daughter Nancy wrote on a pension application that her father now had "no property to dispose" and listed as the reason for requesting government support that the old man was "physically . . . run down and worn out." Asked how Crow had supported himself during the previous year, a family friend said, "He tries to farm . . . he and his wife managed to make [a living] such as it was." Asked what property they owned, the answer was "none."

All over north Georgia, the war had left devastation in its wake, and the decades after the surrender at Appomattox brought a crippling shortage of credit to a region still struggling to recover. The crop-lien system instituted during Reconstruction meant that a man like Isaac Crow—who farmed land inherited from his father but lacked the cash to pay for labor, seed, and supplies—financed each spring's planting by borrowing against the fall harvest to come. But if there was a drought, or a killing frost, or some other stretch of bad luck, he could find that he had absolutely nothing to show for a year of backbreaking labor.

When farmers like Isaac Crow went to the banks looking for help, they could often borrow against their land, but many creditors made loans contingent on a shift from food crops to potentially more lucrative cotton—even in mountain counties like Forsyth, which were not nearly as well suited to it, in terms of climate and soil, as the southern half of the state. With so much cotton on the market, prices plummeted, squeezing small farmers even further and making it nearly impossible for them to repay loans charging 12 to 13 percent interest. As a Forsyth farmer put it in 1888, "It is said that 36 percent . . . of Forsyth county farms are mortgaged . . . and not one in fifty borrowers [are] ready to pay the principal. . . . This is the great danger that threatens us." The combined effect of all these forces was that throughout the 1880s and '90s, many north Georgia families literally bet the farm every time they planted, and it took only a few bad years before the banks foreclosed and they lost their land forever.

In only a single generation, the Crows went from working fields their ancestors had owned before the war to being tenants and sharecroppers—plowing, planting, and harvesting for only a share of whatever they produced. In the wake of emancipation, this meant competing not just with other white renters but with a whole new class of free blacks, who many owners saw as more appealing tenants and employees than poor whites. In a Jim Crow South where African Americans were disenfranchised at the polls and powerless in the courts, landowners could hire and rent to poor blacks, secure in the knowledge that if there was ever a dispute over rent payments, crop shares, or wages, the white man's word was sure to prevail.

AFTER BIDDING AZZIE CROW a pleasant afternoon, census taker Ed Johnson made his way out through a yard teeming with children and spent the last few hours of daylight knocking on the doors of Buices and Gravitts, Dunaways and Hemphills, and the rest of the families that made up the village of Oscarville, which had a total population of just sixty-three people. The faces that appeared out of the shadows of kitchens and barns and the folks who hailed Johnson as they walked out of the corn rows were, almost without fail, white—at least until Johnson came to the end of Durand Road, where he knocked at one of the few black households on his route. There, just past the Waldrips, Johnson stood nodding and scribbling in his ledger for the last time that day, as he spoke with a fifty-eight-year-old man named Buck Daniel.

Born in 1852, Daniel left only one record of his existence prior to emancipation: whatever anonymous tally mark represents him in the 1860 census of Georgia slave owners. But by 1875, there is evidence of the Daniel family's resilience—or at least some combination of the industry and luck that helped them make their way as free people. In the tax records from that year, Buck Daniel and his father, Adam, had amassed what must have seemed like a small fortune to two former slaves: $100 in personal property.

Whether that sum represented savings from wages, profits from a stretch of good crops, a gift from a former master, or some combination of all three, by 1890 it was gone, and the tax collector reported that Buck Daniel had a "total estate" of five dollars. All that remains to hint at the story of his boom and bust in the postwar years is the fact that he moved several times, from one side of the Chattahoochee to the other, crossing the county line between Forsyth and neighboring Hall. At a time when black laborers were bullied and cheated with impunity by their white employers, it's likely that Daniel's trail back and forth across the river represents his willingness to move anywhere there was work, and his struggle to find terms that could support a growing family.

The turn of the century found Daniel on the Hall County side of the river, working for a white man named Calvin Wingo, one of the most prosperous landowners in the area. At forty-eight Daniel was then on his second marriage, to a woman named Catie Marr, with whom he fathered six children, including Jane Daniel and her younger brother Oscar. As if feeding all those mouths wasn't burden enough, Buck and Catie had taken in four relatives in the late 1890s, when a younger sister named Nettie was widowed at twenty-two and left alone with three small children: Charlie, Erma, and Ernest Knox.

It was with this large clan in tow that at some point between 1900 and 1910 Buck and Catie moved to the little cluster of farms known as Oscarville, on the eastern edge of Forsyth County. Oscarville was overwhelmingly white, but there was decent land to rent, and plenty of work for "hired men" on the farms of the biggest landowners. Buck and Catie's two oldest sons, Harley and Cicero, nineteen and seventeen, were hired out to a white man named William Bagby, while the rest of the family rented a place a mile north of the Oscarville crossroads, at the end of Durand Road. They worked land owned by Marcus Waldrip, whose own hired man, living next door to the Daniel family, was one of the few other black people in that section of the county. His name was Rob Edwards—a tall, strongly built man in his twenties. Not long after they arrived, "Big Rob" began courting Buck's pretty teenage daughter Jane, who by 1912 had become his common-law wife.

As white farmers like Bud Crow labored on in the long economic shadow of Reconstruction, they kept a wary eye on black neighbors like Rob Edwards and Buck Daniel. For longtime residents like the Crows, whose people had lived in Oscarville for so long that it was often referred to as "Crowtown," the arrival of Edwards, Daniel, and Daniel's crew of strapping young sons meant competition for scarce work, and even more options for white landowners when it came time to choose the next year's laborers and tenants. As Ed Johnson closed his census book, wished Buck Daniel a good evening, and walked back down the hill, he would have passed Tom Crow's general store, Mt. Zion School, the Oddfellows Hall, and the clean white spire of Pleasant Grove Church. In May of 1910, as Johnson unhitched his horse and headed back toward Cumming, Oscarville must have looked like any other quaint little farming village in north Georgia.

NOT LONG AFTER the Daniel clan moved into Forsyth, something happened to Nettie Knox, for she disappears from the archival records without a trace, leaving her three children—Charlie, fifteen, Ernest, fourteen, and Erma, twelve—to fend for themselves. George Jordan's daughter Ruth was fourteen in 1912, and she recalled that Nettie's children "had become homeless" not long after they moved into the county and were barely surviving even with whatever help their uncle Buck and aunt Catie could afford to give. "I remember passing these children," Jordan said, when it was very cold and seeing these poor kids huddled together outside [an] old abanden [chicken] coop . . . with 2 or 3 joints of old stove pipe for a chimny. They was burning chipps and sticks and roasting red wormes . . . we called them fish wormes. These children had picked cotton for my father many times.

Charlie, Ernest, and Erma must have been living on the edge of starvation, especially during the lean winter months, when there was no cotton to pick and little to scavenge or hunt. At some point Buck Daniel asked his sons Cicero and Harley to see if their white employer, William Bagby, had any work for their cousin Ernest, and in 1910 Bagby's son Gilford offered to make Knox his "hired man." The term itself was an exaggeration, given that Ernest Knox was only fourteen years old when Buck Daniel said he would now live and work at Mr. Bagby's place. The Bagbys offered his best chance for a warm bed at night, a dry roof overhead, and better meals than roasted "fish wormes."

Ernest Knox, October 2nd, 1912

On Monday, September 9th, 1912, Ruth Jordan woke to the news
that Mae Crow, a close friend of her older sister Alice's, had gone
missing in the woods outside of Oscarville. "I [went] to schoole that
morning," Jordan recalled,

> but no one except the teacher was there. So she and I both
> left and started out to join in the serch [for Mae]. But we had
> not gone very far before we seen a big crode coming. We
> stoped while the car that had the girl passed. At that time
> most cars was Fords, Moadle Ts. They had made some kind
> of stracher, and layed it on the top of the back and frount
> seat. We didn't have many hospitals in our county so they
> carried her home.

Falling in with a group of people trailing behind the car, Jordan found the crossroads in Oscarville suddenly transformed into
a crime scene, swarming with reporters who had driven up from
Atlanta, law officers like Bill Reid and Sheriff William Crow of Hall
County, and hundreds of whites from both sides of the river.

As people milled around the little village, Jordan said, their
attention soon turned to a group of black boys who sat watching all
the excitement from the yard of Pleasant Grove Church. Given that
Grant Smith had barely escaped a lynch mob just two days before,
these boys had good reason to keep an eye on the growing crowd of
whites "wrought up" over the attack. "Almost everyone living in a
100 miles was there," Ruth Jordan said,

> and the colord boys wer laying on the grass at the church . . .
> [when] one of the leading citisons of the county . . . walked
> down wher they wer and talked with them a while. They all
> liked this man. He was nice to everyone. After a while the
> man started to go, then he turnd around and sayd, "I found

this merro. Dos it belong to either of you boys?" Then he
showed the glas to them. "Yes sir," Ern Knox sayd, "It's mine."

According to the *Atlanta Constitution,* this "merro"—that is,
mirror—had been found in the woods near Mae Crow's body, and
a label on the back "indicated that it had been bought at Shackelford's store, and Mr. Shackelford identified it as having been pur-
chased by [Ernest Knox]." The discovery of the hand mirror was
seen by many whites as the smoking gun of the case, and taken as
proof that it was Ernest Knox who had attacked Mae Crow. But neither the newspapers nor prosecutors mentioned that when he was
first questioned, Gilford Bagby's young "hired man" freely admitted that the mirror was his and made no attempt to conceal that he
had bought it from Mr. Shackelford. Knox seemed to have no idea
that claiming it might implicate him in a crime.

Once the "leading citison" heard that the mirror belonged to
Ernest Knox, he decided to continue their conversation in private.
"The man ask Ern if he would ride over to a nearby house for some
water," Jordan said,

> [and] after they had got away frome the crowd the man stopped
> his car and told Ern to get out. He then told Ern that he knew
> that Ern had don the crime, but he had to tell who was with
> him. At first the black boy denyed that he knew.
>
> Then this man taken the rope of the well and tyed it around
> Ern's neck, then the boy seen if he didn't tell the whole thing
> he would be hung.

Soon newspapers all over the state would claim that Ernest Knox
had freely admitted to attacking Mae Crow, but what the journalists failed to mention was that this so-called confession occurred
during a form of torture known as a mock lynching.

During the first decades of the twentieth century, newspapers often reported with amusement on the tactic of terrorizing black suspects until they confessed. During the same month that Knox was lured to the well in Oscarville, for example, a Minnesota paper ran the headline "Mock Lynching Extorts Truth" and told how Sheriff Andrew Stahl of Kenosha, Wisconsin, had used "novel means to frighten [a] negro." According to the story, after a black man was accused of grand larceny, "a 'mob' was organized by Sheriff Stahl in a realistic manner. The negro was overpowered and apparently about to be strangled when he broke down and confessed."

For victims of such interrogation, there was little difference between real and "mock" violence, since a ruse arranged to fool a suspect could—and often did—change mid-performance into a summary execution, especially if the victim refused to cooperate. Attacked by white men who quickly turned from a play-acting "mob" into an actual one, the African American man in Kenosha did the only thing that might save his life: he confessed to whatever crime his white attackers claimed he had committed.

Ruth Jordan's letter is the only surviving account of the minutes that led up to Ernest Knox's "confession," and her story leaves little doubt that Knox was presented with the same desperate choice as the man in Kenosha. Knox had every reason to think he was about to die when a man "taken the rope of the well and tyed it around [his] neck," and he knew that a white man could do anything he pleased to a poor black teenager—particularly one who stood accused of attacking a white girl. It is easy to imagine that, as the rope tightened around his throat, Ernest Knox finally opened his mouth and, between gasps, agreed with everything the man said. When the "leading citison" told people in Oscarville what Ernest Knox had admitted at the well, reporters ran off in search of the nearest telephone. By the next morning, news that the killer had

"Confessed His Crime" was splashed across the front pages of the *Atlanta Constitution* and the *Georgian*.

BUT GIVEN THAT rape accusations often led to castration, torture, and burning alive for black suspects in Jim Crow Georgia, is it even plausible to think that a black teenager who had raped and bludgeoned a white woman would choose to spend the next morning watching hundreds of people flood into Oscarville, rather than running as far and as fast as the night could take him? If Knox were guilty, would he have simply gone back to bed at Gilford Bagby's place, then spent the morning watching the sheriff and his deputies comb the area for clues?

By all accounts, the investigation had turned up nothing until a rich white man draped an arm around Knox's shoulder, then led him off to get a drink of water from a nearby well. By the time they returned, Sheriff Reid, Mayor Harris, and the rest of the white people of Forsyth had exactly what they needed: a "barefooted, fiendish-looking" black rapist who had admitted to "the dastardly assault."

Even decades later, in 1980, Ruth Jordan was careful not to reveal the identity of Knox's attacker at the well, but he was almost certainly a man named Marvin Bell. The *Georgian* reported that Bell was among a large group of Cumming men who drove to Oscarville "eager to unearth a clue that might unravel the mystery," and the *Gainesville News* said that soon thereafter, "Knox confessed and was rushed here in an automobile by Mr. Marvin Bell." As a scion of one of the county's oldest and wealthiest families, the thirty-five-year-old Bell certainly fit Ruth Jordan's description of a "leading citison" who was well liked by everyone.

While he had made a name for himself as a star of the Cumming baseball team, Marvin Bell was also widely known as a cousin to Hiram Parks Bell, one of Forsyth's founding fathers and its most revered statesman. Hiram Parks Bell had been toughened

U.S. Representative Hiram Parks Bell

by a childhood spent helping to clear and fence his family's home-
stead in the 1830s; he went on to become a leading politician of his
day, and an embodiment of the ideals of many white southerners.
Elected to the Georgia senate in 1861, he resigned to enlist in the
Confederate army, where he rose through the ranks from private to
colonel of the Forty-third Georgia Regiment. "Colonel Bell," as he
was known ever after, was a delegate to the Confederate Congress
in 1864 and 1865, and in 1873–75 and 1877–79 he represented
Georgia's Ninth District in the U.S. House of Representatives.

Bell was also an unrepentant white supremacist, and while serving in Washington he railed against the Civil Rights Act of 1866,
which gave African Americans citizenship, calling it a "legislative
folly . . . intended to harass and humiliate the white people." Bell
considered himself one of the "able and patriotic" men who, after
forcing black leaders from office in the 1870s, "established a Constitution that secured white over black domination."

When Marvin Bell—cousin to the famed Hiram Parks Bell—arrived in Oscarville, he would have trailed behind him an unmistakable air of power, money, and authority. And in that moment when Bell coiled the bucket-rope into a makeshift noose around Knox's neck, the two extremes of Forsyth's social castes were momentarily locked in a terrible embrace: Bell at the very highest reaches of the white power structure, Knox at the very bottom of the black underclass. No surprise, then, that when Marvin Bell put his mouth to Ernest Knox's ear and demanded a confession, a confession was precisely what he got.

That Bell was from one of Cumming's most powerful families may also help explain why, having come close to lynching Knox himself, he did not hand his prisoner over to a mob of Oscarville farmers. These were men whom Bell saw as far beneath him, and as they stoked a bonfire and pleaded for a chance to burn Ernest Knox at the stake, Marvin Bell quickly turned from Knox's tormentor to his rescuer.

"If the prisoner had not been spirited away," said a reporter for the *Constitution,* "nothing short of troops would have prevented a burning." The *Gainesville News* emphasized that it was not just the attack on Crow that fueled this new lynching fever but also the men's frustration at having been run out of town by government troops just two days before, and prevented from lynching Grant Smith and Toney Howell. "On account of the intense feeling . . . in Forsyth County last Thursday," one witness said, "it was almost certain that the negro [Knox] would have been lynched had he been carried to Cumming." But having held Knox's life in his hands just a few minutes before, Marvin Bell now cranked his Model T and shoved the terrified boy inside.

Bell headed east out of Forsyth, across the Chattahoochee River at Browns Bridge, and into the neighboring town of Gainesville, the seat of Hall County. There, he delivered Knox into the custody of Sheriff William Crow. According to the *Gainesville News*, "when it became known that the negro was in jail [in Hall County] and had confessed, there became wild rumors of lynching." Soon the Gainesville jail was surrounded by Hall County men who had heard that a black rapist was locked inside, as well as people from Forsyth County who had pursued Knox and Bell in buggies and on horseback, arriving just as darkness fell. A reporter for the *Constitution* described how "rumor was passing freely that a lynching would result" when Judge J. B. Jones ordered that the prisoner be moved for his own safety—this time all the way to Atlanta.

At seven-fifteen p.m. on what was surely the longest day of his short life, Ernest Knox found his wrist once again in the iron grip of a white man. When he heard the clatter of Deputy Henry Ward's key in the lock, he must have feared that he was about to be thrust out the front door, into the hands of a lynch mob. Instead, Deputy Ward snuck the prisoner out through the back, and Knox, who before that day had in all likelihood never ridden in an automobile in his life, was once more pushed into the back seat of a car with its engine racing. Knox heard the crunch of gravel, the roar of the engine, and fading shouts shrinking behind him in the dark. The next day's paper told readers that Deputy Ward, fearful that he was being pursued, covered "the distance from Gainesville to Atlanta in [the] almost record time of three hours," at moments reaching the jaw-dropping speed of forty miles per hour.

Knox slept that night in the Fulton County Jail, which was known all over Georgia as "the Tower"—an imposing stone fortress that had been designed to keep Atlanta's worst offenders in and its most determined lynch mobs out. When groups returning from Gainesville reported that Knox had been transferred to the Tower, men in Forsyth realized they'd been outmaneuvered. But that didn't mean they'd given up. After midnight, a reporter at the *Constitution* was busy tapping away, recounting the day's events. "The white people of the mountain section around Gainesville and Forsyth county are incensed," he wrote. "And even though the guilty negro is imprisoned 53 miles away . . . more race trouble is feared." As sixteen-year-old Ernest Knox struggled to sleep with the sounds of the city humming all around him, many people in Forsyth stayed up late, too—venting their shock at the week's second attack on a white woman, and their disgust at the slow machinations of the law.

4

AND THE MOB CAME ON

Bill Reid was in a foul mood when he got to work on Tuesday morning. Upstaged by Marvin Bell, and humiliated by the fact that the "confessed rapist" had been delivered not to Cumming but to the Gainesville city police, Reid was under pressure to make more arrests, particularly after a rumor circulated that Ernest Knox was not alone when he attacked Mae Crow. Overnight, the initial reports of Crow's injuries had been elaborated into a kind of horror story. "Those men had raped [Mae] many times," Ruth Jordan said years later. "They bit her on the legs . . . and cut her and chewed the nipples off her bristes. In an hour all the people in the county had armed ther selves and was just waiting."

Reid and Lummus rode out to Oscarville first thing Tuesday and found that a group of white men had already surrounded Marcus Waldrip's property and taken prisoner one of Waldrip's field hands—the young black man known as "Big Rob" Edwards, who had been seen with Knox on the day of the attack. Knox may have been the "confessed rapist" whose name was in all the Atlanta papers, but he was also far out of reach in the Fulton Tower and under the protection of the Atlanta city police. Unable to lay a finger on him, whites in Oscarville now directed their wrath at Rob

Edwards, who, just like Toney Howell, was conspicuous as an out-sider in the small, isolated community of Oscarville, having been raised in South Carolina.

When Reid and Lummus arrived on the scene, the *Georgian* said, they "went immediately and took the negro from his captors," who were planning to lynch and burn him right there on Waldrip's place. After placing Edwards under arrest on suspicion of rape, Reid and his deputy hurried back toward town, trailing behind them a grow-ing crowd of white men with shotguns and pistols in their hands. Having watched Grant Smith, Toney Howell, and Ernest Knox escape the noose in the past few days, many in the crowd had lost all patience with the law and now saw it as their duty to defend the white women of the county from further attacks. A reporter described the atmosphere as they followed Edwards all the way into Cumming:

> The country roads were dotted with mounted and armed men all hurrying toward the county seat . . . as though some wire-less telegraphy had spread the news of [Edwards's] capture. The men of Forsyth . . . had been gathering all day, bearing rifles and shotguns under their arms, others with coats bulg-ing where a heavy revolver filled a hip pocket. They were silent for the most part, but they gathered in little knots at the cor-ners of the streets . . . and waited.

The *Journal* agreed that "mob spirit [was] at fever heat" when Reid and Lummus finally brought Edwards to the Cumming square, forced their way through the throng, and managed to lock him inside an iron-barred cell. When they peered out through a window, a mob of more than two thousand men swarmed around the little brick jail.

When the lawyers, merchants, and gentlemen farmers of Cum-ming looked up from their desks and shop counters to see what was causing all the commotion, they found the same chaotic scene with which the "race troubles" had begun the previous Saturday. Now, as then, hundreds of whites were screaming themselves hoarse in the public square, demanding that officials hand over an accused black man. Like Smith, Howell, and Knox before him, Rob Edwards would have been able to pick out individual voices in that crowd—men whose names and faces he knew well from having worked shoulder to shoulder with them in the orchards, cotton fields, and corn rows of the county. When these men threatened to slit his throat, castrate him, and roast him like a hog, Edwards knew they meant every word. A big, lumbering man of twenty-four, Edwards could only watch silently as Lummus came and went with his ring of jangling keys.

IT IS AT this point in the story that Bill Reid committed the most incriminating act of his entire tenure as Forsyth County sheriff—which was to simply disappear. A reporter noted his absence as if it were a minor detail, writing that the sheriff "left the jail as soon as he had lodged his prisoner there, and Deputy M. G. Lummus was left in charge."

But given the ongoing political rivalry between the Forsyth County sheriff and his deputy—Reid defeated Lummus in the 1912 election, and would face him again in 1914—it is almost certain that Reid's disappearing act was the result of a careful calculation. The governor had ordered local lawmen to stop the spread of mob violence in Forsyth, but as a future Klansman himself (whose name appears on a list of local KKK members in the 1920s), Reid was no doubt sympathetic with the crowd chanting for Edwards to be handed over, and as eager as they were to see a black man punished for the attack on Mae Crow. To help them get what they wanted, all Reid had to do was nothing. And so, as the mob swelled, and as the threat of a lynching grew more and more serious, Reid called Lum-

mus over and told him to take command of the little jail. Then he
rose from his desk, adjusted his hat, and walked out through the
packed square, with no explanation but for the occasional nod to
friends and relatives as he passed.

By leaving Lummus in charge at the moment of greatest crisis,
Reid neatly sidestepped what was, for him, a political train wreck—
and thrust his rival directly into its path. If the young deputy failed
to hold off the lynchers, it was now his head that would roll when
the governor called from Atlanta. And if Lummus somehow succeeded in repelling the lynch party, it was he who would be remembered, come election time, as a "nigger lover" who'd stopped the
white men of Forsyth from avenging a dying girl.

AS HE AMBLED home down Castleberry Road, Reid couldn't have
failed to understand the dire situation in which he'd left Gay Lummus and Rob Edwards. In 1912, in Georgia, mobs regularly stormed
county jails and abducted black prisoners—and it had happened
many times before in Cumming. Fifty years earlier, in 1862, the
Daily Constitutionalist had reported that a "negro boy belonging to
Judge E. Lewis, of Forsyth County, was taken out of the Cumming
jail and hung on last Saturday night by four men, for improper
advances toward a lady. The men were relatives of the lady, and
at home on furlough at the time the deed was committed." The
matter-of-fact tone of the report suggests just how unremarkable it
was for a black man to be taken from police custody and lynched
in the public square: "[There has been] no excitement among the
people on the subject."

In 1870, the *Chicago Tribune* reported that three other black
residents of Forsyth were "summarily hung one morning by the
roadside, in front of their own dwelling . . . old man Hutchins sus-
pended to the limb of a tree by an old ox chain . . . and his two
sons by green withes cut from the bushes." Sixteen years later, in

1886, a Forsyth man named Pete Holmes was accused of raping a ten-year-old white girl and was locked up in the Cumming jail. The *Atlanta Constitution* called Holmes "a jet black, greasy negro, just fifteen years of age," and reported that "when intelligence of the crime began to spread, the friends of the [girl's] family became terribly stirred up, and before night a strong mob had been organized to lynch Holmes." Even when, the next day, he was sentenced to fifteen years in the penitentiary, "people did not think the sentence sufficient," and Holmes was only saved from a lynch mob when the county sheriff spirited him out the back of the jail and rushed him to safety in the Fulton Tower.

Such scenes were common enough in post-emancipation Forsyth that in 1897 Judge George Gober made a special trip from Atlanta to Cumming in order to try a man named Charley Ward, who stood accused of raping a prominent famer's fifteen-year-old daughter. "Gober gave him the limit allowed by law, twenty years," said the *Macon Telegraph*, and "a speedy trial was had to prevent a case of lynching, which had been planned to take place Christmas day."

These earlier lynchings and near lynchings suggest that rather than yielding to a sudden, irresistible passion—as lynchings were usually portrayed—the men pounding on the door of the Cumming jail on Tuesday, September 10th, 1912, were taking part in a time-honored ritual. Many would have heard tales of past lynchings from their fathers and grandfathers, and when Rob Edwards was arrested on suspicion of rape, they saw their chance to finally join that grand tradition: to show that they, too, were men of honor, and no less committed to the defense of white womanhood.

IF REID'S SOLUTION to the problem of a lynch mob was to pretend it did not exist, his strategy worked, at least in the short term. According to one witness, Lummus "stood his ground bravely against the assault and was warned to get back and save himself." Hearing the shouts and curses of hundreds of men who now viewed him as nothing but an obstacle to be overcome or passed through, Lummus reportedly "locked the doors of the jail and put the heavy bars in place." He positioned himself between his prisoner and the mob, and through the barred door he pleaded with mob leaders to settle down, go back home, and let the Blue Ridge Circuit court take care of Big Rob Edwards.

But outside a murmur was passing through the crowd, and soon a man who'd been sent to a nearby blacksmith's shop was ushered to the front—a long crowbar clenched in one hand, a sledgehammer in the other. As the front door creaked and splintered under the first blow of the sledge, Lummus drew his pistol, spread his arms, and backed toward the row of cells. At the second blow, daylight streamed through a gash in the wooden planks, and just like that, the *Georgian* said, "the mob came on." A reporter told how

> farmers known to all the countryside were in front of the band, which advanced in broad daylight, without a mask, without the slightest fear of what the future might bring. The barred doors . . . gave way under a few heavy blows and the leaders rushed in, followed by as many men as could crowd into the corridors.

Having risked his life to protect Edwards, Lummus was shoved aside as dozens of men stomped over the wreckage of the door and headed straight for the row of cells at the rear of the building. Inside one of them stood Big Rob Edwards, his back against the red brick wall.

WHEN LEADERS OF the mob emerged from the jail with a black man, they were cheered by thousands of whites who had rushed into town in hopes of witnessing exactly such a spectacle. "Out into the sunshine came the negro," said the *Georgian*, "gray in his terror, his eyes rolling in abject fear." Edwards "muttered prayers and supplications to the mob," one reporter noted, but these were soon drowned in the rain of blows which fell upon him. A rope was brought from a nearby store and a noose dropped around the negro's neck. The mob was fighting for a chance to get at its victim, and only the certainty of wounding or killing a friend kept the drawn pistols silent.

Across the street and up to the public square hurried the mob, its victim at the fore. The negro had lost his feet by this time and was being dragged by the rope, his body bumping over the stones. At the corner of the square a telephone post and its cross-arm offered a convenient gallows. The end of the rope was tossed over the arm, a dozen hands grasped it and the negro, perhaps already dead, was drawn high into the air.

After a week of frustration, the abduction and killing took only minutes. There is no way to know whether Edwards died from a gunshot wound, a crowbar to the skull, or strangulation as he was dragged around the Cumming square—but when his limp, blood-slick body finally rose into view high over the crowd, thousands of people joined in. As they loaded their weapons and took aim, rebel yells and howls of celebration rose from the crowd. "Pistols and rifles cracked," a witness said, "and the corpse was mangled into something hardly resembling a human form."

The *Marietta Journal* claimed that "as soon as the guns of those composing the mob were empty the crowd quietly dispersed and returned to their work," but other accounts suggest that many in the crowd looked up at Edwards's corpse and felt not satisfied but more hungry than ever. They had finally killed one of the accused rapists, and now their thoughts turned to the five young men arrested in connection with the Grice assault. Those prisoners were only forty miles south in Marietta, and even as people stood gawking at Edwards's body, leaders of the mob waved men into cars bound

Charlie Hale, Lawrenceville, Georgia, 1911. Hale died twenty miles south of Cumming and, like Rob Edwards, was abducted from the local jail and hung from a telephone pole on the town square.

for the Marietta jail—where they hoped to do to Grant Smith and Toney Howell exactly what they'd just done to Rob Edwards.

SHERIFF REID EMERGED only once "the excitement" was over—when he could claim to have had no idea that Rob Edwards wasn't still asleep in his cell. Having left Lummus in command, Reid could now shake his head and tell reporters he didn't know who'd broken down the jailhouse door, who'd fired the first shot, or how exactly his young deputy had failed to protect the prisoner. After learning that some of the lynchers were speeding out of town, Reid made a phone call to Judge Newt Morris in Marietta, warning him that "the mountaineers were threatening to come . . . and storm the jail there." In response, Morris ordered Cobb County Sheriff J. H. Kincaid to move the Grice prisoners yet again, this time to the one jail in the area that could stop any mob: Atlanta's Fulton Tower, where the night before Ernest Knox had been sent for safekeeping.

In the end, the cars from Forsyth turned around just outside Marietta, when a local farmer told them that the Grice prisoners had already been transferred to the Tower. Pulling back into the Cumming square after dark, they rolled slowly past the splintered door frame that just a few hours before had been ripped to pieces with sledges and crowbars. On a corner near the courthouse, they passed the mutilated, almost unrecognizable corpse of Rob Edwards, still hanging from the yardarm of a telephone pole. A reporter for the *Georgian* took a last glance at the scene before heading back south to Atlanta. "[Edwards's] body swings there to this hour," he wrote, "riddled with bullets, dangling in the wind as a warning to frightened negroes, who are hurrying from the town."

As the last of the crowd drifted toward home, Reid ordered Lummus to cut Edwards down and drag him to the lawn of the Forsyth County Courthouse. There, the *North Georgian* said, "his body lay [out] all night, without a guard, and it was not touched." The next morning, county coroner W. R. Barnett knelt over the stiff corpse, examining the lacerations on Edwards's swollen neck, the hundreds of holes from bullets and buckshot, and the deep impact wounds in his skull. Barnett's report concluded that the twenty-four-year-old black man had suffered multiple gunshots and blunt trauma to the head. Despite eyewitness accounts saying that "farmers known to all the countryside" had come "unmasked [and] threw

West Canton Street, Cumming, c. 1912

off all attempt at concealment," Barnett wrote that Rob Edwards died at the hands of "parties unknown."

In the days that followed, Georgia newspapers were quick to declare that the bloody ritual had been an end, not a beginning, to Forsyth's "race trouble." "The provocation of the people of Forsyth was great," said the *Cherokee Advance,* "and they simply did what Anglo-Saxons have done North, South, East and West . . . where negroes have outraged white women. They formed a mob and took the law into their own hands."

The *Atlanta Journal* agreed that, as gruesome as the killing was, whites had now exhausted their rage and "no further trouble was expected" at Cumming. An editorial in the *Gainesville Times* went further, congratulating the white mobs of Forsyth for having done no worse, and for having lynched no more. "Two criminal assaults in one week wrought up the people to a high pitch," the editors said, "[and] they controlled themselves with remarkable self-restraint."

5

A STRAW IN THE
WHIRLWIND

While the public whipping of Grant Smith had put the entire black community on edge, the sight of Rob Edwards's corpse hanging over the public square sent whole wagon trains of refugees out onto the roads of the county; they fled south toward Atlanta, east toward Gainesville, and west toward Canton. African Americans in Forsyth knew that nothing they said or did was likely to convince Bill Reid to pursue those who had murdered Rob Edwards. And if anyone still held out hope that, in the wake of the killing, whites might leave their black neighbors in peace, they learned otherwise the next morning, when tensions rose over the burning of a building near Cumming.

When they heard that the storehouse of a white man named Will Buice had mysteriously caught fire in the night, whites concluded that it was the work of black arsonists, retaliating for the lynching. The *Georgian* reported that "the clouds of race war which have hung over Forsyth . . . threaten to break into a storm of bloodshed today." The fire was taken as proof that, just like in Plainville, Cumming was now on the brink of a black insurrection. "Rumors that the negroes . . . are rising and arming themselves have led almost to a panic among the women of the little town," one observer wrote, adding that

> even the conservative men fear that the lynching of yesterday and the burning of a store today are merely the first movements in a race war which may sweep the county and bring death to many. Citizens are arming for trouble.

But despite all the rumors, most black residents were too busy trying to protect their families to think about retaliation. Like African Americans all over the Jim Crow South, they understood that even the mildest forms of resistance or the faintest hint of protest could trigger a new wave of white violence. Many would have heard about the black woman in Okemah, Oklahoma, who, in 1911, had been killed for no crime other than defending her fifteen-year-old son against a lynch mob. Newspapers reported that when Laura Nelson confronted the white men who had accused her boy of stealing, Nelson was dragged from her house and repeatedly raped before she and the son she'd tried to protect were hanged side by side from a bridge over the Canadian River.

If anyone in Forsyth's black community thought of publicly naming the leaders of the mob that had killed Edwards, they would have understood the terrible risk. Only a few years later, in 1918, a pregnant woman named Mary Turner would be killed in Lowndes County, Georgia, for having openly grieved for her husband, Hayes. When she threatened to swear out warrants against the men who had abducted and lynched him, the response was swift and savage, even by the standards of Jim Crow Georgia. According to historian Philip Dray, "before a crowd that included women and children, Mary was stripped, hung upside down by the ankles, soaked with gasoline, and roasted to death. In the midst of this torment, a white man opened her swollen belly with

The lynching of Laura Nelson, 1911

a hunting knife and her infant fell to the ground, gave a cry, and was stomped to death."

Like Mary Turner, Jane Daniel must have carried an almost unbearable burden of grief, rage, and fear once she learned— hardly a day after her cousin Ernest had been taken prisoner— that her husband, Rob, had been hanged on the Cumming square, his body gawked at by whites, and torn apart by hundreds of bullets. But if Jane was tempted to go to county officials seeking justice, or to raise her voice in lament, she knew that to do so could have deadly consequences. It had happened many times and would happen again in Georgia: after lynching a black victim, mobs often turned their attention to surviving family members—for crying out in grief, or calling for arrests, or for simply knowing who it was who had pulled a trigger or lobbed a rope over a tree limb. Like thousands of other widows of lynched black men, Jane Daniel knew that her only chance at safety was silence.

Not even that was enough in the end, for on Wednesday, September 11th, newspapers reported that Jane Daniel, her brother Oscar, and their neighbor Ed Collins had been arrested in connection with the Crow assault. According to the *Constitution*, "Another lynching at Cumming [was] narrowly averted" when "a mob formed to take . . . these negroes . . . and swing them up to the same telephone pole on which their partner in crime swung yesterday." This time, though, Mayor Charlie Harris was ready, and before the mob could organize a second siege of the county jail, he had Reid and his deputies "slip [the prisoners] out of the jail and [make] a run . . . in automobiles for Atlanta."

HAVING SAFELY DELIVERED Jane, Oscar, and Ed Collins to the Fulton Tower and added them to a group of prisoners that now included eleven black residents of Forsyth, Bill Reid took time Wednesday morning to speak with Atlanta reporters. Under the headline "Graphic Story of Terror Reign," the *Georgian* gave Reid center stage, introducing him to readers as "the picturesque sheriff of Forsyth county" who came to Atlanta with a carload of black prisoners and tales of a mob run wild in the Georgia foothills. Squinting down at a crowd of reporters with their pencils poised, Reid quickly warmed to his role: as the mustachioed, six-shooter-carrying country lawman fighting a "race war" on the north Georgia frontier. "The people of Cumming have been sleeping with one eye open," Reid began.

The fall of night has brought fear and dread to the town and surrounding county, for there [is] no telling what might happen—it's the dread of treachery, the torch, and the knife stab in the back. We could easily handle any emergency in the day time. The white people are armed and would promptly crush any uprising on the part of the blacks. Excitement has been high, and an uneasy feeling pervade[s] the community.

Given that raids on black churches and homes were already driving many families across the county line, Reid's account of the situation in Forsyth now seems not just distorted but downright delusional. He describes a white population in terror of an impending "uprising on the part of the blacks" and fearful that they might wake to "the knife stab in the back"—when in truth the only real "uprising" was being carried out by white vigilantes and arsonists. Yet even as black families stood guard over their homes, listening for the sound of approaching hoofbeats or the ominous snap of a twig, whites were the ones in a state of constant paranoia, unable to shake their deepest, oldest fear: that the sins of their forefathers would finally be avenged by the children and grandchildren of slaves.

When reporters turned to the subject of Rob Edwards's lynching, Reid hit his stride as a star in the tabloid drama. On the day of the lynching, the sheriff had gone to great lengths to extricate himself from the thorny problem of opposing a mob that included many of his own relatives, friends, and political supporters. But once he got to Atlanta, he didn't miss an opportunity to recast himself as the hero who had tried in vain to save Rob Edwards.

"I was at my home when the mob began to form," Reid said, "and feeling against the negro burst forth in all its fury." Though newspaper reports all agreed that it was Lummus who was left to "lock the doors of the jail and put the heavy bars in place," Reid now claimed it was he who had bravely tried to thwart the lynchers:

I realized it was too late to attempt to get [Edwards] out of the jail and spirit him away. There was but one thing to do—I hid the jail keys. I did this as I knew that even though I should be overpowered, the mob would still be handicapped.

At a single stroke, Reid's revision of the story solved two problems. He erased the genuine bravery with which Deputy Lummus had stood his ground, and claimed that it was actually he, Forsyth's crafty old sheriff, who had slowed the rioters. Such quick thinking had not ultimately saved Rob Edwards, Reid implied, but that was not because he hadn't done his darnedest. "A few minutes" after he hid the keys to the jail, he told reporters,

a crowd of fully 100 men called at my home and demanded the keys. I told them they could not get the keys and begged them not to attempt violence . . . then at a signal the crowd went [back] to the jail. There was no jailer on duty there, as I have to look after the jail and care of the prisoners myself.

By whitewashing Lummus out of the scene, and skipping over the fact that he himself had abandoned his post, Reid implied that he was the last line of defense. "The mob poured wildly into the jail, smashing locks as they came to them," he said, adding just enough detail to help readers forget that he had not, in fact, been present at the time:

Breaking down Rob Edwards' cell door, the infuriated men yanked the cringing negro into the corridor . . . someone struck him on the head with a sledge hammer, fracturing his skull. Then someone else shot him.

As a final flourish, Reid said that "several friends kept [me] in [my] home" while the jail was under attack. Then he reminded readers that even had he been there, "the big sheriff" would have been unable to save Edwards:

> Of course, it would have been all the same if I *had* been there
> . . . Even though I do carry about a lot of flesh and muscle, I
> would have been like a straw in the whirlwind against that
> crowd.

The sheriff had hardly finished his tale when a reporter for the *Georgian,* recognizing a scoop when he heard one, ran off to file his story. Reid had managed, in one rambling, Falstaffian interview, to claim that he'd ingeniously hidden the jail keys; that he had been held prisoner by the mob; and that he would have been unable, despite his great strength and muscular physique, to have stopped the lynchers even if, by some superhuman effort, he had managed to escape his captors. With that, the future Ku Klux Klansman and self-proclaimed "straw in the whirlwind" of the lynching climbed into a car and drove off. He was anxious, he said out the window, "to be on the scene when darkness came."

THE STORY OF the "race riot" in Forsyth disappeared from Georgia's newspapers almost as quickly as it had appeared. In a single week, Cumming had witnessed the near lynching of Grant Smith; the arrival of the Marietta Rifles to quell an imagined race war; the discovery of Mae Crow's bloody body; the killing of Rob Edwards; and the imprisonment of nearly a dozen young black suspects, who were now awaiting trial in the Fulton Tower. As Reid drove back north on the afternoon of September 12th, editors in Atlanta were proofing the last of the stories they would run about Forsyth for almost a month. "Quiet reigns in Cumming," they assured readers. "No disorder of any kind."

When Reid went to work the next morning, he found the town

square humming with activity for the first time in days. Wealthy wives of the county were finally willing to brave the streets, and visions of a black revolution were fading into the background as Cumming returned, for the most part, to business as usual.

Everyone knew that the prisoners would be brought back from Atlanta to stand trial, and that their return would whip "the violent element" of the county into another fury, particularly if witnesses were called—as they surely would be—to testify about Mae Crow's injuries. But all of that lay in the future, and in an effort to defuse the situation, Judge Newt Morris announced that both the Grice and Crow cases would be postponed until the next regular session of the Blue Ridge Circuit court, scheduled for late October. This left white residents in a state of uncertainty, particularly since Bud and Azzie Crow's daughter was still unconscious out in Oscarville, in critical condition from her head wounds. Mayor Harris and Deputy Lummus wouldn't have been the only Cumming residents who looked warily toward the future, wondering just what sort of mayhem news of her death might unleash.

BUT FOR HUNDREDS of black people in the county, the worst kind of trouble had already begun. Though it would take weeks before reports reached Atlanta, in the days after the attack on Crow a nighttime ritual began to unfold, as each evening at dusk groups of white men gathered at the crossroads of the county. They came with satchels of brass bullets, shotgun shells, and stoppered glass bottles of kerosene, and sticks of "Red Cross" dynamite poked out through the tops of their saddlebags. When darkness fell, the night riders set out with one goal: to stoke the terror created by the lynching of Edwards and use it to drive black people out of Forsyth County for good.

In 1907, W. E. B. Du Bois had put into words what every "colored" person in Georgia knew from experience, which was that "the police system of the South was primarily designed to control slaves. . . . And tacitly assumed that every white man was *ipso facto* a member of that police." In the first decade of the twentieth century, the days when all white men had been legally empowered to pursue and arrest fugitive slaves were only fifty years in the past, and the fathers and grandfathers of many locals would have been part of such posses in the days of slavery.

So it must have seemed natural to many whites when, each night around sundown, a knock came at the door and the adult men of the family were summoned to join a group heading out toward the clusters of black cabins scattered around Forsyth—along the Chattahoochee out in Oscarville, in the shadow of Sawnee Mountain north of Cumming, and south, toward Shakerag and Big Creek. It would take months—and, in a handful of cases, years—before the in-town blacks of Cumming were finally forced out, since many lived under the protection of rich white men, in whose kitchens and dining rooms they served. Instead, it was to the homes of cotton pickers, sharecroppers, and small landowners that the night riders went first, and it was these most vulnerable families who fled in the first waves of the exodus.

Written traces of the raids are few and far between and consist mostly of vague reports of "lawlessness" after dark. Since journalists only started writing about the expulsions once the wagon trains of refugees grew too large and too numerous to ignore, it is hard to say precisely what took place on those first nights of the terror. Some of the attacks later made headlines in Atlanta ("Negroes Flee from Forsyth," "Enraged White People Are Driving Blacks from County"), and it's likely that similar raids had been happening since the discovery of Mae Crow's body in early September. The night riders fired shots into front doors, threw rocks through windows, and hollered warnings that it was time for black families to "get." But of all their methods, torches and kerosene worked best, since a fire created a blazing sign for all to see and left the victims no place to ever come back to. In mid-October, the *Augusta Chronicle* reported that "a score or more of homes have been burned during the past few weeks . . . and five negro churches."

The arsonists must have been terrifying wherever they struck, but for Forsyth's poor black farmers, the burning of churches was a true catastrophe, striking not just at the community's spiritual home but at what Du Bois called "the social centre of Negro life." In 1903, sitting in his Atlanta University office, just forty miles south, he had described Georgia's rural black congregations as "the most characteristic expression of African character" in the entire community. "Take a typical church," Du Bois wrote.

> [It is] finished in Georgia pine, with a carpet, a small organ, and benches. This building is the central club-house of a community of Negroes. Various organizations meet here— the church proper, the Sunday-school, two or three insurance societies, women's societies, secret societies, and mass meetings of various kinds. Entertainments, suppers, and lectures are held. . . . Considerable sums of money are collected and expended here, employment is found for the idle, strangers are introduced, news is disseminated and charity distributed. At the same time this social, intellectual, and economic centre is a religious centre of great power. Depravity, Sin, Redemption, Heaven, Hell, and Damnation are preached twice a Sunday after the crops are laid by.

The erasure of such places from the map of Forsyth was complete. Today, all that's left are a few scant details about the dates on which churches were founded, lot numbers for the land on which they stood, and the names of a handful of ministers and worshippers who once gathered there. Backband Church, out near Oscarville, was where Buck and Catie Daniel sat on Sunday mornings—surrounded by their sons Cicero and Harley, their daughter Jane, and their youngest boy, Oscar—listening to the sermons of a local farmer and preacher named Byrd Oliver. Stoney Point, down in Big Creek, was where on some Sunday in August of 1912 Harriet and Morgan Strickland took their visiting nephew, Toney Howell, to meet the congregation and be welcomed into his aunt and uncle's church. Shiloh Baptist, founded by Reverend Levi Greenlee Sr., lay just outside of town on Kelly Mill Road and was home to many of Cumming's maids, cooks, servants, and butlers.

Faint traces of other black churches are tucked away in handwritten ledgers at the state archives at Morrow; in the collections at the University of Georgia in Athens; even in the basement of the Forsyth courthouse, where a cardboard box atop a metal filing cabinet still holds deeds for the land on which black residents once founded Mt. Fair, Shakerag, and Stoney Point—about which nothing is known but names and approximate locations. All that can be said for certain is that, again and again in the fall of 1912, white men sloshed gasoline and kerosene onto the benches and wooden floors of such rooms, then backed out into the dark, tossing lit matches as they went. All over the county, beneath the ground on which black churches stood, the soil is rich with ashes.

IN THEIR RACE to outdo one another, and to further sensationalize the story, journalists had been reporting Mae Crow's death almost from the moment she was discovered in the woods. "GIRL MURDERED BY NEGRO AT CUMMING" the front page of the *Augusta Chronicle* had blared on September 9th, in an article that informed readers that "the negro's victim died at her home near Cumming tonight." The *Macon Telegraph* went further, claiming that when Ernest Knox attacked Crow, he "beat her into unconsciousness and then threw her over [a] cliff." Once a single false report of Crow's death appeared in print, other editors felt compelled to follow suit, and a typical article in the *Constitution* closed by informing readers of the sad fact that "although every effort was made to save her life, [Crow] died late Monday afternoon." By the beginning of October, interest in the story had grown so intense that the *Georgian* upped the ante, writing that Cumming was in an uproar over "the death of two white women at the hands of negroes."

Meanwhile, Ellen Grice was alive and well out in Big Creek, no doubt busy with the work of running a household and a small farm with her husband, John, and keeping a low profile after all the trouble her allegations had stirred up. Mae Crow lay in her bed in Oscarville, watched and prayed over by her parents, Bud and Azzie, but still very much alive. In the first few days after she was found, Dr. John Hockenhull even told reporters "she will likely recover."

For many locals, Mae became an object of fascination during her sickness, and at least two men were so desperate to get a glimpse of the beautiful, bedridden girl that they made a drunken pilgrimage. According to Azzie Crow, "when our darling daughter was living here at the point of death . . . one Sunday Wheeler Hill and another man came up to our house intoxicated." Hill and his friend, Crow said,

> wanted to see *what the negroes had done* . . . They hung around awhile, and before we knew it, they had gone to the back of the house . . . then pushed open the door and climbed up and were in the room where our precious daughter lay.

As much as they were offended by Hill's intrusion, Bud and Azzie made it clear in a letter to the *North Georgian* that they were not opposed to the raids being waged in their daughter's name and were as anxious as everyone else to be rid of "those fiends of hell, negroes."

As September waned and as the first cold breezes rippled across the Chattahoochee, Mae grew weaker from her injuries, despite everything the doctors of the county had tried, and despite her mother's prayers. At some point during the second week of her coma, Dr. George Brice told Bud and Azzie that their daughter had contracted pneumonia. On September 23rd, 1912—two weeks to the day from when she was first found in the woods—Mae Crow died.

MAE'S FUNERAL WAS held at Pleasant Grove Church, a short walk from the house where she grew up, and in the center of a whole community of Crows. According to her schoolmate Ruth Jordan, the sight of Mae's coffin being lowered into the ground was almost more than the white people of Oscarville could bear. "After she was buried it seemed like all hell broke loose," Jordan recalled. Soon "the night was filled with gunfire [and] burning cabins and churches," and the Jordans could hear whites "shooting at any black they could find."

George Jordan and his wife, Mattie, were poor sharecroppers, like most other whites in Oscarville, but all her life Ruth had heard the story of how, when her mother's mother died at a young age, "a black woman that lived nearby . . . became a mother-figure [to Mattie], teaching her to cook, keep house, and care for the younger children." And so, as they listened to the crack of gunshots and smelled the smoke of distant fires, George and Mattie Jordan feared for their black neighbors.

At one point, Ruth's father went out to check on an African American couple named Garrett and Josie Cook, who owned twenty-seven acres not far from the land George Jordan was working as a sharecropper. George told his wife that he was going out "to get news of the goings on," but with gangs of night riders on the move, Forsyth had become dangerous even for a forty-four-year-old white farmer like Jordan. As he "walked down the road that night,"

Ruth remembered, "he was drawn on by a group of armed white men [and] it scared him so bad he came home."

At first light, George Jordan walked toward Garrett Cook's place. "Pa went to check on them," Ruth Jordan said, and he found that their house "had been shot so full of holes that all the legs on the tables, chairs, and bed had been shot off." When George called out, Garrett and Josie Cook finally emerged, having spent the night hiding in the woods:

> Pa told this man to go back to his farm so the two of them could defend it against anyone that tried to take it from him. . . . The man replied, "George, that would just get us both killed," and he left Forsyth County forever.

For days afterward, the Jordans could hear the sounds of the night riders each evening at dusk, and this went on "every night," Ruth Jordan said, "until no colored was left." Asked whether her father was ever challenged by locals for having tried to help his black neighbors, Jordan answered that to her knowledge "the subject was never again brought up by any of the whites involved."

ISABELLA HARRIS, THE eight-year-old daughter of Cumming mayor Charlie Harris, also remembered that September as a terrifying time, particularly once she learned that the night riders were not "mountaineers" from outside the county but gangs of ordinary white men, well known to all. Harris recalled that one day as she walked home from school in Cumming, "a group of men, part of a mob, passed me in the dirt side walk." As they stormed past, Harris said,

> They looked ahead of them, their eyes angry, their faces impassive with anger and determination. I was so frightened

that . . . I climbed to the top of a rail fence and clung there
until these men with their horrible faces had gone by.

Such mobs may have been on the other side of Du Bois's "color
line," but they were far from strangers to the black people they terrorized in the weeks after Mae Crow's death. When black residents
like Garrett and Josie Cook woke to the sound of a rock smashing
through a window or the jangle of bridles outside their door, the
order to leave was usually delivered by men whose voices they had
heard many times before: employers and landowners for whom
they had plowed and picked cotton; merchants with whom they
had traded; and white neighbors they had lived and worked with
for years.

And whereas in early September, men from the church picnic
had been bold enough to try to stand up to the white men pursuing
Grant Smith, after the lynching, and in the wake of Mae Crow's
death, it didn't take much to "run off" the few black residents still
in the county. Joel Whitt, a local white man who was twenty-three
in 1912, said that in the beginning, the night riders used gunfire
and torches, just as Ruth Jordan remembered. But later, Whitt
recalled, "Certain men would go to a black person's home with
sticks tied up in a little bundle [and] leave 'em at the door." By late
October, if you made such a thing and placed it outside the cabin
of some last, proud black farmer, by sunup he and his whole family
would be gone.

6

THE DEVIL'S OWN HORSES

ven as refugees flooded into neighboring counties, many residents bristled at criticism of Forsyth and offered a simple explanation for the "lawlessness" that was making headlines all over the state. A "violent element" had come from outside, they told reporters, and "but very few residents . . . participate in the demonstrations." Asked about the makeup of the lynch party that had dragged Rob Edwards out of the county jail, one Cumming man claimed that "the members of the mob live in the hill country" north of Forsyth and came "from adjoining counties and the mountains."

During the century that followed, generations of whites have continued to blame Forsyth's recurring episodes of racial violence on "outsiders," like when, in 1987, County Commissioner David Gilbert claimed that the men who'd attacked African American peace marchers were all from outside the county—despite the fact that seven of the eight men arrested had Forsyth addresses. "The real thing that upsets me," Gilbert told reporters, "is that this whole thing was sprung by outsiders. It's just a bunch of outsiders trying to start trouble in Forsyth County."

The further one gets from 1912, the more frequently whites have

tried to deflect attention away from the county's long history of bigotry by pointing to a specific group: the Ku Klux Klan. It's easy to understand the appeal of such an argument, since it exonerates the ordinary "people of the county" from wrongdoing during the expulsions and implies that they themselves were the victims of an invasion by hooded, cross-burning white supremacists. The only trouble is that in the America of 1912, there was no such thing as the KKK.

WHEN PEOPLE HEAR of that group today, the organization that comes to mind is actually the second incarnation of the Klan—the first having been stamped out in 1871 after the passage of the "Ku Klux Klan Act," which enabled victims of racial violence to sue in federal court and gave President Ulysses S. Grant the right to suspend habeas corpus in pursuit of racial terrorists. Empowered by Congress to suppress Klan activity during Reconstruction, the U.S. Justice Department arrested and convicted many of the group's earliest, most violent members. As a result, the Klan's first grand wizard, former Confederate general Nathan Bedford Forrest, was already calling for the organization to disband in the early 1870s, and by 1872 federal prosecutions had rendered the original KKK all but defunct.

For more than forty years after those original prosecutions, there was no Ku Klux Klan as we now know it. And when it was reborn, the "modern" version of the Klan came to life not in the woods and fields of the rural South but in Hollywood, where in 1915 D. W. Griffith's film *The Birth of a Nation* portrayed costumed "white knights" as the defenders of white womanhood and the saviors of an idealized antebellum world. Griffith found inspiration for his night riders not only in the Reconstruction-era "Ku Kluxers," but also in the romances of Sir Walter Scott, whose heroic highlanders burned crosses to summon their fellow clansmen to battle.

Griffith's groundbreaking motion picture, based on Thomas Dixon Jr.'s play *The Clansman,* was pure fantasy, but millions of white moviegoers saw it as "history written with lighting," as President Woodrow Wilson was famously—and apocryphally—said to have remarked when the film was screened at the White House. As *Birth of a Nation* took the country by storm, life began to imitate art, and when it opened at the Fox Theater in Atlanta in 1915, the streets around the movie house filled with men dressed up in sheets and pointy hoods, many riding horses draped in white cloth, like the heroes of the film. Once inside, moviegoers were mesmerized by a story of chaste white women being stalked by savage black rapists. *The Birth of a Nation* lit up movie houses with the most vivid fantasy of southern whites: a black rebellion, which in Griffith's telling was both political and sexual. As the film's mulatto villain Silas Lynch tells one of his white victims, gesturing out the window at rampaging black soldiers, "See! My people fill the streets. With them I will build a Black Empire and you as a Queen will sit by my side!"

But given that in 1912 Griffith's film, and the birth of the second-wave Klan, still lay three years in the future, it is simply impossible that the black people of Forsyth were "run out" by gangs of white-sheeted Ku Kluxers. Groups of mounted men did appear out of the darkness and terrorize black families in 1912, but they were not robed "white knights," and they did not wear pointy white hoods. Instead, Forsyth's gangs of night riders were farmers and field hands, blacksmiths and store clerks, and, in all likelihood, even a few elected officials like Bill Reid. The whites of Forsyth didn't need klaverns, kleagles, and fiery crosses to organize a lynching in the fall of 1912. All it took back then, as Ruth Jordan said, was "people of the county."

If the mobs were not made up of masked Klansmen, just well-known local men "with their horrible faces," it is natural to won-

der how those ordinary people first coalesced into gangs of night riders. How, that is, did a bunch of farmers decide to set fire to churches led by respected men like Levi Greenlee Jr. and Byrd Oliver, and to train the beads of their shotguns on the houses of peaceful landowners like Joseph and Eliza Kellogg? How did they summon the nerve to threaten the cooks and maids of even the wealthiest, most powerful whites in Cumming? Given that it required an organized effort, kept up not just over months but years, and given just how much will it took to sustain the racial ban for generations—from what source did all that energy come, and in what epic drama did these people think they were at last taking part?

THE LAND NOW known as Forsyth County, Georgia, was once home to Cherokee people, who had lived there for centuries when James Oglethorpe and the first Georgia colonists arrived from England in 1733. As whites settlers pushed farther and farther west during the late eighteenth century, the line separating native land from United States territory was redrawn again and again, as one treaty after another was broken. By the early nineteenth century, the native people of Georgia were confined to an area in the northwest corner of the state known as the Cherokee Territory, which included present-day Forsyth.

The federal government had long sought to "civilize" the Cherokee, and in the first decades of the 1800s the native people of north Georgia were still hoping to live in peace with their new white neighbors. Around 1809, a Cherokee man named Sequoyah began developing the first written alphabet for his people's language, and by the 1820s the Cherokee settlements in northwestern Georgia included Cherokee-built schoolhouses, Cherokee-owned sawmills and blacksmith shops, and vibrant cultural institutions like a tribal newspaper, the *Cherokee Phoenix*. Hollywood may have filled white

imaginations with visions of Indians living in tepees and hunting
with bows and arrows, but by the late 1820s many Cherokee people
in the Georgia foothills had lived alongside their white neighbors
for years and were part of a racially diverse and increasingly integrated frontier community.

When gold was discovered at Dahlonega in 1828, however, it created a renewed push into the Cherokee Territory. Benjamin Parks,
said to have found the very first gold nugget while out deer hunting, told the *Atlanta Constitution* that "once news got abroad" that
there was gold in the Georgia hills,

> there was such excitement as you never saw. It seemed within
> a few days as if the whole world must have heard of it, for men
> came from every state. . . . They came afoot, on horseback and
> in wagons, acting more like crazy men than anything else.

Even as they tried to tolerate all these encroachments into the
Territory, the Cherokee were disenfranchised in the courts, and
they had no legal recourse even when whites stole from them in
broad daylight. As the editor of the *Cherokee Phoenix* put it in 1829,

> Our [white] neighbors who regard no law, or pay no respect to
> the laws of humanity, are now reaping a plentiful harvest by
> the law of Georgia, which declares that no Indian shall be a
> party in any court created by the laws or constitution of that
> state. These neighbors come over the line [between Georgia
> and the Territory], and take the cattle belonging to the Chero-
> kees. The Cherokees go in pursuit of their property, but all
> that they can effect is, to see their cattle snugly kept in the
> lots of these robbers. We are an abused people. [Even] if we
> can receive no redress, we can feel deeply the injustice done
> to our rights.

White prospectors soon moved from rustling cattle to stealing whole Cherokee farms—emboldened by the fact that bogus claims could receive an official stamp of approval from state land agents. After the U.S. Congress passed the Indian Removal Act of 1830, Georgia officials began planning for the future of the Cherokee Territory, anticipating a day when government troops would force all native people west of the Mississippi. In 1832, two land lotteries were held to redistribute former Cherokee lands to Georgia's white settlers.

In theory, those who drew land lots were allowed to take possession only if the property was unoccupied, but in reality, countless whites interpreted their winning tickets as a license to drive off Cherokee residents, including many who owned prosperous farms. In May of 1833, the editors of the *Phoenix* told how

> an industrious Indian had by his steady habits improved his premises to be of considerable value, when it was drawn by one of the lottery gamblers in Georgia. The fortunate holder of the ticket applied to the governor for a [land] grant, which was given him on his assurance that there was no Indian occupant on it. The fortunate drawer . . . loaded his pistols, entered the possession of Ootawlunsta, pointing one [pistol] at him, and drove the innocent Cherokee from his well-cultivated field. . . . The Cherokee are doomed to suffer.

With such white "pioneers" growing more and more bold, and with Georgia officials unwilling to comply with two separate Supreme Court decisions upholding the Cherokee people's rights as a sovereign nation, the stage was set for the Treaty of New Echota. Signed in 1835 by a small faction of the Cherokee— and against the wishes of Chief John Ross—the treaty ceded the entire Cherokee Territory to the United States, in exchange for

reservation land in Oklahoma. In the wake of New Echota, starting in the spring of 1838, the Cherokee people of north Georgia
were rounded up by state militiamen and confined in makeshift
pens, where they waited to start the forced march west. One of
the largest Cherokee removal forts, Fort Campbell, was located in
present-day Forsyth.

It was at Fort Campbell that Cumming mayor Charlie Harris's
grandfather Aaron Smith served under General Winfield Scott,
commander of the Cherokee removals, in a unit known as the
Georgia Guard. The guardsmen were notoriously cruel. Among
them were many men who had come to north Georgia in search of
gold and many who expected to personally profit from the removal
of the Cherokee.

Charlie Harris grew up hearing tales of how his grandfather
had once driven Cherokee families from their homes at gunpoint.
According to Harris's son David, Aaron Smith and other state
militiamen spent the fall of 1838 deep in the pine forests of Forsyth, hunting down the last of the Cherokee holdouts. Smith was
ordered to "search out . . . the pitiful and old Indians hiding and
starving in the woods . . . who would not go willingly to the con-
centration camps for removal." John G. Burnett, an army private
who also served during the Cherokee removals, said that in 1838 he
witnessed "the execution of the most brutal order in the History of
American Warfare. . . . I saw them loaded like cattle or sheep into
six hundred and forty-five wagons and started toward the West.
The trail of the exiles was a trail of death."

In 1839, when the last of north Georgia's Cherokee people set
out on the eight-hundred-mile march to Oklahoma, the newly
depopulated area of the Cherokee Territory was overrun by white
land speculators, gold prospectors, lawyers, and farmers, who had
either won their forty-acre lots in the 1832 land lottery or bought
winning tickets from others.

This is the real origin story of Forsyth. While descendants of the county's oldest families have long celebrated their "pioneer" ancestors, the truth is that early white settlers pushed relentlessly into the Cherokee Territory over the objections of tribal leaders and the U.S. Supreme Court—and found the land "empty" only after military troops rounded up sixteen thousand native people, imprisoned them in removal forts, and then drove the Cherokee out of Georgia like a herd of livestock.

When a new kind of "race trouble" broke out in 1912, Forsyth was a place that had already witnessed the rapid expulsion of an entire people, and many residents, like Charlie Harris, had heard firsthand accounts from relatives who'd taken part in the Cherokee removals. So whenever someone first suggested that blacks in the county should not only be punished for the murder of Mae Crow but driven out of the county forever, the white people of Forsyth knew in their bones that such a thing was possible. After all, many families owed their land and their livelihoods to exactly such a racial cleansing in the 1830s.

IN ONE OF his many books on the history of the county, local writer Don Shadburn claimed that when his ancestors first entered the Cherokee Territory, they had to tame the county's rugged wilderness by themselves. "The crops [of nineteenth-century Forsyth]," Shadburn wrote, "were worked exclusive of slave labor by the hands of the farm families *alone*—this native class of people viewed, then and now, as inherently proud, suspicious, God-fearing, and eccentric."

But Shadburn's paean to the hardworking, God-fearing "native class" of white mountaineers is one of those lies that persists because it is mixed with a kernel of truth. It's true that many small-scale farmers worked Forsyth's red soil without the benefit of slave labor. It's also true that slavery was never as pervasive in the foothills as it was on the vast plantations farther south—where slavery was the foundation of a globally dominant cotton economy. But while a majority of Forsyth's early settlers owned no slaves, there was a sizable minority who did, and when they crossed the Chattahoochee in 1839 and entered the former Cherokee Territory, they brought with them a population of enslaved black men and women whose labor would be vital to carving out a living in the wild, isolated hills.

The largest slaveholders were the Stricklands, whose patriarch, Hardy Sr., had come into the county with the first wave of land lottery winners, in 1832, and had quickly established some of Forsyth's most productive gold mines. In 1840, he owned seven slaves; a decade later, that number had grown to seventeen. By 1860, Hardy's four sons, Hardy Jr., Tolbert, Joel, and Jacob, were the owners of a group of slaves that had now swelled to 113, and they used that massive supply of unpaid labor to grow rich from the bounty of Strickland mines and Strickland plantations, which were among the county's largest producers of corn, wheat, and oats.

The last slave census before emancipation showed that Forsyth was home to a total of 890 enslaved people and nearly 200 different slave-owning families, representing 15 percent of all households. No one else in Forsyth owned slaves on the same scale as the Stricklands, but there were numerous other white men whose farms, mines, and households depended on enslaved workers. Most prominent among them were David and Martin Graham, S. W. Clement, and John Baily, each of whom owned more than thirty slaves.

The men and women Hardy Sr. brought into the hills were listed in the 1840 and 1850 slave schedules as "black," but by 1860 more than twenty-one of the 113 Strickland slaves were recorded by the census taker as "mulatto," or mixed race. Such distinctions based on skin color were not, of course, scientific. Nevertheless, that shift in the way the census takers viewed the growing population of Strickland slaves raises the possibility that some of the exponential growth in the size of the slave community on Strickland farms was due to the rape of African American women by the families' white patriarchs. Even today, descendants of the Strickland slaves tell family stories about light-skinned ancestors who spoke openly of having been fathered by their white owners.

At least one former Georgia slave made it clear to a white listener that plantations like the Strickland farm did not fill up with "mulatto" babies by chance. "Why is [my husband] George so white?" Carrie Mason asked a Federal Writers' Project interviewer in 1937, going on to answer her own question:

> 'Cause his marster wuz er white genemun named Mister Jimmie Dunn. His mammy wuz er cullud 'oman name Frances Mason an' his marster wuz his paw. Yas mam, I see you is s'prised, but dat happ'ned a lots in dem days. I hyeared tell of er white man whut would tell his sons ter "go down ter dem nigger quarters an' git me mo' slaves."

The four adult sons of Hardy Strickland Sr., like the young men in Carrie Mason's account, may have inherited an increasingly "mulatto" population of Strickland slaves because they themselves had fathered many of the slave children they owned. Congressman Hiram Parks Bell, who was a boy when his family moved into the newly opened Cherokee Territory, claimed that in the Forsyth of his childhood, residents "made an honest living by hard labor . . . and did not care whether slavery was established or prohibited." But census records tell a different story; they show that slave labor—and the whole culture of slavery—was no more alien to Forsyth than anywhere else in nineteenth-century Georgia.

GEORGIA'S COLONIAL LEGISLATURE first established a "slave patrol" system in 1757, citing widespread fear of a revolt. The "Act for Establishing and Regulating of Patrols" required that all slave owners patrol the borders of their plantations after dark and ensure that any enslaved person found abroad had written permission. At first the work fell to the planters themselves, but soon many slave owners began hiring others to patrol for them. These "pattyrollers," as they were known to black people all over the South, were usually poor white men whose hardscrabble homes bordered slave-farmed lands, and who were paid to capture and whip any slave caught out of bounds. Resentful of their rich white neighbors and eager to show that they were not at the very bottom of the social hierarchy, many of these earliest "night riders" approached the task with a brutal zeal.

There are few written records of the slave patrols, and none at all documenting the groups that once operated in Forsyth. So most of what is known comes from oral histories, like the stories told by a man named Edward Glenn, who was a slave on the Clinton Brown plantation, near Oscarville, in the 1850s. In 1937 Glenn recalled those days, and confirmed that the patrol system was in full force in antebellum Forsyth. "When a runaway slave" was caught outside the Brown plantation, Glenn said,

> they was punished. . . . I saw a woman stripped naked, laid over a stump in a field with her head hanging down on one side, her feet on the other, and tied to the stump. They whipped her hard, and you could hear her hollering far off.

Glenn described how white patrollers also used the "Gameron Stick," a punishment in which "the slave's arms were bound around the bent knees and fastened to a stick run beneath them. This was [also] called the 'Spanish Buck.' . . . They stripped the slave, who was unable to stand up, and rolled him on one side and whipped him till the blood came." As William McWhorther, a slave in nearby Clarke County, put it, "Paterollers was de devil's own hosses. If dey cotched a Nigger out and his Marster hadn't fixed him up wid a pass, it was jus' too bad; dey most kilt him."

Such scenes are also common in the stories passed down through families forced out of Forsyth. One comes from Anthony Neal, whose ancestors Joseph and Eliza Kellogg became the county's largest black property owners in the 1880s, although they'd begun their lives as slaves. Eliza made repeated attempts to escape during slave times, Neal says, and by the time the Confederate army surrendered, in 1865, and the slaves of Georgia were finally free, Eliza had run off yet again. According to family lore, before she could be told she was free, Eliza Kellogg first had to be coaxed out of hiding from the pattyrollers.

NEWSPAPERS IN 1912 may have portrayed Forsyth's "trouble" as a sudden flare-up of racial violence, sparked by the alleged rapes of Ellen Grice and Mae Crow. But for many whites in the county there was nothing unusual about riding out to violently punish what they saw as black transgressions. Such night riding was a long tradition in many families, dating back to the days when Forsyth's poor white men had been "de devils' own hosses," paid to patrol the roads of the county.

But in the wake of emancipation, that de facto police force of lower-class whites had become obsolete—and in August of 1912, the state legislature redefined vigilante violence as "riot, rout, [and] tumult," which the governor's troops were now empowered to stop with lethal force. To a new generation of whites like Charlie Harris and his partners in the Atlanta Northeastern Railroad, such "lawlessness" was no longer seen as a necessary evil, essential to managing black labor. To them, the mobs that had regulated black workers for so long were shameful, uncouth, and—worst of all— very bad for business.

In such an environment, the old southern power dynamics between rich and poor whites were radically, if invisibly, altered. Desperate to join the economic boom just forty miles south in Atlanta, men like Harris now had an incentive to protect the black labor supply and to dispel any worries that Forsyth was the kind of "lawless settlement" feared by the businessmen of the new South. Two dirt-poor, illiterate black defendants like Ernest Knox and Oscar Daniel were almost certain to "swing for their crime" in Jim Crow Georgia, but it mattered deeply to Harris that they swing not from a tree limb but from a legally constructed, legally sanctioned gallows. To reassure shareholders in the Atlanta Northeastern Railroad, Cumming's young mayor needed to stage a trial that maintained at least the outward appearance of justice.

7

THE MAJESTY OF THE LAW

When news of Mae Crow's death reached Atlanta, murder was added to the "true bill" against Ernest Knox. The trials—of Ernest Knox and Oscar Daniel for the rape and murder of Mae Crow; of Jane Daniel as accomplice to rape and murder; and of Toney Howell for the rape of Ellen Grice—were set to begin on Thursday, October 3rd, at the Forsyth County Courthouse. The U.S. Supreme Court would eventually decide that it was unconstitutional to try African Americans in any place where they were systematically excluded from juries—which violated the equal protection clause of the Fourteenth Amendment. But that decision, in 1935, was still more than two decades in the future. And so in 1912, the fate of the Grice and Crow prisoners would be decided by all-white juries in Cumming, on the same town square where Rob Edwards's bullet-riddled corpse had been left on public display, as a silent warning to local blacks.

With the accused rapists headed back into the heart of the "race troubles," Judge Newt Morris drove to Atlanta on Friday, September 27th, to personally communicate his concerns to the governor. His request: that Joseph Mackey Brown impose martial law for the duration of the trials and once again send state troops to prevent a lynching. Brown responded by declaring Forsyth to be in "a state of insurrection" for the second time in a month, and ordered three companies of the Georgia National Guard to escort the prisoners north.

With military protection in place, Morris turned his attention to a second vexing problem: finding men bold enough—or fool enough—to mount a legal defense. It was, Morris understood, a difficult thing to ask of any white man. Most attorneys in the state knew from experience that defending black clients could lead at best to a quick defeat, and at worst to a visit from the same kind of men who had stalked and killed Rob Edwards.

According to the *Atlanta Georgian,* on October 1st—just two days before the trails were to begin—Morris called eight lawyers before the bench, looked each man sternly in the eye, and asked him to do his public duty. In response, "each one offered an excuse for not defending the negroes." Four of them had a ready answer to the judge's request: they could not serve because they had already been "retained to assist the prosecution."

These four were experienced litigators from Marietta, eager to claim a share of the attention and gratitude that would come to whoever won a conviction. They were led by Solicitor General J. P. Brooke, a friend of Charlie Harris's and a partner in the Atlanta Northeastern Railroad. Also on the prosecution team was Eugene Herbert Clay, the mayor of Marietta, son of U.S. Senator Alexander Clay, and, at thirty-one, a rising political star. After a glance at the list of prosecuting attorneys, many people in Cumming must have nodded and chuckled; seeing his reputation and his railroad threatened by all the negative attention, Charlie Harris had called in an army of powerful friends, and nearly all his political favors.

By contrast, the defense team was made up of small-town lawyers from Cumming and nearby Canton, who were appointed by Morris despite their own objections. Amaziah Fisher, Isaac Grant,

and John Collins were far more experienced with land deeds, contract disputes, and rental agreements than they were with a sen-
sational rape and murder trial, which was now being covered by
newspapers all over the South. Leading the defense was another
Marietta man, Fred Morris (no relation to Newt Morris), who was
known to be a close confidant of many of his opponents on the
prosecution. Two of the attorneys opposing one another, J. P. and
Howell Brooke, were father and son. The latter, at twenty-one, was
barely older than the two teenagers he was assigned to defend.

HAVING DIVIDED THE lawyers into two camps—one stocked with
talent, power, and experience, the other with law students and over-
matched small-town attorneys—Judge Morris prepared to open
the fall session of the Blue Ridge Circuit court. With the ambitious
Eugene Herbert Clay preening for all the photographers and journalists in town, and with the five defenders reluctantly accepting
their no-win assignment, everything was now in place—except for
the defendants themselves.

And so at eleven a.m. on Wednesday, October 2nd, Lieutenant
Rucker McCarty of the Georgia National Guard appeared at the
Fulton Tower and signed forms acknowledging receipt of six prisoners: the four defendants (Ernest Knox, Oscar Daniel, and Jane
Daniel in the Crow case; and Toney Howell in the Grice case), as
well as two material witnesses, Ed Collins and Isaiah Pirkle. Collins was an Oscarville farmer said to have been with Rob Edwards
and Oscar Daniel on the day of Mae Crow's murder, and Pirkle had
been swept up in the earliest wave of arrests back in September,
along with his friend Toney Howell. It is likely that the other five
black men arrested during the hysteria were simply released from
the Tower, but the papers make no mention of their fates.

A photo taken that morning shows McCarty's troops marching
through the streets of Atlanta toward Terminal Station, with Jane

Jane Daniel, Oscar Daniel, and Toney Howell (center, left to right) being led toward the Atlanta train terminal, October 2nd, 1912

Daniel and her brother Oscar walking at the center of the military formation. For the past month, papers had described Oscar Daniel as "the barefooted, fiendish-looking type," but what readers saw in the photograph was a teenage boy, dwarfed by the armed militiamen marching all around him. As hundreds of Atlantans gawked at the procession, Jane clutched the long folds of her dress with one hand and walked beside her brother, their wrists handcuffed together. Over Oscar's shoulder, in his porkpie hat and white shirt, was the slim figure of Toney Howell, who had not been outside the Atlanta jail for nearly a month.

AT TERMINAL STATION, the prisoners boarded a special train, rode a little more than an hour north into the foothills, then got off thirteen miles east of Cumming, in the little whistle-stop town of Buford. The group that disembarked numbered more than two hundred, counting 167 military escorts, the prisoners themselves, members of the press, and lawyers participating in the trial. The military commander, Major I. T. Catron, had appointed "a personal guard of six men" who were to surround the prisoners at all times and defend them from potential lynchers and assassins. With a Southern Railway locomotive steaming and hissing in the background, and troops spilling out onto the tiny platform all around him, Catron raised his arm and ordered a brief stop for lunch.

As the midday sun beat down, and as the soldiers were fed by the kitchen staff of a local hotel, the prisoners got a brief moment of rest, as they too ate a hot meal, then waited on a stack of railroad ties at the very center of the traveling circus. Just before Catron ordered them to rise and begin the day's long march, a photographer extended the black leather bellows of a camera and squinted into the viewfinder. When the shutter clicked, he captured the most indelible image of the Forsyth expulsions, and it was soon churning off the presses of the *Atlanta Constitution*.

The Forsyth prisoners at Buford, Georgia, October 2nd, 1912 (left to right): Jane Daniel, Oscar Daniel, Toney Howell, Ed Collins, Isaiah Pirkle, and Ernest Knox

That afternoon the troops walked through miles of pine forest and river bottom, watched by hundreds of curious locals who came out of their houses, eager to get a look at the troops and their notorious prisoners. Having crossed the Chattahoochee and entered Forsyth, the regiment reached the outskirts of town just as the sun was going down. Catron called the march to a halt, and as his command echoed down the line, the militiamen shrugged off their knapsacks and bedrolls, pitched their white canvas pup tents, and established a camp perimeter on land that had been volunteered, Catron was told, by the local sheriff.

IT WAS WIDELY reported that "the mountaineers of north Georgia" were once again flooding into Cumming for the trials, many of them "armed and prepared to make trouble." So when a group of civilians appeared out of the darkness at the edge of the camp, a nervous sentry called, "Who goes there?" and was surprised to find before him, with their hands raised, not overall-clad farmers but a group of gentlemen wearing the spectacles and fine wool suits of attorneys-at-law. "Tonight," a reporter wrote, "Judge Morris, Sheriff Reid, Fred Morris of Marietta, John Collins, and Howell Brooke of Canton came to the camp" from Cumming. As soon as they were recognized, the men asked to speak privately with the six prisoners.

There are no reports of exactly why such a visit was made, what was discussed, or how long it lasted, but the appearance of Judge Morris and defense attorney Fred Morris at that campfire meeting raises a number of questions. There was nothing unusual, of course, about a judge and an attorney meeting with defendants on the eve of a trial. But this particular judge and this particular attorney are now known to have participated in one of the most brazen acts of mob violence in American history: the 1915 kidnapping and murder of Leo Frank, a Jewish man who was convicted of the rape and murder of a young white girl named Mary Phagan.

Judge Newton Morris, former governor Joseph Mackey Brown, prosecutor Eugene Herbert Clay, and defense attorney Fred Morris were all involved. Newt Morris was, in fact, the mastermind of Frank's abduction from the state penitentiary, but he pretended to have arrived just minutes after the lynching and persuaded journalists, including a reporter for the *New York Times,* that it was he who had prevented the crowd from burning Frank's body. Thus, just three years after the trials in Forsyth, Morris would manage to both lynch a man *and* become famous for having stood up to a mob. Harold Willingham, a local lawyer who knew him well, said that Morris was powerful and widely respected during his lifetime, but in private many people in Marietta knew a very different man. "He was," said Willingham, "a fourteen-karat son of a bitch with spare parts."

Jane, Oscar, and Ernest could not have known that the judge hearing their cases would soon preside over a lynching in the woods outside Marietta, but they must have realized just how unlikely it was that they would ever receive justice from the all-white juries of Forsyth. Even if their lives were spared when Judge Morris handed down sentences, everyone knew that the farmers flooding into town brought with them an unspoken threat: that any outcome other than the death penalty would be remedied by "the will of the people," as one Cumming man put it. In the lead-up to the trials, the editors of the *Gainesville Times* expressed the view of most whites—which was that the Knox and Daniel trials could, and should, lead to only one verdict. "Little time will be required," a reporter wrote, "and, of course, the brutes will be found guilty."

Given the near impossibility of acquittal, the only hope left for the prisoners was to cooperate with Morris and hope that at least some of them might still escape alive. Jane Daniel, Ed Collins, Isaiah Pirkle, and Toney Howell were all in grave danger the minute they crossed back over the county line. But what, they must have

The lynching of Leo Frank outside Marietta, Georgia, 1915. Judge Newton A. Morris (far right, in bow tie and straw hat) stands among the crowd of spectators.

wondered, if the convictions of Ernest Knox and Oscar Daniel could be made to satisfy the white people of Forsyth? What if, somehow, two hangings could be enough?

At a nod from Major Catron, Judge Morris passed through a military checkpoint in Bill Reid's pasture. Then he and the attorneys followed a soldier past rows of glowing campfires, until they reached the little cluster of tents where Jane Daniel and the other prisoners were trying, and no doubt failing, to get some rest.

After a brief fireside conversation with Jane and the accused men, Morris and the lawyers appeared once more at the checkpoint and were escorted back to Cumming by Sheriff Reid. What sort of bargain they had come to offer—and what they'd asked in return—was not reported. But the next day's evening papers shocked readers with news that the sister of one of the accused men had suddenly, and supposedly of her own accord, "turned State's evidence" and agreed to testify for the prosecution. For reasons no one could, or would, explain, the night had wrought a sudden change in young Jane Daniel.

AFTER BREAKFAST ON the morning of Thursday, October 3rd, the soldiers struck their tents and readied the prisoners for the last mile of the march, through the dusty streets of Cumming. The little town, according to one observer, was "crowded as never before in its history" as people all over north Georgia were drawn by the excitement. Surrounded by military guards as they walked up Castleberry Road, the prisoners faced the jeers and howls of "mountaineers [who had] been gathering weapons," according to one reporter, "and making threats that the accused negroes would not be permitted to reach the jail."

To protect them, the governor had ordered out an overwhelming show of military force and armed the guardsmen to the teeth. In addition to the Springfield carbines slung over their shoulders, the *Georgian* reported, the soldiers of the Fifth Regiment were "ordered to discard the usual revolver and equip themselves with the new Army derringer pistols . . . which automatically discharges eleven heavy bullets and can be reloaded in a second." Governor Brown's declaration of martial law had even concluded with a steely warning to people crowding into town for the trials: "While it is the desire of the authorities to exercise the powers of martial law mildly, it must not be supposed that they will not be vigorously and firmly enforced." When Judge Morris was asked about the potential for trouble while walking towards the courthouse, he paused just long enough to remind a reporter that the troops were authorized to fire at will: "any disorder," he said, "[will] have serious, if not fatal, consequences."

Sheriff Reid had summoned eighty-four men for jury duty, so when Morris banged his gavel and opened *State of Georgia v. Ernest Knox*, jury selection was the first order of business. By eleven a.m., fifty-six "talesmen" had been questioned, and twelve jurors agreed upon. Five were struck for being over sixty; as to the other thirty-nine who were disqualified? An Atlanta reporter with a gift for understatement said that "their minds were not clearly unbiased as between the prosecution and defense."

The judge empaneled a jury of twelve white men, eleven of them employed as farmers and the twelfth as "a watchman at the local mill." Among these otherwise unremarkable "people of the county" were two jurors—E. S. Garrett and William Hammond—who would join the Sawnee Klavern of the Ku Klux Klan in the early 1920s. Guarding the door was Sheriff Reid, who would stand beside them as a Klansman, dressed in his own white robe and hood. Seated among the lawyers were two of Leo Frank's future lynchers, Fred Morris and Howell Brooke. And at the very center of the courtroom, directing the whole affair, was Judge Newton A. Morris.

No doubt conscious of all the reporters in attendance, the judge called the murmuring spectators to order, then announced in a booming voice that he would "expedite the trial in every manner possible" and at the same time ensure that the proceedings were "fair and impartial." The purpose of the entire process, Morris said—with a grave and imperious glance around the room—was to "uphold the majesty of the law."

The Cumming Courthouse, c. 1912

If Morris's speech gave even a glimmer of hope to Ernest Knox, it must have faded when the prosecution called the day's first witness: Mr. L. A. "Bud" Crow. Mae's father was listed as the official prosecutor of the case, and he struck a pitiful figure as he sat, hat in hand, and spoke of his beloved daughter; of the morning he'd first looked upon her bloody body; of the two weeks his wife, Azzie, had spent praying at Mae's bedside; and of her recent death and burial, at a funeral attended by many people present in the courtroom. Bud Crow "was compelled to repeat the pathetic story of his daughter's shameful handling," a reporter wrote, "and the recital stirred the depths of [even] the most hardened onlookers."

The two witnesses who followed—Dr. George Brice and Dr. John Hockenhull—made the prosecution's strategy clear. They would ask witness after witness to describe Mae's injuries and stoke the same sense of horror and outrage that had led to the lynching of Rob Edwards. The image of Mae Crow's broken, defiled body was enough, they knew, to make a conviction of Ernest Knox all but inevitable.

AFTER THE DEAD girl's father brought many in the crowd to tears, and after the doctors shocked listeners with their accounts of Mae's fractured skull and lacerated throat, the next witness was Ed Collins, a black farmer from Oscarville, who was among the prisoners brought north from the Fulton Tower. There is no telling what Collins's wife, Julia, knew or didn't know during the time her husband was jailed, but if she had dared to venture into Cumming for the trial, it would have been the first time she laid eyes on him since mid-September. For at least two days during their separation, Collins was mistakenly identified by reporters as the man whose body had hung from a telephone pole on the Cumming square. When Collins rose and walked toward the witness stand, the reason for the mistake was clear to everyone: just like "Big Rob" Edwards, Ed Collins was a tall and powerfully built young black man.

Collins was called not by the defense but the prosecution, because the story he told implicated Knox and Daniel through circumstantial evidence. He said that on the day of Mae Crow's disappearance, Knox and Edwards came to his house in Oscarville and stayed until about ten p.m. Most importantly for the state's case, Collins testified that "they borrowed a lantern . . . and [said] they were going in the direction of the Crow home, which was about two miles away."

Thus began the prosecution's attempt to prove allegations that had been racing from storefront to storefront all month. After Ernest Knox met Mae Crow on Durand Road and beat her over the head with a rock, the story went, he dragged Crow's unconscious body into the woods, then went to find Rob Edwards and his cousins Jane and Oscar, and led them back to the scene. There, all three men were said to have spent the night repeatedly raping Crow.

This narrative justified the prosecution of Daniel as well as Knox, explained the arrests of Ed Collins and Jane Daniel, and,

Ed Collins, October 1912

most importantly, redefined the lynching of Rob Edwards as a just
punishment for a heinous crime. As a prosecutor turned his back
to Ed Collins, he told the jury that Knox, Daniel, and Edwards had
borrowed Collins's lantern not because they had stayed later than
intended, not because it was dark, and not because they had a long
walk home. Instead, the jury heard, it was because a beautiful white
girl was lying out there unconscious in the woods, and they needed
a light to find her.

If anyone in the courtroom had doubts, the prosecution's next
witness presented what seemed like irrefutable evidence: a confession that came from Ernest Knox's own lips. Whatever else he
said on the witness stand, it's clear that Marvin Bell left out the
fact that Knox had confessed while in the midst of a mock lynching. Bell reiterated what was now the widely accepted story: that
on Sunday, September 8th, Ernest Knox had met Mae Crow while
she was walking on the road between her parents' and her aunt's
house, bashed in her skull in the throes of a sexual rage, left her
unconscious body in the woods, then returned with Edwards and
his cousins, Jane and Oscar. Bell said that Jane was forced to come

along by her brother, her cousin, and her husband—to "hold the lantern" while the three men took turns raping Crow.

By the time Marvin Bell sat down, most whites in the gallery were nodding in agreement with a patently unconvincing story, which the next day's *Constitution* deemed "one of the most revolting rape cases in the annals of the state." As Ernest Knox sat stone still beside his team of reluctant defense attorneys, Newt Morris rose from the bench, tapped his gavel, and announced a midday adjournment.

8

FASTENING THE NOOSE

Sheriff Reid took the recess as an opportunity to once more strike the pose of a brave country lawman. At one point, as he threaded his way out through the dense crowd surrounding the courthouse, he leaned into a circle of journalists and whispered that he'd just received an urgent message from Atlanta. The sheriff warned, one reporter said, that "1,000 rounds of ammunition are en-route to Cumming . . . [though] he declined to give the source of his information."

If the writer sounds skeptical about the sheriff's tale, perhaps it is because there are no other references to such a shipment, and no evidence that any such threat ever existed. But that moment gives a clear picture of Reid on the day of the trial: desperately playing to the crowd, trying to somehow keep himself center stage—particularly as photographers focused their cameras on the dashing soldiers of the Fulton Blues. When a reporter asked Reid to elaborate on the story, the sheriff confessed that "he [did] not believe this report to be true," but hurried to add that he was "making arrangements to intercept any such shipment should it be en-route."

No matter how broadly Reid played his role as guardian of the county, Judge Morris was the real ringmaster on the day of the trials, and Catron's soldiers were stars of the show. One reporter noted that while there were "enough determined men in Cumming today . . . to overpower a sheriff's posse and hang the accused men to the nearest tree," those "who felt that the two rapists deserved immediate death [were stopped by] the businesslike look of the men behind the army rifles."

As hundreds of whites milled around the courthouse and tried to catch a glimpse of the prisoners inside, the signs of martial law were everywhere. According to the *Constitution*, the military guard kept "at a safe distance a crowd that would have otherwise made short work of the accused negroes." The *Georgian* said that "Major Catron has 24 men stationed in the court room, while squads are on duty in the corridors, on the stairways, in the court house yard and around the fence surrounding the building. Other soldiers are patrolling the streets of the town, while a reserve force is held in readiness to move at a moment's notice, should there be any demonstration." The article was accompanied by a photograph showing a guardsman, rifle at the ready, perched on a ledge of the courthouse wall, lest anyone attempt to take a shot through the window.

WHEN IT WAS time for the trials to resume, sentries of the Fifth Regiment admitted only "court officers, attorneys, newspaper correspondents, talesmen summoned for jury service, witnesses . . . and a few prominent citizens." Those prominent citizens included Mayor Charlie Harris, members of wealthy clans like the Bells, the Hockenhulls, and the Stricklands, and others from the moneyed families of Cumming. It was these men who had convinced Governor Brown to send troops in the first place, and they who had the most to gain from a quick and convincing trial.

In that first week of October, corn, cotton, and tobacco leaves waited in rows all over the county, ripe and ready to be picked. Yet one field after another stood empty of the workers who were usually busy with the fall harvest. To the merchants, planters, and large landowners who showed their passes at the courthouse fence and took their seats for the afternoon session, it mattered little whether the harvest had come to a halt because black families were being driven out or because poor whites were all in town to see the Fulton Blues. For such "prominent citizens," what mattered more than anything else was getting the trials over with, and the pickers of the county back into the fields.

Even Charlie Harris—who had stared down a lynch mob on the courthouse steps—had a stake in expediency, since he had now sold stock in the Atlanta Northeastern Railroad Company worth $1.2 million. After a month during which the Atlanta papers were filled with stories of rape, murder, lynchings, and arson in Forsyth, Harris and his partner J. P. Brooke, lead prosecutor in the trials, were eager to show investors, potential clients, and government regulators that the foothills were no longer the outlaw territory of old but a quiet, profitable place in which to do business. And like so many upper-class whites in the Jim Crow South, they seem to have decided that if the price of peace was sending a couple of black teenagers to the gallows after a one-day trial—well, then so be it. As the trial resumed and proceeded at a record pace, it must have become clear to the prisoners that these elegantly dressed white men were no less dangerous than the crackers and "mountaineers" out on the square—and no less intent, in their way, on fastening a noose before sundown.

JUDGE MORRIS HAD planned to decide the Knox, Daniel, and Howell cases in a single day, but as people settled into their seats after the recess, they could sense that the proceedings still might not satisfy the mob outside the courthouse windows. "Civil and military officials are afraid," Angus Perkerson wrote in the *Atlanta Journal,* that if "all of the negroes are not convicted and sentenced to hang the crowd will be inflamed to a dangerous point." The trouble, Perkerson said, was that while Knox, Daniel, and Howell could be sentenced to death if convicted on rape and murder charges, Jane Daniel was charged with an accessory crime and faced a maximum penalty of imprisonment. Ed Collins and Isaiah Pirkle were held only as witnesses.

As Catron took his place next to the bench and scanned the returning crowd, he was already playing out in his mind a worst-case scenario: that the mob would accept nothing short of the death penalty for all six prisoners and, failing that, would try to take them by force. "If any one of the six [fell] into the hands of the crowd," Perkerson wrote, "it is admitted by everyone . . . that he would be lynched immediately." As the trial resumed, Catron ordered his men to have their rifles loaded and bayonets fixed.

The subpoena list for *State of Georgia v. Ernest Knox* includes a number of witnesses the audience expected to hear from during the afternoon session. Among these were Sheriff Reid and four white neighbors of the Crows: Joseph McClure, W. R. Stovall, Roysten Smith, and C. O. Wallis. These men could be counted on to describe the all-night search for Mae and the discovery of her body in the woods outside Oscarville. By calling them, the prosecution planned to forge ahead with its simple plan: have witness after witness recount Mae's gruesome injuries and drive home the fact that on the morning she was found, Ernest Knox had "confessed his crime."

But the prosecution's parade of circumstantial evidence never even began, for as soon as Morris took his seat, Solicitor General J. P. Brooke rose and announced that instead of the planned group of white farmers, the prosecution wished to call one Jane Daniel, colored, of Forsyth County. As a petite young woman walked toward the front of the courtroom, a stir passed through the crowd. "Jane Daniel was a complete surprise," the *Constitution* reported, "even to her own counsel, who conferred with her yesterday afternoon as usual and were told nothing by her. This morning, however, she narrated the entire revolting story of the crime to Sheriff Reid, and to Herbert Clay, assisting prosecuting attorney."

But if Jane Daniel had freely chosen to testify against her brother and cousin, as the papers claimed, is it really plausible that she would have volunteered that story to Bill Reid and Eugene Herbert Clay? Reid, the man who a month earlier had abandoned his post as a mob was threatening to lynch Jane's husband, Rob? And Clay, an attorney for the prosecution? These were men Jane Daniel had every reason to fear, and it seems far more likely that during their late-night conversation in Reid's pasture, the judge and lawyers had made Jane Daniel an offer she couldn't refuse: that she might save herself and some of the other prisoners if she would only take the witness stand, look into the eyes of the people who had murdered her husband, and tell them exactly what they wanted to hear.

ACCORDING TO THE *Constitution*, once Jane was been sworn in, she told a hushed gallery how her cousin Ernest Knox had met "a crowd of negro friends returning from Sunday afternoon church services, [then] went home with them." She confirmed earlier testimony that Knox had spent the evening of September 8th at Ed Collins's house, and that as he and Rob Edwards left, they asked to borrow a lantern, then headed off "in the direction of the Crow place."

But it was here that Jane departed from what the audience had already heard, and seemed to offer, for the first time, an eyewitness account. According to the papers, Jane told prosecutors that earlier in the evening Ernest had "accosted [Mae] on the road [where] she was dragged into the woods, and knocked insensible with a rock. . . . Her body was dragged to a point 120 yards away from the road and there, after being cruelly treated, she was left for dead."

Jane went on to tell how late that night Oscar, Ernest, and her husband, Rob, appeared before her, their faces lit by the glow of the lantern. She claimed that they forced her to walk to a secluded place in the woods, where all four stood staring down at Crow's unconscious body. The men threatened to kill her, Jane said, if she did not hold the lamp as "the negroes satisfied their lustful passions on the insensible body of the victim." It is easy to imagine the howls that erupted in the courtroom—as Judge Morris banged his gavel and called for order, as reporters scribbled frantically, and as the guards surrounding Jane's chair gripped the stocks of their rifles and glanced nervously at Catron.

Jane's story horrified whites, but it must have also filled many with relief, since her account allowed all those who had taken part in the killing of Rob Edwards to decide once and for all that the lynching had been not a gruesome communal murder but a case of old-fashioned frontier justice. Anyone could see how young Ernest Knox was as he sat listening to his cousin's story, but Jane's testimony convinced the crowd that however harmless he looked, Knox was one of Forsyth's bloodthirsty black rapists, and a murderer who would soon "take [his] departure from Cumming to hell."

THERE IS NO indication that Knox's court-appointed lawyers cross-examined Jane or in any way challenged her testimony. But there are a host of questions a defense attorney might have asked. If Knox had indeed encountered Mae Crow on the road and for some reason assaulted her, would he not—in the world of Jim Crow Georgia— have simply run for his life? Is it within the realm of possibility that he would have walked several miles in order to find Rob Edwards, Oscar Daniel, and Jane Daniel, then led them back to the scene of the crime, with the purpose of gang-raping Crow's unconscious body? Surely if he had told Rob Edwards and Jane Daniel of such an attack, their first move would have been to get Ernest Knox as far away from the mobs of Forsyth as possible. Instead, the next morning found him watching all the excitement on the lawn of Pleasant Grove Church—looking for all the world like a boy with nothing to hide.

Jury deliberations lasted nineteen minutes. Then, at 4:08 p.m., the door to the courtroom opened, and the twelve white men of the jury filed back toward their seats. When Judge Morris called for their verdict, foreman Tom Pool rose and said, "We the jury find the defendant guilty." Morris quieted the boisterous crowd, then informed Knox that in the morning he would be sentenced for the rape and murder of Mae Crow.

HAVING SHOCKED THE courtroom once, Jane Daniel was forced to give an encore during the second prosecution of the day, though this time her performance was witnessed not by a packed gallery but two small teams of lawyers, a dwindling row of reporters, and a handful of weary militiamen. After at last hearing the horror story they'd craved, and cheering the conviction of Ernest Knox, hundreds of white people who had come to see the trials streamed out of town, hurrying to make it home before dark. By sundown it was so quiet on the Cumming square that as Oscar Daniel's trial ground toward its inevitable conclusion, a reporter could hear the crackle of the Fifth Regiment's campfires through the open windows, and the clank of spoons on tin bowls, as "the choice tenors of the regiment . . . crooned sentimentally."

The journalists, too, were losing steam as they listened to the day's eighth hour of testimony, and as Jane was forced to repeat the whole lurid tale: of three black men raping and killing Mae Crow, of her brother Oscar's role in the attack, and of how she stood holding the lantern while he, Ernest, and her husband, Rob Edwards, took turns raping Crow. The few spectators left surely jeered and hissed at Oscar, as they had at his cousin Ernest, and the closest anyone came to sympathy was when a reporter described the eighteen-year-old Oscar Daniel as "a shade more human-looking than Knox."

Unlike his cousin, who'd "confessed his crime" to Marvin Bell, Oscar Daniel maintained his innocence throughout the trial, and would continue to do so for the rest of his life. And in Jane's story, Oscar was only later drawn into a plot that had been begun by Knox and Edwards. Even to whites eager for a hanging, Oscar seemed the least culpable of the three. As he sat in his handcuffs, watching his sister through the candlelight and listening as her words quietly sealed his doom, at least a few jurors must have seen before them not a fiendish black rapist but a frightened teenage boy.

The jurors in the second case deliberated for nearly an hour. When Morris finally asked for a verdict, foreman Ed Johnson announced, "We the jury find the defendant guilty." It was 9:20 p.m., and even the low murmur of the soldiers in their tents had fallen silent. A hoarse-throated Morris rose and declared that Oscar Daniel, guilty of rape and accessory to murder, would be sentenced first thing in the morning.

After more than twelve hours, both cases were closed, and as the judges and lawyers gathered their things and walked out onto the Cumming square, they passed the last spectators heading home, as well as a few of Major Catron's sentries, still patrolling the deserted streets. For their own safety, Ernest, Oscar, Jane, and the rest of the prisoners spent the night not in the rickety old jail but deep inside the courthouse, at the center of the Fifth Regiment's bristling ring of protection. Judge Morris, who had complained to a reporter that he had been denied his customary morning nap, finally settled back into his bed at a local boardinghouse.

In an adjacent room, another of Leo Frank's lynchers, Eugene Herbert Clay, must have felt pleased with how the day's surprises had unfolded. Not only had both men been convicted, as expected, but Jane's testimony had given the whole town the eyewitness account they'd been longing to hear for more than a month. Politicians in Atlanta could criticize Forsyth all they wanted for the lynching of Rob Edwards. But Clay knew—in light of Jane's lurid tale—that if such a thing had happened to their own daughters, they, too, might have picked up a crowbar.

A TREMENDOUS RAINSTORM passed over Cumming a few hours after the trials, and, according to one reporter, "All things changed at midnight . . . as water trickled under the [militia's] tents and sentries stood guard soaked to the skin." The next morning, as Judge Morris walked toward the courtroom, he found that where thousands of people had swarmed the day before, now there were only muddy puddles and a few weary, rain-soaked sentries. They stood at attention as he passed, and Morris, himself a former captain of the Marietta Rifles, was so impressed that he decided to devote a majority of the morning's session to praising what he called the "courageous and gentlemanly" conduct of the troops.

But first there was the business of sentencing two black convicts to die, which Morris dispensed with in short order. Taking the bench at nine a.m., he told Ernest Knox to rise, then ordered that Knox be "hanged by the neck until he is dead and may the Lord have mercy on his soul." Morris sentenced Oscar Daniel to die in the same manner. Georgia law required a waiting period of at least twenty days between conviction and execution, and Morris granted the men exactly one extra day of life, setting October 25th as the date for the double hanging.

The judge then turned to his main subject for the day: the exemplary conduct of the Fifth Regiment. As Knox and Daniel were led out of the courtroom, they passed the square-jawed Major Catron, standing at attention as photographers jostled for position and as the judge turned in his seat and spoke directly to the commander. The two boys ducked their heads and shuffled out into the hallway, and the last thing they heard from the man who had condemned them to die were words of praise for the white community's "admirable restraint" and his sympathy for all that the soldiers had endured during their service. "It speaks well for the citizens of Forsyth," Morris said, "that they should have exercised the degree of restraint that they did." He ended with an encomium to the Fulton Blues that was reprinted in all the papers. "I want to thank both officers and men," Morris said. "Every member of this detachment has been courageous and gentlemanly. They have endured much hardship . . . and they came here at a sacrifice."

WHEN COURT WAS adjourned, at ten-thirty a.m., the soldiers broke camp, formed up ranks around the prisoners, and began the long, soggy march back to Buford, where they would catch the train to Atlanta. On their way out of town, they passed through what Angus Perkerson of the *Journal* described as "a crowd of several hundred men [who] neither expressed nor attempted violence." This new calm may have reflected whites' satisfaction with the trials and the two death sentences. Or perhaps it was a product of exhaustion, which seems to have been the prevailing mood, even among the militiamen. "Every man of the whole detachment," Perkerson wrote, "was wet through and they began to march . . . worn and bedraggled."

Asa Candler, a captain of the regiment, later told reporters that as they walked the muddy roads between Cumming and Buford and crossed the swollen creeks and branches of the Chattahoochee, at one point Ernest Knox surprised everyone by speaking up. When Candler asked what the trouble was, Knox glanced at the soldiers around him, then asked for permission to "make a run for it." The captain couldn't help but laugh and pointed out that there were "a score of men in the battalion who could pick off a man running at 1,000 yards." Knox nodded and said he understood what he was asking: for a chance "to be killed right then." Candler refused, and Knox walked the rest of the way to Buford handcuffed to Oscar Daniel.

When the train arrived back in Atlanta, the officers in charge did something surprising. Having deposited Knox and Daniel safely in their cells, they led Jane Daniel, Ed Collins, and Isaiah Pirkle to the front of the Fulton Tower, unlocked their handcuffs, and said that they were free to go. All three disappeared into the city and vanished from the pages of the Atlanta papers—eager, no doubt, to begin the search for their families, who were scattered among the hundreds of refugees who had fled Forsyth.

The one prisoner not released was Toney Howell, who Judge Morris had hoped to try for the attempted rape of Ellen Grice. But on the day Knox and Daniel were sentenced, with no other business before the court, Sheriff Reid had informed the judge that none of the black witnesses summoned to testify in the Grice case had appeared. Neither, apparently, had Ellen Grice herself. Morris was left with no choice but to "pass [Howell's] case to the next term of court in February . . . because of the absence of witnesses," and he ordered that Howell be held in the Tower along with Knox and Daniel. Reporters noted that when he gathered his things and prepared to leave the courtroom, Morris looked openly annoyed with Bill Reid. How was it was possible, he must have wondered, that in all of Forsyth County, not a single black witness could be found?

9

WE CONDEMN THIS CONDUCT

Byrd and Delia Oliver lived two doors down from Ed Collins and his wife, Julia, and not far from the cluster of houses where Rob Edwards, Oscar Daniel, and Ernest Knox had lived before the "race troubles" began. Having seen three of his neighbors arrested and one of them lynched on the Cumming square, Oliver must have realized, in October of 1912, that his days in Forsyth County were numbered. In the weeks after the trials, he watched the black community grow smaller and smaller, as one family after another decided it was better to risk the uncertainties of the road than to take their chances with the armed and increasingly dangerous white people of the county.

Forsyth's vigilantes eventually caught the attention of the national press, and papers as far away as New York told readers of a mass exodus and a black population "In Terror of Night Riders." "The anti-negro movement began in Forsyth," a correspondent wrote in the *New York Times*. Unchecked by local law enforcement, he said,

the crusade against the negroes is being conducted by bands of mounted men, who ride through the country at night and leave notices at the homes of the negroes warning them to leave at once. . . . In many instances respectable, hard-working negroes have been frightened into sacrificing their property and fleeing.

As a renter in the overwhelmingly white community of Oscarville, Byrd Oliver was just such a "respectable, hard-working negro" when he, his wife, Delia, and their seven children, ages three to fourteen, set out on foot, heading east toward the Chattahoochee River. They were bound, like so many of their fellow refugees, for the railroad town of Gainesville, in Hall County.

The Oliver family's flight from Forsyth was similar to what hundreds of their neighbors endured, but unlike those who left no trace of the journey, Byrd Oliver used to tell his daughter Dorothy all about it. "Every so often, he would sit on the doorstep and talk. . . . He could talk about it 15 or 20 years later," she said. "He would always sit with his chin in the palm of his hand and the tears would run down his sleeve. He has cried about it many a day." When Forsyth once again made national headlines in 1987,

Byrd Oliver, date unknown

seventy-seven-year-old Dorothy Rucker Oliver recounted her father's memories for the *Gainesville Times*.

"My Dad saw everything" in 1912, she said, referring to the arrests of Knox, Daniel, and Collins, the burning of black homes and churches, and the ultimatums delivered in the night. "They knew everything that was going to happen . . . it doesn't take bad news long to spread." Byrd Oliver told his daughter that many black families were forced to leave behind "drums of syrups, canned goods, family keepsakes, and most important, farmland." And when, as a child, Dorothy asked her father if he had *really* grown up in "all white" Forsyth, Oliver told how his family banded together with other groups of refugees for safety, then set out across a landscape teeming with white mobs:

> [He] traveled with a group of about 75 people . . . they would walk so far and then count [everyone in the group]. Just before they got to the river, three of his relatives were missing. But you couldn't turn back to look for them.

According to family lore, Byrd and his wife, Delia, got separated somewhere along the road, with the three oldest daughters following their mother, and the four youngest making the eleven-mile journey to Gainesville with their father. Byrd and these four children reappear in the census of 1920, living with Oliver's second wife, Beulah Rucker, who he met once they had resettled in Hall County.

It's not clear whether Byrd and Delia chose to part ways when they fled Forsyth, or she and the older children never made it to a planned reunion, or they suffered some violent attack along the road. But the records confirm Byrd Oliver's story of losing half of his family on the journey out of Forsyth, never to be seen again. While he and his second wife, Beulah, would go on to become leaders in the black community of Gainesville—and founders of one of the most successful African American schools in the state—according to Dorothy, her father never forgot about all he'd left behind in Forsyth. And like so many others, his life was divided between what happened before and what came after the fall of 1912.

AS MORE AND MORE hardworking, law-abiding people like Byrd and Delia Oliver abandoned their homes, the county's white landowners began to feel deeply concerned about the future. A report in the *New York Times* makes it clear that as the violence spread, the night riders began threatening not just black residents but many of their white employers:

> Recently warnings have been sent to white planters who employ many negroes and who have announced that they intend to protect their employees. To these planters the night riders have sent notices stating that unless they cease to protect the negroes their barns and homes will be burned.

Everyone knew that arson was no idle threat among the white people of north Georgia, and as the terror escalated, Cherokee County, which borders Forsyth to the west, saw a sudden influx of refugees. "Three wagon loads stopped here last week," a witness said, "and we are informed that several more are in and around Canton." Residents of Hall County saw long lines of displaced families walking along the roads leading out of Forsyth, and the *Savannah Tribune* ran an article with the headline "Gainesville Invaded," describing the arrival of "hordes of Negroes from Forsyth and neighboring counties, who have been driven from their homes by indignant whites." The story went on to tell how

> anonymous letters have been sent [to] almost every planter in the hill country. . . . These missives threaten arson and dynamiting

of the houses in which the Negroes live as penalty for disobey-
ance. In many instances, mobs of whites appeared at the Negro
homes on farms and openly demanded evacuation.

A. J. Julian, a longtime resident of Forsyth, was an old friend of
Joseph Mackey Brown's, and after hearing reports of such "lawlessness," he wrote directly to the governor, to make sure Brown understood that the convictions of Knox and Daniel had not brought an
end to mob violence, and that the situation was growing worse by
the day. "My Dear Gov," Julian began,

> A very important matter I desire to call your attention [to] is
> the protection of the citizens of Ga. & especially of Forsyth. . . .
> There is a gang of night marauders . . . that have run off about
> all of the negroes . . . & they are bold in their operations. It
> seems that the Sheriffs are cowards and fearful.

Julian told of one raid on a group of young black women and their
infant children, who were visited by night riders only after whites
made sure that all the adult men were away and the women unarmed:

> Last Sunday week five men went to [a] Negro House. . . . They
> sent a young man up to see if the Negro men were gone & ask
> the women if they had any guns. When they found the men
> gone & no pistols, they went up [and] ordered the women to
> leave, one with right young baby & it pouring rain. After they
> left they shot the dogs, taken all their furniture, clothes, &
> bedding, piled it out in the yard [then] set fire & burned it,
> dogs & all.

Julian clearly meant to shock the governor with the image of a
young mother, babe in arms, being driven out into a storm, as her

family's whole household was burned "dogs & all." He also knew Brown would be troubled by news that rich farmland lay abandoned and unplanted due to the violence:

> Hundreds of acres of land . . . will not be cultivated [this year], which will be a loss in taxes to both state & counties. Labor now can not be found to hire or rent. Is this state of affairs to go on? It will end in race war if some check is not put on these outrages.

The "check" Julian proposed was simple: pursue and arrest the offenders, and prosecute them vigorously in the courts.

When Brown wrote back, he offered a fifty-dollar reward to anyone who could identify the perpetrators of violence against black citizens and said he, too, "deplore[d] the action on the part of the lawless element who are committing so many outrageous crimes on the people of that section." But while Brown shared Julian's anxiety about the financial consequences, he was steadfast in his view that this was a problem to be solved by local people themselves whenever possible, not state or federal authorities. "The law-abiding element," Brown's reply to Julian concluded, "will have to by concerted efforts run down these people and bring them to justice."

In mid-October, a group of Forsyth whites tried to do just that, when they announced that a mass meeting would be held at the Cumming courthouse, to address the "lawlessness" that was driving black residents out of the county. The problem was clearly not going away on its own, and on the evening of Wednesday, October 16th—a little more than three weeks after "all hell broke loose" on the night of Mae Crow's funeral—concerned citizens gathered to discuss actions "the law-abiding element" might take to stop, and hopefully reverse, the exodus. Many surely felt a moral, Christian duty to speak out against the violence and in defense of black families who had lived in their homes, cooked their meals, and nursed

The children of Jeremiah and Nancy Brown, who were expelled from Forsyth in 1912. Left to right: Harrison, Rosalee, Bertie, Fred, Naomi, and Minor Brown, c. 1896

their children for generations—in some cases going all the way back to the days of slavery. As one local man put it, "They drove out a cook who raised seventeen children out of my kitchen!"

Present at the mass meeting were planters, mill operators, and mine owners, as well as members of rich white families who could hardly imagine life without their black "help." All these people had in common an urgent goal, and that was to stop the intimidation as soon as possible, lest they wake to find that every black field hand, overseer, driver, cook, and washerwoman in the county had vanished into the night. Cumming mayor Charlie Harris presided over the gathering, and its secretary was John F. Echols, a twenty-four-year-old who had grown up in Cumming, gone to school in Atlanta, and recently returned to serve as a clerk in Harris's law office.

The official resolution that Echols recorded in his stenography pad shows that many whites in Cumming were deeply troubled by what was happening after dark. Their resolution informed the governor that the violence was not a series of unrelated attacks but part of a coordinated "effort on the part of some unknown persons to drive the colored people from the county, which is evidenced by letters written and dropped at the door of this class of our people, and in their mail boxes, notifying them that they must leave, and containing threats against them as well as letters to some of the white people—all of which is unlawful and detrimental to the interest of the common people." In a cover letter to the governor, Harris added that "Quite a number of black churches have been burned and inhabited houses shot into by persons unknown and letters of intimidation sent through the mails . . . contrary, we believe to the laws."

This last detail, about threats being delivered through the U.S. Postal Service, was no small matter, for it meant that these "persons unknown" were violating not just county and state criminal codes but federal law. The implicit argument was that this was no longer a problem for a part-time mayor and a small county police force but a matter worthy of the attention of the governor and the federal judiciary. As part of their appeal for help, those present affirmed their commitment to peace and order. "We condemn this conduct," they said, "and pledge ourselves to give to the innocent and law abiding colored people in the County the reasonable and lawful protection in our power, and our aid in ferreting out the real perpetrators and bringing them to justice."

The resolution called on Judge William T. Newman of Georgia's Northern District federal court to open an investigation, and reminded state officials that Knox and Daniel were soon to be brought back and hung near the Cumming square. Citizens of Forsyth asked the governor to send the Georgia National Guard to help "in maintaining order and preserving the peace as well as suppressing evils already existing." Finally, the resolution called for "immediate action" from Governor Brown and Judge Newman and stressed the key role Bill Reid would have to play in stopping the violence. "We pledge ourselves to stand by Sheriff Reid," the document concluded, "and give him our support in protecting the innocent citizens of our county." Given Reid's complicity with the mob that had already killed Rob Edwards, this now sounds like a case of tragically wishful thinking.

THE PROCLAMATION OF the October mass meeting was a clear and unequivocal call to end the violence, and it provides evidence that only three weeks into the expulsions many white residents understood what was happening around them and tried to stop it. Rather than sitting idly by, they called upon those with state and federal power to "investigate these depredations and bring the guilty parties to justice."

The answer Governor Brown sent back to Cumming, five days later, was just as clear and unequivocal as Mayor Harris had been in his plea for help. "I am in receipt of your letter . . . asking my aid in restoring peace and order in your county," the governor wrote.

> In reply [I] will state that this is a matter for the judge, sheriff and other local authorities to handle; the Governor has no authority to take any steps to give protection until the local authorities advise that they are unable to enforce the laws and properly protect life and property. I sincerely hope that the good people of Forsyth County will cooperate in giving protection to all who peaceably pursue their avocations and obey all the laws.

Judge Newman also failed to act, even though the Cumming resolution implored him to launch a federal investigation and to use his office to arrest those making terrorist threats. Instead, Newman was busy playing his part in America's original "war on drugs": prosecuting thousands of poor, small-time moonshiners, who were arrested in large numbers after Georgia passed one of the earliest Prohibition laws in the nation, in 1908. With corn prices depressed for much of the first decade of the century, and with much of north Georgia unserved by railroad lines, thousands of upland farmers had realized that it was far easier to transport a wooden crate of mason jars than it was to move heaping bushels of corn over the rocky roads out of the hills. Once those jars of "white lightning" reached places like Gainesville and Atlanta, they fetched far more on the black market than any wagonload of produce ever could. Pound for pound, ears of corn were no match for white corn liquor, no matter the risk of arrest by federal "revenuers."

The massive leather minute book of Judge Newman's Northern District court is filled with convictions of one poor white distiller after another in the fall of 1912, usually on charges of federal tax evasion. What it doesn't contain is a single case brought against the night riders who, during those same months, were using the U.S. mail to make terrorist threats against African Americans. It was a federal offense for a man to stand in some shady hollow of Forsyth and quietly fill a jar with liquor, and the government sent a virtual army of revenue agents into north Georgia to arrest moonshiners and break up their stills. But when those same white men spent their nights shooting, bombing, and burning black residents out of their homes, the federal government, like Governor Joseph Mackey Brown, turned a blind eye and a deaf ear.

IN THE SUMMER of 1915, W. E. B. Du Bois, editor of the NAACP's magazine, *The Crisis*, sent a journalist named Royal Freeman Nash to Cumming, to investigate reports of a wholesale exodus of blacks from Forsyth County. The resulting article, which appeared in November of 1915, gives us one of the only written accounts of these events that comes from outside the southern point of view. Nash was a social worker and secretary of the NAACP, but as a white man, he could walk through places like Forsyth in relative anonymity, and years of investigating racial crimes had honed Nash's gift for getting people to talk.

After interviewing whites all over Forsyth, as well as members of the black community who had fled to neighboring counties, Nash described how whites had exploited the desperate situation of their black neighbors in 1912 and had swooped in with offers to buy livestock and farm implements at a fraction of their real value. "A negro would receive an anonymous letter giving him twenty-four, thirty-six hours, occasionally ten days to quit the county," Nash wrote,

> and that meant precipitate flight and abandonment of everything owned in the world. In other cases it meant a sale at a few days' notice, during which a cow worth $25 would bring $8–9, and hogs worth $15–20 sold for $4–6. House and land brought nothing. If the Negro owned a mule he moved out his furniture, otherwise it burned after his departure.

Nash went on to tell of the dire consequences if black residents tried to hold out, and he spoke with one family who'd received their ultimatum not from grown men but two white children:

> Failure to vacate on the date set meant a stealthy visit in the night and either dynamite or the torch. The result was a state of terror which caused one Negro family to accept a twenty-four hour notice [delivered by] two children aged five and six respectively, who had learned the game from their elders.

As Forsyth's white children learned "the game" of terrorizing black neighbors and driving them from their homes, a small group of African Americans tried to continue living peacefully in town, hoping they might be protected by their close connections to rich whites. Nash spoke with one black employee at a Cumming board-inghouse and told how even "after repeated notices . . . the owner kept her on until January, but let her go then for fear he could no longer protect the servant's life." Nash heard similar stories about longtime employees on the farms of the county, whose white bosses only dismissed them, often with regret and apologies, after repeated threats from the mobs. Asked if he knew of any cases where blacks were defended by whites, a Forsyth farmer told Nash that

> Old Man Roper yonder had a nigger he well nigh couldn't live without, knew every stone and stump on the farm. The boys warned him time and again to get shet of him, but Roper would keep him on. So one night they jest had to put a stick of dynamite under the nigger's house. . . . No, it didn't kill him, but it started him for Hall County right smart. . . . I reckon they won't be back. You see, the young fellers are growing up sort of with the idea that this is a white man's county.

Farm by farm, cabin by cabin, the last black residents who dared to remain in Forsyth after the death of Mae Crow were rooted out, and those who defended them were taught, with dynamite and torches, the cost of resisting the new "whites only" rule. Whatever Sheriff Reid knew about the men behind such terrorism, and whatever role he played in the violent performances that took place after dark, there is no record of a single warrant or arrest for any of the crimes committed against the property and people of black Forsyth in 1912. By mid-October, the editor of the *Dahlonega Nugget* could claim that "A gentleman of Forsyth County, who was here last week, said every Negro who lived in it was gone. Not a single one is left to tell the tale."

10

CRUSH THE THING
IN ITS INFANCY

Just a few miles east of Oscarville, across the Chattahoochee, there was another predominantly white county, with its own poor and exploited black population and its own white underclass. In Hall County, too, race hysteria spread in the fall of 1912, and residents there witnessed a similar spate of attacks on black workers and black homes. But what happened as a result could hardly have been more different.

Whatever racial tensions existed in Hall prior to the Forsyth exodus, they were aggravated by the arrival of hundreds of displaced families, who camped along the roads leading into Gainesville, and crowded into the homes of friends and relatives in the African American sections of town. The "influx of negroes," the *Constitution* said, "has created a wave of resentment throughout the hot-tempered and lawless element."

The *Gainesville Times* told of a morning that October when "a crowd variously estimated at from a dozen to one hundred went to Mr. M. A. Gaines' building near the city hall and ordered the negro brickmasons to quit work. . . . The negroes left the job as soon as they could get away and have not returned, [so] the building remains in an unfinished state." Soon local farmers were getting

similar visits from men who demanded that black workers be fired
and leave Hall County for good. The *Constitution* reported that on
October 14th,

> a mob of whites appeared at the home of Joe Hood, a negro,
> living about three miles north of Gainesville. A spokesman
> demanded Hood's removal from the vicinity [but] the negro
> slammed the door in the white man's face. A fusillade of shots
> was fired by the crowd into the house. Hood, his wife, and
> family barricaded themselves behind mattresses and bed-
> ding, and escaped unhurt, although their home was riddled
> with bullets. Large holes were rent in the sides of the build-
> ing, showing the effect of shotgun shells, and the entire side
> was peppered with pistol and Winchester bullets.

Just as in Forsyth, such attacks were part of a sustained effort
to drive out the black population and, especially, black labor competition. "Not only has the entire section suffered from the aban-
donment of farms and loss of labor from the fleeing negroes," a
journalist wrote,

> prominent businessmen of Gainesville have received . . .
> attacks by hostile whites. Many black chauffeurs of the city
> have been ordered to give up their jobs, and anonymous letters
> demanding the dismissal of negro employees have been sent.

While "cooler-headed" residents hoped that the violence would
remain a local matter and not damage Gainesville's reputation as a
center of trade, on Saturday, October 12th, the mobs of Hall County
made headlines all over the state when the Southern Railway's flag-
ship New York & New Orleans Limited stopped to take on water at
Flowery Branch, at the southern edge of the county. As the train

idled, passengers en route to Atlanta looked out their windows and were startled to see a mob dragging a black man down off the train. The man, named W. A. Flake, worked in the mail car, and it seems that the mere sight of him in his uniform was enough to enrage local whites. "Cursing the negro and surging dangerously around the car," one witness said, "the crowd frightened Flake until he cowered in a corner of the coach. D. P. White, chief clerk on the train, stepped to the doorway, and ordered the mob away, threatening to shoot the first [person] who attempted to mount the car."

Such an ambush makes it clear that Hall County was not immune to the waves of white terrorism that were transforming Forsyth in 1912. But while that October saw numerous attacks against blacks in Hall, by the time winter arrived things had calmed down, and the bands of night riders gave up their efforts to create another "white man's county" on the eastern bank of the Chattahoochee. Given that the racial cleansing succeeded on one side of the river but failed on the other, it is natural to wonder what made the difference. Why was the expulsion of African Americans part of Forsyth County's identity for nearly a hundred years, but only a brief episode in the history of Hall?

THE ATTACK ON Bill Hurse provides some clues. Hurse was a black sharecropper who lived and worked in Hall County, on the property of a wealthy white planter named Raymond Carlile, whose farm was not far from the railroad siding where W. A. Flake had narrowly escaped a lynching. The *Gainesville News* reported that on Monday, October 14th—just two days after the train was ambushed—"five nightriders went to a negro house on Mr. Raymond Carlile's place" and tried to force Hurse and his family to flee. But unlike in Forsyth County, the paper noted,

the nightriders met with such opposition as all like marauders ought to meet with—a shot gun at the hands of the

property-owner. The shooting occurred at about 10 o'clock
. . . at the house of Bill Hurse, coloured. Mr. Carlile lost no
time. . . . He made up his mind that his croppers should not
be run off. . . . When he heard the shooting at his tenant's
house, [Carlile] grabbed his shotgun and went to the place
to protect his negroes and his property. He returned the fire
and followed the marauders, winding up with the capture
of Tobe Tullus, and securing information enough to identify
[other] participants in the outlawry.

When the shooting was over and Carlile knew that Hurse and
his family were safe, he delivered his prisoner, Tobe Tullus, to Hall
County sheriff William Crow, and gave a full report. The next
morning, Crow and a posse of deputies rode out in pursuit of the
other night riders who had attacked Carlile's black tenants.

The men alleged to be in the party [of night riders] are Will
Jenkins, Bud and Jess Martin, Tobe Tullus and Wash Phagan,
warrants for each of whom are in the hands of officers.

Tobe Tullus was the only one captured [on the night of the
attack] and he is languishing behind the bars of Hall County
jail, while officers are looking for the other men, all of whom
will be captured if they do not get out of the county.

Just before the *Gainesville News* went to press, the editors added
a last-minute update. "Bud Martin, Will Jenkins, and Wash Phagan
were arrested," readers learned,

by Messers. Lon Spencer and John Tanner . . . and brought
to Gainesville on train No. 12 and lodged in jail. Mr. Spencer
was sworn in as a Deputy by Sheriff Crow . . . and returned
to Flowery Branch to take active charge of the situation. He

will apprehend any others who may engage in night-riding or the commission of other unlawful acts. The officers and the people are going to put an immediate stop to the depredations . . . the night-riding and warning of good negroes to leave must stop—and stop at once.

Though Sheriff Crow was himself a distant cousin to the white girl who had been murdered just across the river, he told reporters that he had every intention of finding and arresting whites who engaged in violence against black families. "We don't need any military," he later said, "because we're going to break this thing up ourselves." Tobe Tullus, Bud Martin, Will Jenkins, and Wash Phagan were tried and convicted for the attack on Hurse, and soon thereafter five more white men went to jail for driving bricklayers off W. A. Gaines's jobsite in downtown Gainesville. Once again, the names of the perpetrators appeared on the front page of the *Gainesville Times*: "Horace Smith, Tom Hall, Newt Strickland, John Strickland, and Tolman Strickland" were convicted "for interfering with persons engaged in lawful pursuits."

These prosecutions stand out, against the backdrop of Jim Crow Georgia, as rare instances in which white offenders were punished for violence against blacks. One witness to the raids in Forsyth later said, "If we could have gotten a few detectives in here right at the start . . . and convict[ed] one or two of [the night riders], the rest would have been frightened." By pursuing and jailing the first, boldest offenders in Hall, legal officials sent a message that whites in Forsyth never had to consider: that the power of the locally elected government would be brought to bear on "lawless" white men, even when their victims were black. As Royal Freeman Nash put it in *The Crisis,*

When the crackers in Hall County started to . . . make a sweep of their own county, at the same time, the word went out, according to local gossip, to spend ten thousand dollars if necessary to crush the thing in its infancy. . . . Eleven arrests were made within twenty-four hours after the terrorization started, and it was subsided in just a few days.

Georgia was still Georgia, and in 1912, emancipation's guarantee of freedom was still in many ways an empty promise. But when hundreds of Forsyth refugees crossed Browns Bridge and stepped onto the eastern bank of the Chattahoochee River, they were right to feel some small measure of relief. In Hall County, at least, it was still a crime to kill a black man.

11

THE SCAFFOLD

The most prominent spokesman for the Forsyth expulsions was a wealthy Cumming doctor named Ansel Strickland, who was descended from Hardy Strickland, the largest slave owner in antebellum Forsyth. In the weeks after Rob Edwards was lynched, Dr. Strickland wrote an angry letter to the *North Georgian*, full of indignation at Atlanta editors who suggested that "lawlessness" had run rampant in Forsyth County. "Now what *is* the law?" Dr. Strickland asked readers. "The law is the will of the people. . . . [If] the citizens of the county are satisfied," he said, "that ends it. The people make the law." Not surprisingly, as the date of the Knox and Daniel executions approached, Dr. Strickland volunteered to host the double hanging on his own property.

Judge Morris had been clear in his directive from the bench: the death sentences were to be carried out "within one mile of the county courthouse . . . in private and witnessed only by the executing officer, a sufficient guard, the relatives of the defendant[s] and such clergymen as [they] may desire." Morris knew just how easily a public hanging could become a "temptation to mob violence," and so he ordered a stately, discreet affair—then turned plans for the hanging over to Bill Reid.

When the sheriff first walked down a grassy slope behind Strickland's house and stared out across the doctor's lower pasture, he must have recognized the possibilities right away. With its proximity to the courthouse, the site technically complied with the judge's order, and could be reached on foot with just a short stroll down Maple Street. At the same time, as Reid squinted up at the ridges rising on three sides, he could see that they formed a kind of natural amphitheater, with a horseshoe of hills surrounding the wide, level field. Thousands of people could gather on those hillsides, with their quilts, their children, and their picnic baskets, and every last one of them would have a clear view of the proceedings. Once the hanging proper began, Reid knew they would cheer for him as he sent two convicted black rapists to their doom.

When Morris learned that the gallows was to be erected in such a public place, he ordered that the site at least be concealed behind some kind of blind. The wooden fence Reid's men built in response rose fifteen feet in the air and formed a thirty-foot-square enclosure in the middle of Dr. Strickland's pasture—the whole thing designed to comply with the judge's demand that the scaffold, and the dying men, be shielded from view.

But in the days leading up to the hanging, people came from miles around to watch the carpenters work, and as they sat on the grassy hillsides, it was easy to see the flaw in Newt Morris's plan. If anything were to happen to that fifteen-foot fence—if, say, it were to somehow catch fire—the hanging would become not the dignified, private affair Judge Morris had envisioned, but a gruesome bit of theater in the round.

On Thursday, October 24th, as the little town filled with people eager to witness the county's first legal execution in fifty years, Ernest Knox and Oscar Daniel were just beginning their final trip north. If the two cousins held out any last hope as they lay on their cots inside the Fulton Tower, the appearance of a deputy, handcuffs at the ready, brought home their situation: they were going home to die, surrounded by the same whites who had whipped Grant Smith, lynched Rob Edwards, and driven almost everyone they knew out of Forsyth County. At an order from the deputy, they rose, held their wrists out to be manacled, and shuffled out through a gauntlet of photographers, emerging one last time into the glare of Butler Street.

Having been convinced by Mayor Harris that Bill Reid was not the sort of man to oppose a lynch mob, Brown signed an executive order declaring Forsyth to be once more—for the third time in six weeks—"in a state of insurrection" and directed the Fifth Regiment to escort the prisoners on the now-familiar trip to Cumming. Knox and Daniel again found themselves at the center of a military parade, as they marched along Hunter Street to Terminal Station. Along the way, a reporter who had struggled to get close to the prisoners darted into an office building, climbed the stairs to a high floor, and aimed his camera out a window. The result is a god's-eye view of the scene, and the last known photograph of sixteen-year-old Ernest, and his eighteen-year-old cousin, Oscar.

The Fifth Regiment boarded a four-thirty Southern Railway train and arrived at Buford at six o'clock that evening. After a pause for supper, they began the march toward Forsyth. According to the unit's chief medical officer, Dr. Arnold Lindorme, "The weather was ideal, cool and bright moonlight, [and] we made good time. At 1:30 a.m., the command reached the courthouse, in Cumming."

Sheriff Reid was waiting on the square, and after arranging for the prisoners and their guards to spend the night inside the courthouse, Reid and Catron spoke about plans for the next day's executions. Unfortunately, the sheriff told Catron, there had been an accident involving the court-ordered fence.

A reporter for the *Keowee Courier* told the story of how, just a

The Fifth Regiment en route from Fulton Tower to Terminal Station, Atlanta; the arrow indicates the prisoners Knox and Daniel.

few hours before the militiamen arrived, a mob had gone "to the scene of the scaffold, tore down the high fence and made a monster bonfire of the lumber and timbers." The pasture lay almost within sight of Ansel Strickland's house, and certainly within earshot, so it is likely that as he settled into bed that night, the Cumming doctor could hear the sound of the revelers celebrating their triumph. Defying Judge Morris's order of privacy was clearly the point, since vandals dismantled the fence and set it ablaze but were careful not to lay a finger on the gallows where Knox and Daniel would hang. "This morning only a heap of charred embers was left" where the fence stood, said the *Courier*, but "the scaffold itself was not molested."

When he learned that no guards had been stationed to protect the fence, Major Catron began to sense that Bill Reid was a large part of the problem in Forsyth County. In his report, Catron expanded on his worries about the county sheriff:

> I ask[ed] him if he did not intend to have [the fence] rebuilt, but he said he could not get lumber for that purpose. I had noticed a stack of lumber on our way into town and I told him

I would have [it] put on the ground and furnish him any number of men from my command to put it up, but he declined
this offer without comment.

When Judge Morris got wind of the fire the next morning and
ordered county ordinary Herschel Jones to have the fence rebuilt,
one Cumming merchant after another refused to sell the lumber.
A story even circulated—no doubt told with a wink and a nod—
that it was illegal for the sound of a hammer to be heard on the day
of a hanging.

Catron suspected that Reid had openly colluded with the men
who'd burned the fence and had plotted to make the execution into
a public spectacle:

I had every reason to believe that the Sheriff was entirely in
sympathy with the would-be mob, [and] that he selected the
place for the gallows solely that the fence might be torn away,
and that the spectators might have a good view of the execution. I believe [Reid] connived with the mob in tearing away
the wall and that his own henchmen actually did the work.

He promised that the execution should take place early
in order that the crowd would not have time to gather and
possibly get boisterous and unruly. [But] at the same time he
advised the doctors who were to be witnesses to the execution
not to come until 12 o'clock . . . I believe that he was playing with the law for political advantages and would have welcomed an opportunity to openly espouse the side of the mob.

What Catron had discovered, it seems, is that Bill Reid's con-
duct during the hangings was no less calculated than when he gave
Deputy Lummus the politically toxic job of guarding Rob Edwards.
Now that his role as county sheriff was not to control the mobs of

Forsyth but to treat them to a public hanging, Bill Reid seized his moment and took center stage.

After breakfast on the morning of Friday, October 25th, Reid made his way to the middle of Strickland's pasture and began waving to the families who were staking out prime locations on the grassy banks. Dr. Lindorme, who was there to ensure that the hangings were carried out in a humane manner, was just as appalled as Catron:

> The ground selected by the Sheriff . . . could not have been better for the purpose—to let the thousands of people who gathered to see it well done by him, THE SHERIFF. It made on the writer the impression of an execution as was indulged in in the early times of the 18th century.

As mules, horses, and buggies clogged Tolbert Street and Kelly Mill Road, and as thousands of new arrivals took their places on the hillsides, Catron's men used barbed wire to create a one-hundred-yard cordon around the gallows. The only people allowed inside, said Catron, were "newspaper men, some two or three Sheriffs from adjoining counties, and a few relatives of the Sheriff of Forsyth County." Basking in the attention of the crowd, and having used his position to give "a few relatives" the most coveted seats in the house, Reid filled the hours between daybreak and the arrival of the prisoners by showboating for the crowd and whipping them up for the hangings to come. "He was boisterous and went out where everybody could see him," Catron reported,

> and [he] wrestled with a young man, dragging him down the hill by the foot and in other ways [tried] to create a scene. The mob around the fence were constantly calling to him to let them know when he needed them, and he would call

back to them that he would do so. He was constantly yelling to the people around the fence outside. The Sheriff so conducted himself that if the sentence of the court could have been carried out without him I would have placed him under arrest for inciting to riot. . . . [He was] openly in accord with insurrection.

As the anticipation built, more and more people "took up their position on the hills above the pasture and waited," witnesses said, "like eager crowds waited for a circus parade." The audience included many "fathers and mothers with children on their arms" who "had full view of the execution . . . [since] the wooden fence around the scaffold was burned [and] every detail of the gruesome program could be seen from the hills."

While Catron was disgusted by the "festive mood," at no point were his troops challenged by members of the crowd, who seemed to realize that a lynching was now redundant, since Reid had arranged for them to witness all the pomp and drama of a state-sponsored killing. Still, as Knox and Daniel made the half-mile walk from the courthouse, their dread of the gallows must have been matched by a sense that at any moment the mob might grow impatient. As Catron put it, "Most of these people were merely idle spectators, but there was a large element of vicious and lawless people . . . and we had no way of distinguishing them."

BEFORE THE HANGING could begin, there was one more group of guests to be led through the military checkpoint and seated inside the deadline. When they appeared at the edge of the pasture, a hush fell over the crowd, and for the first time all morning the raucous men quieted down, mothers shushed their children, and even Bill Reid stopped hamming long enough to take off his hat and assume a somber pose.

More than five thousand people watched as a solider led Bud and Azzie Crow to their seats at the base of the gallows—where, as the bereaved parents of the victim, they would have the honor of seeing Knox and Daniel die before their eyes. They were followed by their twenty-year-old son Major, Mae's oldest brother, then her younger siblings Ed, Lee, Rinta, the twins Obie and Ovie, seven-year-old Bonnie, and the baby of the family, eighteen-month-old Esta. This was the row of children Mae, the eldest daughter, had been on her way to fetch almost seven weeks earlier, when someone attacked her in the woods outside of Oscarville. For those gathered on the hillside, the sight was heartbreaking: Mae's grieving mother and father, and their long line of mournful children trailing behind.

As was customary, the condemned prisoners were offered a chance to speak before they were led up onto the scaffold. Accounts of their last words differ. The *Forsyth County News* claimed that "shortly before his death Knox confessed, but Oscar Daniel carried his secret of the crime through the trap, denying his guilt to the moment of his death." But another eyewitness said that "neither negro had a word to say [and] they went stolidly to their death, apparently unmoved by the fate that awaited them."

According to a story passed down in the Crow family, soon after he was led through the barbed-wire cordon, Oscar Daniel turned and looked directly at Azzie Crow. Oscar held her eye, perhaps hoping to silently communicate to Azzie that whatever terrible thing had happened to her daughter, he'd had nothing to do with it. Either the newspapermen weren't close enough to witness that fleeting exchange or they chose not to report it. And so, for forty years the story was a secret Mae's mother kept to herself. Only in 1952, on her deathbed, did she admit to her daughter Esta that she still remembered the look on Oscar Daniel's face, and had carried all her life a terrible fear that the boy was innocent.

Even if she had wanted to stop the executions at that point, there is probably little Azzie could have done. The hillsides were packed with thousands of people who had come to see a double hanging, and Major Catron and his troops had strict orders: to ensure that a court-ordered death sentence was carried out. Whatever Azzie thought in that instant when her eyes met the eyes of Oscar Daniel, she said nothing, and a moment later Sheriff Reid and the two attending physicians rose and took their places. At a nod from Reid, Deputy Lummus led Knox and Daniel up a narrow wooden stairway and onto the scaffold, where two thick nooses hung at eye level.

IN 1912, HANGING convicts "by the neck until dead" was still the primary means of execution, and it would be more than a decade before courts moved to the newly invented electric chair—which gained favor precisely because killing someone with a rope is not as simple as it sounds. American legal authorities had been hang-

Azzie Crow, mother of Mae, c. 1950

ing prisoners as far back as the Jamestown Colony, but botched executions were common well into the twentieth century. State law stipulated that Forsyth County ordinary Herschel V. Jones design a scaffold and prepare nooses appropriate for the hanging of Knox and Daniel. Mobs may have simply thrown the end of a rope over a tree limb or the nearest telephone pole, but to play his role in the pageant of capital punishment, Jones had a number of problems to overcome.

The goal was to drop the prisoner from such a height that as the slipknot tightened and the body reached the end of the rope, forces multiplied enough to fracture the spine. If all went according to plan, such a hanging was the most humane form of execution available at the time, resulting in instantaneous and bloodless death. But there were two unsavory risks: decapitation and strangulation. If the force generated by a fall was too great, the spine might be not just broken but completely severed. Many people on the hillsides overlooking the gallows must have recalled the 1900 hanging of a Georgia man named Benjamin Snell, whose execution went so awry that the *Atlanta Constitution* gave a lengthy account:

> The heavy rope cut through the neck of the murderer and severed the windpipe and blood vessels, and practically pulverized the bones of the neck. The tough muscles at the back of [Snell's] neck saved the total severance of the head from the body. Blood gushed from the severed arteries almost instantly, and dyed the white linen shirt and collar, and then flowed down the clothing, extending to the shoes. It was a spectacle that was most revolting . . . had the drop been four inches lower decapitation would certainly have resulted.

Clearly, whoever planned Snell's hanging had gotten the figures wrong. The most common reason for such errors was a desire to avoid the equally gruesome alternative to decapitation: the sight of

a prisoner writhing, gasping, kicking, and moaning at the end of a rope, as he or she died a slow and noisy death by strangulation. This happened when the drop was too short and the forces were not enough to fracture the vertebrae. In such cases the prisoner eventually choked to death, but it could take as long as half an hour.

When, in early October, Herschel Jones had sketched the scaffold through which Knox and Daniel were to fall, he would have consulted a "table of drops" that was widely used to calculate the length of the noose, based on a convict's body weight. The key fact for Jones was that the two prisoners to be hung in Forsyth were not grown men but adolescents. For Knox and Daniel, the charts would have recommended a nine- to ten-foot drop—a height normally reserved for hanging women. To snap their necks, Herschel Jones needed a high scaffold and two unusually long ropes.

AFTER WEEKS OF tension and violence, the ritual up on the platform took less than a minute. Theo Wills, the pastor of Cumming's First Baptist Church, led the crowd in a brief prayer, during which even the rowdiest spectators fell silent. According to the *Forsyth County News,* when Wills finally opened his eyes and looked up at the heavens, "Deputies Gay Lummus and Monroe Jones assisted in tying the hands and feet of the negroes, and in placing the noose about their necks." The last thing Knox and Daniel saw before black sacks were placed over their heads was a hillside dotted with thousands of white faces—young and old, rich and poor, men, women, and children. Squinting into the midday sun, they would have seen the rooftops of the fine houses on Kelly Mill Road, the spires of a dozen little churches poking up through the treetops, and, on the edge of town, in the hazy gray distance, the familiar humpbacked silhouette of Sawnee Mountain.

They may have even seen, among the chauffeurs and buggy drivers on the margins of the crowd, a few of the last remaining black

people of Forsyth. By October 25th, the only families left were a few property owners reluctant to leave their homes in town, as well as those who worked as servants for Cumming's wealthiest white residents. If such "town negroes" had known Knox and Daniel at all before their arrest, it would have been as illiterate, barefoot field hands from the farms out in Oscarville. What Knox and Daniel did not see was anyone from their own families: not Jane Daniel, not Buck or Catie, not Oscar's older brother Cicero, Ernest's sister, Erma, or his long-vanished mother, Nettie Knox. Side by side, as they'd been so often over the past month, the two cousins stood on the wooden platform as Deputy Lummus fixed the hoods that would shield their eyes—and hide their dying faces from the crowd. He lowered the nooses over their heads and cinched the slipknots tight.

With his usual flair for the dramatic, Reid let the prisoners stand for a long moment over the trap doors, which were held closed by a rope that ran under the gallows, ending in a knot around a post where the sheriff stood. Reid raised one arm, then, as the voices of thousands of whites gathered and roared down from the hillsides, "cut the rope trigger with a hatchet." There was a "quick ker-thrash," the *Forsyth County News* said, as "the souls of the negroes were rushed into eternity."

Bud and Azzie Crow stared silently as the two bodies plunged into the shadows, jerked violently at the bottom of their ropes, then spun several times in one direction and slowly back the other way. "The trap was sprung at 12," Dr. Lindorme said, "[and at] 12:11 the heart stopped beating." Lindorme's time line suggests that Herschel Jones had gotten his figures right, since eleven minutes is within the normal range of time it takes a prisoner's heart to stop after the spinal cord has been severed. The crowd on the hillsides cheered and shouted their approval when, fifteen minutes later, the doctor signaled for the prisoners to be cut down. A legend passed down for generations says that when the bodies of Knox and Daniel were laid out, and their hoods removed, Bud and Azzie Crow sat only inches away, at the center of the front row of spectators. An eighty-two-year-old Ruth Jordan remembered that "the famely of the murderd girl all had ringside seats" and said that when Reid "cut the rope that threw the boys, they fell almost at [their] feet."

Having stood over his mutilated daughter just weeks earlier, and having seen Rob Edwards laid out on the courthouse lawn, Bud Crow found himself facing a corpse for the third time that fall. He rose from his chair and paused briefly over Knox and Daniel before a soldier led him and his family back out through the barbed-wire fence.

Hundreds of postcards and lynching photographs from the Jim Crow era attest to the fact that whites often gathered keepsakes from a lynching—and it was no different that day in Ansel Strickland's field. The line of militiamen prevented spectators from slicing fingers and toes off the corpses as they filed past, but Major Catron couldn't stop Reid and his men from cutting up the two hangman's nooses and handing out small pieces as souvenirs.

While most of these vanished long ago, one remnant was put on a kind of public display in the Forsyth County Courthouse. Well into the 1980s, it could still be found tucked between the pages of a big leather-bound volume of superior court minutes from 1912. And so when, in 1987, descendants of Forsyth's expelled African American families finally came searching for records of the Knox and Daniel trials, they found the page they were looking for quite easily. For as long as anyone could remember, it had been marked with a dusty and disintegrating—but still recognizable—piece of old hemp rope.

ANSEL STRICKLAND HAD already hosted one bonfire in his lower pasture, and now Major Catron feared that "if the bodies of the prisoners were left at Cumming they would be burned." After all that had transpired over the previous month, the last thing Catron

wanted was a bunch of drunken whites dancing around the burning bodies of two black men. So he ordered his soldiers to place the
corpses inside two pine boxes provided by the local undertaker, and
had them loaded onto a hired wagon. Dr. Lindorme then "called
Dr. Selman over long distance phone and arranged to bring [them]
to Atlanta . . . at the expense of the State Anatomical Board and for
their use."

When, well after dark, a detachment from Catron's unit turned
onto Luckie Street in Atlanta, William Selman was waiting in
his long white coat, outside the Baptist Tabernacle Infirmary. He
ordered assistants to store the bodies in a basement morgue, in
case some relative or friend appeared to claim them. But as Dr. Selman made his rounds the following day, no one came to the front
door or the back, asking after the two convicted rapists. So there
was no one to object when, Friday morning, they were washed
and prepared for "use." At a nod from Selman, a group of young
surgical students lowered their head mirrors, lifted their scalpels,
and began examining the lacerations and cracked vertebrae of two
anonymous black cadavers.

12

WHEN THEY WERE SLAVES

Not long after the hanging, somewhere in Georgia an amateur photographer lifted a negative out of its fixing bath, held it up to the light, and peered at the only known photograph taken on the day of the executions. The photographer had scrambled to high ground, unfolded the bellows of a camera, and taken a shot looking back over the jumble of buggies lined up on Tolbert Street, as thousands of people spilled out of Ansel Strickland's pasture and headed back toward Cumming. Two men in the foreground stare directly into the lens, with an expression common to so many lynching photographs of the Jim Crow era: somber but self-assured, earnest yet openly content.

But the most startling thing about the image is that in the bottom right corner, three young black men can be seen standing among the crowd. On a day when the overwhelming majority of Forsyth's African American residents had already fled across the county line, these men were part of the small group of holdouts in Cumming, who still hoped they might weather the season of violence and hold on to whatever it was that had kept them in Forsyth, despite the obvious risks.

One of the men sits in the driver's seat of a buggy, having

unhitched his mule and allowed it to graze by the roadside. The other two are caught in conversation. The man on the left wears a rumpled hat, a white shirt, and a simple coat, but the other, in the center of the group, is dressed like a man of means—with his crisp bowler, long topcoat and bow tie, and a gold watch chain looping down from the buttonhole of his vest.

With his elegant attire and air of wealth, this figure belies the stereotypical image of the 1,098 banished people of Forsyth. A great many of them were indeed poor, illiterate field hands and hired men, like Rob Edwards, Ernest Knox, and Oscar Daniel. Still, there were others who had managed—through skill, patience, luck, and decades of hard work—to not only survive in post-emancipation Forsyth but thrive there. These successful black residents, like the dapper gentleman in the photograph, were among the very last

A crowd near the gallows where Knox and Daniel were hung, with Sawnee Mountain in the distance, October 25th, 1912

Three witnesses to the Knox and Daniel hangings, October 25th, 1912

African Americans to leave the county—not because wealth and property were any protection from the mobs but because they had more than anyone else to lose.

ONE SUCH MAN was Joseph Kellogg, the largest black property owner in the county. When emancipation finally reached Georgia, in 1865, Joseph's parents, Edmund and Hannah, had begun building a new life, as free citizens of Forsyth. They were more fortunate than most former slaves, given that they had eight adult children, including six strong young sons, and had been staked to a small parcel of land by their former owner, a white merchant named George Kellogg, who had moved to Georgia from Hartford, Connecticut. By 1870, only five years after the South's surrender at Appomattox, the sixty-two-year-old Edmund could report to the tax collector that his "total estate" was $125—an impressive sum for a man who had been enslaved for more than sixty years. Four years later, he owned multiple lots near Sawnee Mountain, north of Cumming, totaling eighty acres, with a reported value of $345.

Edmund's oldest son, Joseph, had also been the legal property of a white man when he was born. But he was just twenty-three when freed, and so the early years of Joseph's adulthood were marked not by the hopelessness of slavery but by one new milestone after another. There was the day—July 2nd, 1867—when Joseph and his younger brother Lewis stood in line at the Forsyth County Courthouse, shoulder to shoulder with white men who two years earlier might have bought and sold them like livestock. When they signed oaths of allegiance to the United States government, scratching small X's above their names, they became for the first time in their lives "Qualified Voters." There was also the day—July 21st, 1868— when they learned that Georgia had ratified the Fourteenth Amendment, granting in theory, if seldom in practice, "equal protection of the laws," regardless of color or "previous conditions of slavery or involuntary servitude." And then there was the day in 1870 when they celebrated news that the right of black men to vote had been enshrined in the Fifteenth Amendment to the U.S. Constitution.

It would take more than a century of struggle to even begin to realize the promises that federal lawmakers made to the Kelloggs during these early years of Reconstruction. But as Edmund, Joseph, and the rest of the Kelloggs harvested one successful crop after another in the 1870s, and as they reinvested their earnings in acquiring more and better land in Forsyth, they had good reason to hope that going forward the protections of law and government might actually be available to them. Looking out over their farm at the base of Sawnee Mountain, they surely believed that Forsyth would always be their home.

Filled with that hope, on a crisp fall morning in September of 1871, a twenty-nine-year-old Joseph Kellogg asked eighteen-year-old Eliza Thompson to be his wife. When she said yes, rather than "jumping the broom," as blacks had done to consecrate marriages in the days of slavery, they walked together toward Cumming, accompanied by a local minister named Silas Smith. As it happens, Reverend Smith was the father of Grant Smith, the man who would be horsewhipped on that same town square four decades later. But the expulsions of 1912 were still far in the future on the day of Joseph and Eliza's wedding, and when Reverend Smith signed their marriage license and dated it September 7th, 1871, they must have all had great expectations for this new America—in which black people had the right to receive fair wages for their labor, own land, vote, and even hold elected office.

It's true that the majority of African Americans in Forsyth still worked on the same farms where they had been enslaved, and that like black people all over the South, they were widely exploited and cheated by whites under the new contract labor system. But for the first time in their lives, people like Joseph and Eliza Kellogg had the right to protest the injustices whites committed against them, and at least the possibility of legal remedy. The face of the law in Forsyth, which had always been the local sheriff, now included the county's own representative of the United States government, who had an office located right on the Cumming square. Over its door hung a sign that read "BRFAL." The acronym stood for the Bureau of Refugees, Freedmen, and Abandoned Lands—though everyone in town, whether in bitterness or gratitude, called it simply "the Bureau."

ABRAHAM LINCOLN HAD established the Freedmen's Bureau as part of the Department of War, intending it to operate for one year after the Confederate surrender, with the express mission of helping protect the rights of people like Joseph and Eliza Kellogg as they made the difficult transition from slavery to freedom. The bill Lincoln signed into law on March 3rd, 1865—just a month before his assassination—gave the Bureau power to rule on disputes between blacks and whites "in all places where . . . local courts . . . disregard the negro's right to justice before the laws."

Federal officials quickly recognized that Forsyth County, Georgia, was just such a place. The Freedmen's Bureau office at Cumming opened in March of 1867, headed by a man named Alexander Burruss Nuckolls. The thirty-seven-year-old Nuckolls, a local Baptist minister, was typical of the first group of Freedmen's Bureau agents in Georgia, who were appointed by Brigadier General Davis Tillson. Tillson is best known as the man who reversed Sherman's Field Order 15, which had given freed slaves a share in the vast abandoned plantations along the Georgia coast. Having reneged on the promise of "forty acres and a mule," Tillson went on to appoint a whole class of Freedmen's Bureau agents like Reverend Nuckolls, who were ill-suited to the job of imposing federal law on resentful local whites. These were local men with strong connections to former slaveholders and a deep personal investment in the status quo.

To make matters worse, under the original arrangements of the Freedmen's Bureau, agents were not given government pay; they were compensated by the white landowners for whom they certified labor contracts. The system was abused all across the South, and when Tillson was replaced as commissioner of the Freedmen's Bureau in Georgia, his successor, Colonel Caleb Sibley, realized just how corrupt the Bureau had become—and just how woefully it had failed to protect vulnerable African American communities. As Sibley put it, the "power delegated to these resident white appointees [was] shamefully abused. . . . And [t]hey occasionally inflicted cruel and unusual punishment."

Sibley fired most of the original Bureau agents in 1867 and replaced them with northern military men, in the hope of establishing impartial legal tribunals that would give freed slaves their first taste of real justice. On April 1st, 1867, Nuckolls was relieved of command of the Cumming Freedmen's Bureau office and replaced by Major William J. Bryan, who hailed from North Carolina, and who owed his $1,200 annual salary—and his allegiance—not to local white property owners but to the United States government.

As a small cog in the great machine of the Bureau, Agent Bryan focused his efforts in Forsyth on disputes brought by black workers whose employers refused to honor verbal and signed labor agreements. Like former slave owners all over the South, the white planters of Forsyth were frequently ordered to appear before the Freedmen's Bureau court for withholding crop shares and payments to black field hands, who for the first time in the history of the state had to be paid a fair wage.

Records of the cases heard by Major Bryan are peppered with the names of the same white men who feature most prominently in the lists of Forsyth slave owners in the 1850s and '60s. Tolbert Strickland, scion of the Hardy Strickland family, which had owned more than a hundred slaves in 1860, appeared before Bryan six times in a single week in October of 1867, charged by his employees with refusing to pay wages owed and refusing to give tenants a share of crops they had spent the entire year planting, tending, and harvesting.

In case after case, Bryan found in favor of black plaintiffs. Most of his judgments ordered white employers to honor prior agreements, usually after black laborers produced documents detailing what they were owed "according to contract." It is also clear that, absent court orders, many whites would do everything possible to avoid paying. When one man, Newton Harrell, was sued by a black employee listed only as John, Harrell presented a document in which the man seemed to agree to work for nothing but room, board, and clothing. Upon closer inspection, it became clear that Harrell had forged the agreement, and Bryan ruled that "the contract was a fraud."

On days when black workers did prevail in court, they frequently suffered for the victory after dark. When one group of white planters was forced to pay black workers, the Bureau's judgment was followed by a night of terrorism. The whites who lost the case, Bryan said, retaliated by "breaking into the house [of one man] and shooting at the complainant in the night. . . . Another [black family was] burnt out. . . . All this in Forsyth County."

Bryan also had the power to review and reverse civil court judgments involving freed people, and many of these cases involved the practice of legally "binding" minor children to white masters. In theory these agreements were a kind of social welfare, meant to provide shelter, food, and clothing to black children orphaned and left destitute by the war. Many former slave owners in Forsyth offered to take in such children as "apprentices" and teach them a trade, in exchange for years of labor. But in reality the apprentice system was highly corrupt, and Bryan found in case after case that such contracts were a thinly veiled form of reenslavement, with black children "bound out" to the white masters who had owned their families before emancipation, and for whom they now worked for little or no pay. The youngest "apprentice" in Forsyth was John A. Armstrong, who was not yet five years old when he was bound to M. C. Chastain until the age of twenty-one.

Historian Eric Foner has written that all over the South "ideas inherited from slavery displayed remarkable resilience" during Reconstruction, noting that "for those accustomed to the power of command, the normal give-and-take of employer and employee was difficult to accept." Such was undoubtedly the case among the former slave owners of Forsyth, as they fought to preserve the pre-emancipation social order even long after the war. In March of 1866, for example, Hardy Strickland went to the Freedmen's Bureau office in order to "bind" a sixteen-year-old named Thomas Strickland. After laying out the terms under which Thomas would continue to live in a slave cabin on the Strickland plantation, the document stipulated that Thomas had to faithfully obey Hardy Strickland's command and keep his master's counsel:

> Thomas . . . binds himself to live with [and] continue to serve
> . . . until he arrives at the age of twenty-one years . . . obeying
> the commands of the said H. W. Strickland . . . behaving him-
> self faithfully, neither revealing his secrets nor at any time
> leaving or neglecting the business of the said Strickland.

Most of the children "bound out" in this way were not orphans at all but prisoners to their former owners, still enslaved long after emancipation. A black mother named Jenny complained to the Freedmen's Bureau about John Hockenhull Sr. (the father of Dr. John Hockenhull Jr., who would dress Mae Crow's wounds and testify against Ernest Knox and Oscar Daniel). After speaking with Jenny, Agent Bryan wrote that Hockenhull "now holds without consent her two sons . . . and refuses to let her have or see them." Charity Ramsey reported that her three children were being held by their former owner "without consent and without compensation." Thomas Riley put it even more bluntly when he begged the Bureau for help retrieving his "stolen child."

After hearing and ruling on such cases for nearly a year, an exhausted and frustrated William Bryan appended a personal note to his monthly report for October 1867. At the bottom of a page filled with cases of white masters holding black children prisoner, of employers mistreating and defrauding black workers, and of vigilantes threatening to burn down "a school for colored children," Bryan acknowledged the desperate situation of the freed people of Forsyth. It was a place where powerful whites rejected black citizenship on principle and resented the very idea of paying for black labor. "I am fully satisfied from observation," he wrote, "that if the Freedmen's Bureau did not exist [then] in my district colored people would stand no chance of getting any more for their labor than when they were slaves."

Bryan was alarmed not just at the hostile environment African Americans faced in Forsyth but by what he saw as a downward spiral of violence, made all the worse by the Bureau's contraction in the face of opposition from southern Democrats in Congress. A year later, he wrote another letter to Bureau officials, this time warning that

> affairs are in a worse condition than at any time in the last 20 mos. There appear to be . . . robbers, murderers, and house thieves at large in Cherokee and Forsyth Counties, who are a terror to good citizens both white and black. . . . Complaints are frequent of persons refusing to divide crops with freedmen who have been working on joint account. I fear things are growing worse very fast.

If Bryan sounds anxious about what would happen in Forsyth if his office closed, he seems, in hindsight, to have been sadly prophetic. For these are among the last written records of the Freedmen's Bureau in Cumming. After that burst of activity between 1867 and 1868, when black laborers could use the power of the federal government to receive what was owed to them—and when distraught mothers could come to Major Bryan for help rescuing their "stolen children"—in January of 1868, the Cumming Freedmen's Bureau office closed for good.

That month Cumming saw the last of Major Bryan, who was a despised figure to many whites for having used his position exactly as Lincoln had intended. "Until the freedmen are protected by Government officials," Bryan said in one of his last letters to superiors in Atlanta, "their freedom is only a name, without its benefits." Bryan was reassigned to Marietta as the Bureau, underfunded and

losing support in Washington, struggled to continue its work with
fewer agents and fewer offices. In late 1869, the Marietta office
closed as well, and by 1872 the entire federal Freedmen's Bureau
had ceased all operations, as legal authority fell back into the hands
of local sheriffs all over the South.

IN 1906, THE *Gainesville News* interviewed an old white man
named George Harris Bell, who reminisced about his childhood
in Forsyth in the 1870s and '80s. Bell's recollections leave little
doubt that Major Bryan was right to have worried about what
would happen to black residents once he was gone. As Bell strolled
around Oscarville, he told a reporter about the "Taylor boys" and
how they had

> terrorized [Forsyth] just after the War and in the 1870s. Woe
> be unto the man who gained their enmity, for he was certain
> to be paid a visit. It was their favorite pastime to go at night to
> the home of someone they disliked and shoot into the house,
> throw rails and rocks into the well, tear down fences and out-
> buildings, cut open feather beds, and sometimes carry away
> guns, pistols and other things they took a fancy to. Living, as
> we did, only a short distance from their home, often have we
> seen them returning on Sunday morning, tired and worn out
> after making a raid on Saturday night.

Bell remembered groups of white night riders expelling black
people from the county long before 1912, such as the time "a number of citizens . . . whipped a Negro and treated him to a free ride
upon a rail to the Chattahoochee River at Williams' Ferry, set him
across the river, and told him never to return."

Against the odds, and without legal protection once the Bureau
was disbanded, Joseph and Hannah Kellogg slowly built a prosper-

ous life for themselves during those first decades of freedom. By the 1890s, nearly all the advances of congressional Reconstruction had been reversed by the oppressive codes of Jim Crow, and yet the Kelloggs were busy heeding the advice Booker T. Washington and his Tuskegee Institute gave to southern blacks at the end of the nineteenth century. Intellectuals like W. E. B. Du Bois viewed the South as a wasteland for black people and saw the industrial North as the only hope of safety and equal treatment under the law. But in his famous "Atlanta Compromise" speech of 1895, Washington declared that the corn rows and tobacco fields of the South would always be home to African Americans. "One-third of the population of the South is of the Negro race," Washington said, and

> to those who underestimate the importance of preservating friendly relations with the Southern white man who is their next door neighbor, I would say: "Cast down your bucket where you are." Cast it down, making friends in every manly way of the people of all races, by whom you are surrounded.

The road to betterment, Washington argued, was paved with hard work, savings, and thrift, and African American farmers, laborers, and tradesmen would be truly safe only when they became highly productive members of the community, deeply interconnected with white prosperity. Washington might as well have been describing Forsyth's black Kellogg family when he wrote that

> the Negro . . . should make himself, through skill, intelligence, and character, of such undeniable value to the community in which he live[s] that the community could not dispense with his presence. . . . In proportion as the Negro learn[s] to produce what other people want and must have, in the same proportion [will] he be respected.

Joseph Kellogg had inherited the family land when his father, Edmund, died in 1874, and he was exactly the kind of tireless and productive black farmer Booker T. Washington idealized. Joseph improved the family property such that, including machinery, buildings, and livestock, it had a total value of close to $600 in 1880. Records show that by 1890 Joseph had purchased an additional fifty acres, and by the 1900 census, the Kelloggs were themselves landlords—renting to other black families and using the proceeds to accumulate more and more land each year.

So when, in April of 1910, census taker Ed Johnson walked north out of Cumming, he found the white-bearded sixty-eight-year-old Joseph Kellogg, who had been born into slavery in 1842, presiding over a two-hundred-acre farm. Such a spread, stretching out over rolling hills in the shadow of Sawnee Mountain, was the envy of people all over the county, and especially the poor and property-less white men who sometimes stopped and admired it from the road—shaking their heads and narrowing their eyes at the luck of old Joe Kellogg.

13

DRIVEN TO THE
COOK STOVES

M any whites in Forsyth spent the days after the hangings defending Bill Reid against criticism in the Atlanta papers and congratulating him on a job well done. He had presided over an execution with all the excitement of a country fair and had gone out of his way to ensure that Ernest Knox and Oscar Daniel died not behind a fifteen-foot blind but in full view of the people. Having filled the arena and sprung the trap with one swift blow of his hatchet, Reid was now one of the county's most celebrated heroes.

Some Atlanta editors, however, railed against the sheriff for having arranged the spectacle in the first place, and against Major Catron for having allowed it to continue. "After going all the way to Cumming," the *Constitution* said, "at an expense to the state . . . to guarantee [against] just this thing . . . the execution took place before the gaze of a multitude of about 5,000 people specially gathered for the event." General William Obear, head of the Georgia National Guard, criticized Catron for not delaying the execution until the fence could be rebuilt. When Governor Brown got wind of what had taken place, he blasted both the military commanders and Reid himself—calling the Forsyth lawman one of Georgia's

"jellyfish sheriffs," too busy pandering for votes to ever stand up
to a mob.

Such indignation is ironic coming from Brown, given that in
only three years he would join Newt Morris's gang of kidnap-
pers and help to lynch Leo Frank in the woods outside Marietta. Clearly when Brown called on sheriffs like Reid to stop
lynch mobs, he did not mean they should stand up to men like
himself and Morris. Instead, what seems to have really offended
Brown was Reid's lack of subtlety. After all, Knox and Daniel
would have died that day whether or not their hangings were
witnessed by thousands of cheering whites, and whether or not
Reid turned the event into a three-ring circus. At the heart of
the controversy was not justice so much as decorum. The *Constitution* agreed that Reid's primary sin was his overt "coquet-
ting with the mob." Such buffoonery, the editors implied, was
bad for Georgia's reputation, and bad for its national aspirations.
"An official may compromise with his own conscience when he
stultifies himself," one critic concluded, but "he has no right to
indict the whole state."

EVEN MORE PROBLEMATIC for Reid was a news story that appeared
just a few days after the hangings. Forsyth was supposed to be
returning to law and order after a solid month of "excitement"
and getting on with the long-delayed work of the harvest. But on
October 29th the *Atlanta Constitution* reported that a white man
named Dabner Elliot, "a wealthy farmer of Forsyth county," had
been attacked the previous night and "today lies at the point of
death with his skull crushed."

People all over the county were disturbed by this news, not only
because Elliot was a rich and well-liked planter but also because of
where his unconscious body had been found, and the modus ope-
randi of his attacker. According to the *Constitution,*

Deputy Sheriff Lummus went to the scene, 7 miles north of Cumming, this morning and is making an investigation. The assault occurred about 10 o'clock last night as Mr. Elliot was driving along a lonely section of the road in his buggy. He had been to Gainesville . . . [but] has been unable to throw any light on the affair, as he has been unconscious . . . apparently [having] been struck by a blunt instrument, the back of the skull being crushed.

While no one in Forsyth dared to say it publicly, there were obvious parallels between what had happened to Elliot and the attack on Mae Crow two months earlier. Whoever appeared out of the darkness had waylaid his buggy "7 miles north of Cumming" and soon after he reentered the county from Gainesville—which is to say, somewhere near the sleepy little crossroads village of Oscarville. And Elliot's attacker had left him in the same condition as Crow: dragged into the woods beside the road, unconscious, and suffering from grave head injuries.

When doctors announced that Elliot had died from his wounds, few whites were willing to even consider the possibility that someone other than a vengeful black assailant had killed Dabner Elliot, presumably in retaliation for the deaths of Edwards, Knox, and Daniel. But privately, some people must have shaken their heads at the fact that Elliot had died in the exact same fashion as Mae Crow and in almost the exact same place—despite the fact that Crow's alleged murderers were now dead and the entire black population of Oscarville had been banished across the county line. Cumming's leaders were eager to put the season of death and violence behind them, and they clearly hoped that the double hanging had brought an end to Forsyth's "troubles." The only problem: there was still a murderer lurking somewhere in the woods of Oscarville.

STILL GRIEVING FOR Oscar, Ernest, and Jane's husband, Rob—
and no doubt haunted by the fact that Jane's testimony had helped
send her brother and cousin to their graves—Buck Daniel's family spent their first days on the road in one of the shantytowns
that had sprung up on the western outskirts of Gainesville, the
seat of Hall County. As a station on the rail line that ran south to
Atlanta and north all the way to Boston, Gainesville had long been
a magnet for rural blacks, who steadily migrated from farmland
to cities after emancipation. In the previous forty years, Gainesville's African American population had grown from sixty black
residents in 1870 to more than sixteen hundred in 1910. People of
color made up almost a third of the city's population in the fall of
1912, before hundreds of Forsyth refugees began appearing on the
streets of Gainesville. Even the more tolerant whites raised an eyebrow at the sheer volume of the migration, and the *Atlanta Constitution* sounded a note of alarm, declaring that "Gainesville is being
invaded as a haven of refuge. . . . The Negro sections have been
flooded with safety-seeking Negroes, and scores of shanties and
dwelling houses shelter as many as six or more families."

Whenever the Daniel family finally made it to town, they entered
a world radically different from the sleepy farms and sharecroppers' shacks out in Oscarville. In 1912, Gainesville was a frequent
holiday destination for affluent tourists seeking to escape to the
cool mountain air of north Georgia. With its grand hotels, bustling railway station, and tourists in gleaming automobiles, the
city employed a whole class of African American nannies, cooks,
drivers, and butlers, who lived relatively stable lives compared to
the dirt-poor laborers of Forsyth. With the completion of the Dun-
lap Hydroelectric Dam in 1908, Gainesville had become the first
city south of Baltimore whose sidewalks were lined with electric
streetlamps.

As they walked those glowing city blocks, Buck and Catie must have recognized, in the blur of unknown faces, at least a few familiar ones, from other families who had "come out of Forsyth," as the refugees put it. It was not just the poor and landless who had been forced out but people from all walks of life: field hands and sharecroppers like the Daniel clan, as well as ministers, land-owning black planters, and educated black schoolteachers. Not long after their arrival, many of these families began to make their mark on Hall County.

Among them were the sons and daughters of Levi and Elizabeth Greenlee, who would go on to found the Greenlee Funeral Home, a landmark in Gainesville for decades, and one of the most successful black-owned businesses in north Georgia. There was Byrd Oliver, who met and married young Beulah Rucker shortly after he settled in Hall and helped her found a Tuskegee-style school for African Americans called the State Industrial and High School, which educated blacks in north Georgia for more than forty years. And there were children like the fourteen-year-old Willie Bryant, who was old enough to remember the attacks of the mobs but young enough to quickly adapt to his new life in the city. By 1920, Bryant was working a union job for the Southern Railway and was well on his way to joining Gainesville's black middle class. Census records show that, like Bryant, many other Forsyth refugees started over in Hall—still struggling to bear the crushing burdens of segregation, but with at least a taste of the electrified, industrialized twentieth century that Charlie Harris had worked so hard to bring to Cumming.

Even Jane Daniel seems to have found some happiness across the river. After she was freed from the Fulton Tower, Jane made her way back north and eventually rejoined her family in Gainesville. By 1913 she had found work as a laundress for one of the rich families in town and had met a young man named William Butler, who, with his panel truck, his uniform, and his job as a driver for the Gainesville Ice Company, must have struck her as a real city boy. Within months, Will Butler proposed to the girl he called Janie. On February 5th, 1914, the two were married, and they set up house in the heart of Gainesville's black community, at 9 Atlanta Street.

Of other families, who fled in other directions, the written traces are faint, and in many cases old stories are all that's left of their journeys down the dusty red roads leading out of Forsyth. Olin Collins was eight years old the night his father and mother, George and Katie, loaded him and his brother Clarence into the back of a wagon, covered the boys with an old quilt, and drove out of Forsyth as fast as their mule could go. With no destination other than the county line, they headed first toward Canton, in neighboring Cherokee County, and eventually to the little town of Tate, twenty miles northwest.

Once there, George Collins was either determined or lucky enough to get an appointment with Mr. Samuel Tate, owner of the town's sole industry, the Georgia Marble Company. Just as the rich men of Gainesville protected blacks who worked in their mills, washed their clothes, and cooked their meals, Sam Tate quickly became both an employer and a guardian of the Collins family. By all accounts, "the Colonel" brought his power to bear quickly and fiercely on anyone who dared to threaten the black workers who were vital to the operation of his pink marble quarries.

Poor blacks like the Collins family left with only what they could carry, but more affluent families refused to simply abandon their property, holding out hope that they might return, or at the very least sell for something close to fair market value. As the largest black landowners in the county, Joseph and Eliza Kellogg were reluctant to sell the two hundred acres they had accumulated near Sawnee Mountain, or even the small lot they owned on the town square in Cumming. While they had no choice but to flee the mobs, before he headed south to Marietta, Kellogg borrowed money from some of his white neighbors, using the deeds to his land as collateral. The benefits were twofold: first, the loans gave Kellogg enough money to support his extended family during their exile, which he still hoped would be temporary. And second, those who lent money to Kellogg now had good reason to look after his property, farm equipment, and outbuildings while he was gone— since they would take possession if the debts went unpaid. This also meant, of course, that Joseph and Eliza Kellogg's white neighbors had a vested interest in keeping them away.

WHETHER THEY JOINED, opposed, or were indifferent to the raids of Forsyth's night riders, for many whites the misfortune of black property owners became a once-in-a-lifetime opportunity. The early years of the new century had seen a sharp rise in the value of real estate in the foothills, as the introduction of chemical fertilizers and mechanized agriculture turned what had always been a marginal region into more productive and more valuable farmland. Spikes in land values and crop yields meant that as the new century entered its second decade, Joseph Kellogg's large spread near Sawnee Mountain came to seem both highly attractive to landless whites and terribly far out of reach.

In a market that was making landowners richer and richer, poor whites in Forsyth must have realized that if they were ever going to climb up from the bottom of the economic ladder, something would have to give. And in the last quarter of 1912, something finally did, when one black family after another was forced at gunpoint to pack up their belongings and leave. As even the proudest, most prosperous black men, like Joseph Kellogg, gave in to the threats, Forsyth County suddenly became—for the first time in living memory—a buyer's market.

Even peaceful whites understood that as the violence escalated, and as more and more of the black community scattered, black owners might be tempted by lowball offers. One owner in Forsyth placed an ad in the *Atlanta Constitution,* offering for sale "200 Acres [in] Forsyth County . . . and [a] business corner lot in Cumming, 100 x 175, on public square." This description matches the two hundred acres and town lot on which Joseph Kellogg paid taxes in 1912, and it seems likely that this anonymous listing was part of Kellogg's last-ditch effort to cut his losses and get something approaching fair value for land he had acquired through forty years of sweat, determination, and keen business sense. By advertising the property in an Atlanta paper, Kellogg may have hoped to find a buyer who wouldn't fully understand, and therefore fully exploit, his desperate situation.

In the last sentence of the listing, the seller added that in the absence of a cash transaction, he would let go of his Forsyth County farm in "exchange for negro property." Implicit in such an offer was the seller's hope of relocating to some new place far from the night riders and arsonists of Forsyth, and free from the inherent risks that came with white neighbors. With this offer to trade his land for "negro property," whoever placed that ad seemed to acknowledge what was fast becoming clear to everyone: regardless of how prosperous and productive he might be, Forsyth County was no place for a black man.

MEANWHILE, UPPER-CLASS WHITES continued to speak out against the violence—and to protest not just the injustice of the purge but its economic cost. While there was nothing all that unusual about poor whites intimidating their black neighbors, it was another thing altogether when violent "crackers" started threatening rich white employers and landowners. In early December, one such planter drove all the way to Atlanta to meet with Joseph Mackey Brown. He warned the governor, "If something is not done to check this movement the labor situation . . . will become quite acute. . . . Our wives and daughters will soon be put to the necessity of doing the cooking, washing, and performing menial labor. In addition the farmers will suffer greatly, for they will be deprived of field hands."

The battle lines were clearly drawn when 1912 came to a close, and in early 1913, in a speech before the General Assembly, Governor Brown acknowledged the larger threat the night riders posed. "I am reliably informed," he said,

> that quite a number of farms in Forsyth County have been practically abandoned this year for lack of labor, which has fled before these threats. . . . There is no reason why farms should lose their productive power and why the white women of this State should be driven to the cook stoves and wash pots.

Brown's call for law and order was above all pragmatic: for white-owned farms to produce a profit, and for upper-class white families to function as they always had—with black men working in their fields and black women tending "the cook stoves and wash pots" of their homes—it was vital that the "outrages" be checked.

But in Forsyth, there were landowners who disagreed with the governor's argument that black workers were a vital part of the state's economy. They argued that farming was fast becoming "a white man's job," as the banker Benjamin Hunt put it in the *Atlanta Constitution*. Citing statistics from "The 'Big Cotton' Counties" in the 1910 census—a category that in his analysis included Forsyth—Hunt declared that the most productive Georgia counties were invariably those that "show an excess of white farmers," while the least productive "show an excess of negro."

There were many explanations for this disparity in the productivity of "white" and "black" counties, including the barriers to credit faced by African Americans, their inability to purchase the best parcels of land, and the myriad ways in which the culture and legal system of the Jim Crow South was stacked against them. Nonetheless, Hunt made a case for viewing Georgia's cotton empire as a product of Caucasian ingenuity and "Caucasian living," as he put it. "We are indebted to the white race for the American success in cotton culture," Hunt wrote, "not to negro slavery nor black labor."

This was a revisionist history that denied what everyone in Georgia could see with their own eyes: that most cotton fields in the state were planted, tended, and harvested by black hands, and had been for as long as anyone could remember. Hunt's argument that cotton was a "Caucasian crop" erased two centuries of toil by enslaved people and ignored the success of black farmers like Joseph and Eliza Kellogg. It also allowed whites to claim exclusive rights in a cotton empire that—at least in Hunt's view—they and they alone had built.

But this still left the question of how landowners were ever going to make their crops in a place where African Americans had been banished, and banned from ever returning. From the earliest days of British colonialism, many whites had argued that forced labor was essential to farming in Georgia's searingly hot, humid, and malarial climate, and that without the institution of slavery, whites would never make it on their own. As colonist Thomas Stephens put it in 1742,

> The extraordinary Heats here, the extraordinary Difficulty and Danger there is in clearing the Lands . . . [and] the poor Returns . . . make it indisputably impossible for White Men alone to carry on Planting to any good Purpose. . . . The poor People of Georgia, may as well think of becoming Negroes themselves . . . as of hoping to be ever able to live without them.

But after two hundred years of dependence on black workers, Benjamin Hunt argued that white farmers could now prosper without them—thanks to technological advances in the early twentieth century. "I desire the world to realize . . . that the economic changes wrought by machinery [have] revolutionized all labor conditions," Hunt said. "To think correctly we must think in terms of this era of free white labor, and not in terms of the black labor of the past."

FACED WITH COMPLAINTS from the women in his own household, Ansel Strickland, the Cumming doctor who had hosted the executions of Knox and Daniel, started thinking along the same lines as Benjamin Hunt in early 1913. As the upper-class families of Cumming struggled to adapt to Forsyth's new "whites only" era, Strickland wrote a letter to the *North Georgian,* offering suggestions for how people unaccustomed to domestic labor could solve basic problems, such as washing clothes. "Well, old man," Strickland began,

> the negro is gone from Forsyth county and you had as well roll up your sleeves and follow me. For the last 33 years I have always hired my wife's washing done by negroes, at a heavy expense, but on the morning of October 22nd, 1912, my negro washwoman informed me that she was going to leave my washing for my wife to do, [saying] that the people did not give the negro proper protection. I told her in so many words that if I had to sell my daughter's virtue to negro boys in order to retain her as a wash woman, she could *get.*

Having fired his servant for daring to protest Forsyth's waves of mob violence, Strickland told readers that he

> at once ordered improved wash pots, tubs, wringers, etc., and prepared to take the hard part of the washing onto my and the boys' shoulders. [This new] wash tub is no play thing. . . . When I saw northern women washing with improved machinery they

made the wash-tub day a picnic [compared to] the old Georgia
way of washing.

Armed with his modern equipment, and reconciled to the fact
that his black servants were gone and would never be coming
back, Strickland proudly declared that his family had "adopted the
cooperative plan of washing at my house, and we are independent
of the negro. . . . I endeavor to make wash day a day of pleasure to
the ladies."

Strickland was clearly proud to be "independent of the negro,"
and he wanted to convince others in Forsyth that new machines
could more than make up for the sudden loss of black workers—
who represented one-tenth of the county's population in the census
of 1910 but a much larger percentage of its labor supply. Just as
Benjamin Hunt imagined new machinery and chemical fertilizers
making up for the loss of black field hands, Strickland presented
to the wives of Forsyth a vision of home life in which the modern
washtub and wringer would more than compensate for the loss of
maids and butlers and laundresses, and make domestic chores "a
pleasure to the ladies."

Rich planters like Strickland and Hunt had reason to feel opti-
mistic in the second decade of the twentieth century, as life on the
American farm was just beginning to be revolutionized by new
technologies. As early as the 1870s, inventors had experimented
with steam-powered farm equipment, but because of their massive weight and high cost, steam engines had never competed seriously with the horse and the mule, particularly in regions like the
Georgia hill country, which was dominated by small-scale farmers, working plots that rarely yielded enough profit for such a major
investment. There were still twenty-one million horses and mules
in the United States in 1900, averaging four per farm, and they
pulled plows, threshing machines, harrows, and reapers and served

Your inauguration . . . is to the colored people a momentous occasion. . . . We black men by our votes helped put into power a man who [can] become the greatest benefactor of his country since Abraham Lincoln. . . . The fight is on, and you, sir, are this month stepping into its arena.

We want to be treated as men. We want to vote. We want our children educated. We want lynching stopped. We want no longer to be herded as cattle on street cars and railroads. We want the right to earn a living, to own our own property and to spend our income unhindered and uncursed. . . . In the name then of that common country for which your fathers and ours have bled and toiled, be not untrue, President Wilson, to the highest ideals of American Democracy.

By forsaking Republican William Howard Taft and endorsing Wilson, Du Bois had helped the new president win more African American votes than any previous Democratic presidential candidate, and the *Crisis* editor clearly wanted to remind Wilson of the debt he owed black America.

It didn't take long for Wilson to reward Du Bois's faith with a stinging rebuke: he soon empowered cabinet members to racially segregate the bathrooms and cafeterias in government buildings and to segregate a civil service that had been integrated since the days of Reconstruction. Wilson ignored African American candidates when making new political appointments, and when, in 1914, the black newspaper editor Monroe Trotter went to Washington to demand that the president "undo this race segregation in accord with your duty as President and with your pre-election pledges to colored American voters," Wilson was unrepentant. Segregation of the federal government "is not humiliating," the president told Trotter and his delegation of black leaders. It was, he said, "a benefit, and ought to be so regarded by you gentlemen." Wilson then had the delegation removed from the White House, saying that if black leaders ever wanted another audience with the president, they would need "another spokesman." He scolded Trotter, a Phi Beta Kappa graduate of Harvard, saying, "Your manner offends me. . . . Your tone, with its background of passion."

Wilson held office from 1913 to 1921, and throughout his two terms he continued to implement Jim Crow codes in Washington, with African American applicants deemed ineligible for most government jobs and both the Department of the Treasury and the U.S. Postal Service segregated by order of senior cabinet members. Wilson documented his own bigotry in 1918 when, in his *History of the American People*, he wrote that "a great Ku Klux Klan" had risen up after the Civil War and helped rid the South of "the intolerable burden of governments sustained by the votes of ignorant negroes."

Having such a man in the White House emboldened white supremacists across the nation and particularly in the South, which Wilson had once called home. Black postal workers and government employees were fired all over the region and were barred from state jobs that had been one of the few paths to the middle class open to people of color. In 1913, the director of the Internal Revenue Services' office in Atlanta left little doubt that Wilson's support of segregation was a devastating blow to all African Americans, and particularly in places like Georgia. "There are no Government positions for Negroes in the South," he said. "A Negro's place is in the cornfield."

YET EVEN AS Wilson reversed the gears of racial progress in Washington, and as Forsyth County men like Ansel Strickland touted the benefits of a racially cleansed labor force, many of the wives of Cumming were growing weary of life without their black "help," and exhausted from replacing all that domestic labor themselves. With the racial purge of 1912 still just a few months old, Laura

Hockenhull had had enough, and she urged her husband, Cumming doctor John Hockenhull, to reach out to his former employees wherever they had fled and somehow lure them back. No doubt enticed by the wages Hockenhull offered, and assured by him that they would be safe, three families—the Blakes, the Smiths, and the Grahams—moved back into their cabins on the Hockenhull property in early February of 1913 and tried to quietly resume their former lives.

Ophelia Blake, a fifty-three-year-old widow, had been the Hockenhulls' maid and cook for many years before the night riders forced her to flee with the two youngest of her eight children, sons Louie and Adkinson, eighteen and sixteen. Before they were forced out, Alex and Flora Graham had also rented on Hockenhull's property, where they were raising sons Leonard, four, and Henry, two. Frank Smith, a farmhand, had lived there with his wife, Annie, and their four children: Byel, twelve, Eddie, eight, Roosevelt, six, and Lula, three.

That Laura Hockenhull's servants agreed to come back at all is a testament to just how bleak the outlook was for the Forsyth refugees, particularly as fall turned to winter, and as the steady work of the harvest came to an end. While they must have taken some comfort in returning as a group, they also lived a precarious existence, completely cut off from the black community they'd once known, and shielded from the white mobs and lynchers only as long as they stayed within the confines of Hockenhull land.

If the quiet that greeted their return gave Ophelia Blake hope that Forsyth might once again be safe, those hopes were soon shattered. The *Atlanta Constitution* reported that on the night of Wednesday, February 19th, 1913, "persons unknown" crept onto the Hockenhull place. They slid bundled sticks of dynamite into the crawl spaces under the "negro cabins" where the Blakes, the Grahams, and the Smiths were sleeping with their children, then unspooled a long coil of fuse and crouched in the dark, where the only visible sign of their presence was the brief flare of a match. According to one witness, the explosion at Dr. Hockenhull's place "aroused practically the entire town . . . [and] the concussion shook many buildings. The negroes . . . who had recently returned to Cumming were terror stricken. The dynamiters made their escape before the townspeople had ascertained what had taken place."

The newspapers make no mention of whether the three families lived or died, and at this point they disappear entirely from written records of the county. Ophelia Blake, Frank Smith, and Alex Graham had tried, however cautiously and however quietly, to come home. The response, delivered in the dead of night, left no room for doubt. Forsyth was now a place for whites only, and even black people born and raised there were forced to heed the warnings of the night riders. Defying them, as the Hockenhulls and their tenants had done, was nothing short of suicidal.

The "negro cabins" at the edge of the Hockenhull property were left in a splintered heap, but the big house in which Hockenhull lived with his wife, Laura, was unscathed. Chastened by a visit from the nameless, faceless night riders, the doctor and his wife seem to have reconciled themselves to living in a racially cleansed world they didn't support but were now too frightened to publicly oppose. There was an outpouring of affection from Forsyth residents when "Dr. John" died in 1922, and a notice in the paper said he had been "gentle, kind, and considerate to even the most humble who chanced to come in contact with him."

FEW AFRICAN AMERICANS were desperate or reckless enough to cross the county line in the years that followed, but on those rare occasions when a black face did appear inside the "whites only" zone, he or she was usually arrested and charged with a crime. In April of 1914, there were reports that a thirty-two-year-old man

named Will Phillips had been caught trying to rob merchants
in Cumming and was "followed by his tracks in the mud from
Cumming to Buford, where he lived." A journalist for the *Atlanta
Constitution* wrote that "the negro was exceedingly clever" and
claimed that

> his method [was] to enter a merchant's house in the stillness
> of the night and steal the keys to his store from the pockets
> of his trousers and then proceed to the store and divest the
> money drawer of its contents.

After hearing such accusations, Deputy Lummus arrested Phillips
at his home in Buford and, just as he had done with the prisoners
in 1912, delivered him to the Fulton Tower in Atlanta.

It is, of course, within the realm of possibility that Phillips did
steal shop keys from sleeping merchants in Cumming, then empty
the registers of stores on the town square. But given Forsyth's reputation as the home of lynchers, arsonists, and shotgun-wielding
night riders, it is difficult to believe that a black man intent on
robbery would have chosen Cumming as his target. Will Phillips
lived in Buford, a station on the Southern Railway, which offered
its own wealth of money drawers stuffed with cash at the close of
each business day. In order to accept contemporary accounts of his
arrest, we have to believe that Phillips instead chose to walk thirteen miles west to Cumming, across a landscape where, only a few
years earlier, thousands of blacks had been shot at and threatened,
their homes dynamited and burned by white mobs.

It seems much more likely that Phillips was simply caught on
the wrong side of the county line, and that his arrest was meant
to drive home a familiar message: Forsyth was now out of bounds
for African Americans. Phillips was brought back north to stand
trial in May of 1914, and he spent what must have been a terrifying

night in the Forsyth County Jail. The next morning, he was found guilty on all charges and given the maximum sentence of forty years on the Georgia chain gang.

A similar case was recorded in October of 1915, when a black man named Joe Smith was accused of burglary in Cumming. According to the papers, a warrant was issued for his arrest, and "Sheriff W. W. Reid, of Cumming, was appointed to bring back Smith, who is said to be in Leon County." Leon County lay just across Georgia's southern border with Florida, but Bill Reid made the long journey anyway. Whatever had tempted Smith to trespass into the "white man's county" of Forsyth, the arm of the law was long enough to reach him, even three hundred miles away.

Prosecutions like these helped cement Forsyth's reputation as a bastion of white supremacy and Georgia's most racist county. While some of the African American residents who returned may have come back seeking revenge, it seems far more likely that they were simply trying to recover their own lost and stolen possessions, whether livestock, furniture, farm equipment, or some other valuable left behind in the rush to escape the night riders. However briefly and however stealthily they tried to return, it was now clear that a black man could be arrested for simply *being* in Forsyth County.

14

EXILE, 1915–1920

The codes of racial segregation grew more rigid and oppressive throughout the South during Woodrow Wilson's two terms in the White House, but no place was more committed to a complete racial cleansing than Forsyth. The county gained wider notoriety as people from other parts of the state found themselves face-to-face with the enforcers of a "whites only" rule that was extraordinary even by the standards of Jim Crow.

In September of 1915, the *Times-Enterprise* of Thomasville, in south Georgia, ran a story meant to shock readers with the fact that in the Georgia mountains there was "A County Without a Negro in It." "Every family was run out of the county," a reporter wrote, "and now an automobile cannot pass through and take a colored servant. This fact has just been ascertained by a physician who went there on a visit." That physician was Hudson Moore, a wealthy Atlanta man who had business at the Forsyth County Courthouse on September 4th, 1915. When Moore drove north to Cumming, he took with him "a colored nurse and colored chauffeur" and left them waiting in the car while he went inside. Witnesses said that while Moore was speaking with officials, "he heard a commotion outside, and rushing out he found a crowd of several hundred gathered around the two servants, threatening them. Mr. Moore took his two employees in his automobile and rushed them out of the county."

What Dr. Moore clearly hadn't realized was that by their very presence on the Cumming square, his black employees were committing what many local whites now regarded as a hanging offense. Not long after Moore's harrowing trip, another group of white aristocrats would make the same mistake, when they took part in an automobile tour of the north Georgia hill country and brought their black chauffeurs onto the wrong side of the Chattahoochee River.

LOOKING TO CAPITALIZE on a recent craze for glamorous driving tours, in the fall of 1915 the Georgia Chamber of Commerce organized an event called "Seeing Georgia," which would lead a group of automobile enthusiasts through the northern region of the state, staying each night in a different town. "Seeing Georgia" attracted the interest of mayors, business leaders, and society women, as well as northern capitalists looking to make investments in the South. The list of participants included many bold-faced names, such as Charles J. Haden, president of the Georgia Chamber of Commerce; James Price, state commissioner of agriculture; and K. G. Matheson, president of Georgia Institute of Technology, in Atlanta. There were also prominent businessmen like A. C. Webb, manager of Atlanta's first Studebaker dealership, and Wylie West, a former racecar driver who was now a regional manager for the Firestone Tire and Rubber Company.

When Cumming mayor Charlie Harris learned that the tour would bring a group of rich and powerful men into the foothills, he used his connections at the Georgia Chamber of Commerce to get Forsyth County added to the proposed route. Harris knew that "Seeing Georgia" was a rare opportunity to promote his home county—

The "Seeing Georgia" tourists en route to Forsyth, October 3rd, 1915

and to show the whole state just how much money could be made there once the Atlanta Northeastern Railroad was complete.

After driving from Macon to Milledgeville and then to Athens, the second leg of the tour entered the north Georgia mountains, where the tourists viewed the colorful fall foliage and spent a night near a state-of-the-art hydroelectric plant at Tallulah Falls. The group was then scheduled to turn back south toward Hall County, and from there to drive west, for a brief stopover at Cumming.

But during their lunchtime break in Gainesville, a group of Hall residents urged tour leaders to decline Charlie Harris's invitation and skip Forsyth County altogether. The reason for their concern: many of the cars, carrying affluent white men and women, were being driven by uniformed black chauffeurs. After hearing warnings about rabid white mobs, several of the drivers asked for permission to go home by train from Gainesville, hoping to avoid the "white county" where Hudson Moore's employees had nearly been lynched just a month before.

According to reporters, when Harris learned that the tourists might cancel their visit, he dispatched a messenger, who drove to Gainesville at breakneck speed. Harris's man arrived just as tour organizers were debating whether or not to take a detour, and he assured the participants that their black drivers would encounter no problems. The mayor of Cumming offered his personal guarantee of safety.

STEADY RAIN ON the morning of Monday, October 4th, turned the red clay road between Gainesville and Cumming into a quagmire, and journalist Emma Martin, covering the "Seeing Georgia" tour for the *Macon Telegraph,* said the long line of automobiles needed frequent help from locals as they made their way west. "The good farmers of Hall county came to our rescue by the dozens," she wrote, "and whenever we skidded they came on foot and on horseback, and went with us to the Forsyth county line."

But as they rounded a curve and saw Browns Bridge coming into view, Martin learned that even the white farmers of Hall now thought of Forsyth as a world apart, and treated the county line as more than just a border between two local governments. "They would not cross the bridge," Martin said,

> because of our negro chauffeurs. Many times we were warned not to enter Forsyth . . . but we had the personal pledge of the mayor of Cumming, and of the better element of the community, that there would be neither trouble nor danger.

Having put their faith, and the lives of their drivers, in the hands of Charlie Harris, the tourists soon realized that they had made a serious mistake. After rattling over the Chattahoochee on the narrow, wooden-planked bridge, the long line of cars rolled into a sleepy little crossroads settlement that the maps referred to as Oscarville. It was exactly the kind of quaint rural village that the organizers had promised the tour would feature. But according to a reporter for the *Georgian,* farmers at [the] hamlet spied a negro chauffeur in the car of W. A. McCullough, of Atlanta, and went after him. One threw a stick of stove wood that passed dangerously near the head of the frightened darky, and also near Mr. McCullough and his guests.

"When McCullough's car hove into sight," said another witness,

one of the men saw the negro chauffeur driving and shouted *"Look yonder, boys, get him, get him."* As the car shot past, one of the men grabbed a stick and let fly. . . . From there on into Cumming there were frequent curses and threats and rocks hurled at the cars.

The tour's genteel passengers came from some of the wealthiest families in Georgia, and it is easy to imagine their horrified faces as they peered out through muddy windshields and got their first look at the cursing, violent white "mountaineers" of Forsyth. Skidding and fishtailing over the rain-soaked roads, the black drivers raced out of Oscarville, and toward what they hoped would be a safe haven at the county seat.

A smiling Charlie Harris was waiting for them on the Cumming square, and after hearing reports of the "trouble" out in Oscarville, the mayor assured everyone that their ordeal was over, and that the black drivers were now perfectly safe. The *Constitution* said Harris was "most cordial and reassured the tourists that there would be no harm done to any one . . . [as] school children lined up and sang songs." But when word spread that there were black men sitting in a row of cars lined up outside the Cumming courthouse, "mob spirit" boiled up all over town. The children had just finished their performance and the tourists were hurrying to get back on the road when "things took on a more serious aspect." According to one reporter, several men gathered around the Rome car and threatened to take from it the negro chauffeur. . . . One man caught hold of the negro's arm and said "I've got his arm. Somebody take his legs." Mr. Simpson warned them not to execute their threat and ordered the negro to speed up, [until] the car shot out of line and forged past the others.

After months of anticipation, "Seeing Georgia" had finally brought to Forsyth exactly the kinds of businessmen and deep-pocketed investors who could help Charlie Harris transform Cumming into a prosperous railroad town. But all he could do was watch in horror as one car after another roared down Main Street at full throttle, pursued by a mob of screaming, rock-throwing whites.

Emma Martin told readers that she and several other ladies on the tour were "transferred to a speedy Ford . . . and shot through the town and county like a bullet out of a 12-centimeter . . . to avoid the rocks and profanity being hurled." With their car now being driven by one of the white tourists, the black chauffeur "sat on the seat with me," Martin said, "while Mrs. Wall, her hand on a pistol, sat in front."

Martin hunkered down below the height of the doors as they sped toward the county line, and when she looked over she saw that the black man next to her "was quite pale" with fear. Finally, she said, "we passed a cabin on the porch of which sat a negro woman." At that, "the driver sprang up and said: 'I know we's back in God's country now' . . . and we were."

THERE WAS GREAT indignation when reports of the attacks reached Atlanta, and many of the participants in "Seeing Georgia" vowed to speak out against the mobs who had tried to lynch their employees. When the tour stopped for supper in Tate, a lawyer and former superior court judge named Wright Willingham addressed report-

ers and called on state leaders to take action against Forsyth's racial
ban. "A sense of duty," Willingham said,

> will not permit me to remain silent over a liability which
> thrust itself upon us in the beautiful county of Forsyth . . .
> where we were confronted with a spirit on the part of many of
> the citizens of that county which [is] the antithesis of all the
> virtues we have discovered elsewhere. And this because every
> negro man, woman, and child has been exiled from their
> homes and because a few of our tourists had negro drivers . . .
> culminating in an effort at Cumming on the part of Forsyth
> county citizens to take one of the negro drivers from the car
> and to do with him the Lord knows what.

Had one white passenger not "reached for his revolver," Willingham said, there might have been another lynching on the Cumming square—in full sight of the mayor, the "Seeing Georgia"
tourists cowering in their cars, and the schoolchildren standing
with songbooks tucked under their arms. "Conditions like this,"
Willingham went on,

> can no longer be regarded with calm satisfaction but must
> commend themselves to the patriotic men of our state. The
> Governor of Georgia, the men who represent this state in the
> legislature, the judges of the superior courts cannot pass in
> silence over this state of anarchy which is being bred in this
> commonwealth. . . . Ultimately, unless checked, [it] will bury
> its fangs in the body politic.

As he sat in his office at the Cumming courthouse, scanning
the headlines on the morning of October 5th, 1915, Charlie Harris
must have been despondent. Only a day earlier, reporters visiting

north Georgia for the first time had described how "the wonders of this section fill one with an inexpressible sense of having been through a land of resources [and] . . . a profound respect for the possibilities of the country." Businessmen all over the South read about the mineral riches of Dahlonega, "the enchanted country of the Nacoochee Valley," and the network of paved roads that was being built in Hall County. But on that Tuesday morning, after Harris had worked for months to ensure that the tour passed through Cumming, journalists told a very different story about Forsyth. All over the state, people read about wives who held off the mobs with drawn pistols. Newspapers as far away as Kentucky, Ohio, Indiana, and New York spoke not of the resources and business opportunities in Harris's home county but of its widespread bigotry. "Georgia Crackers Rock Negro Chauffeurs," one headline read. "Stoned by Georgia Mob," said another.

The message to his investors in Atlanta was unmistakable. Harris had tried since 1912 to reassure them that Forsyth was the ideal terminus for a rail spur linking the state capitol to the foothills. But the very first delegation of business leaders who'd gone there, at the invitation of the mayor and the Georgia Chamber of Commerce, had been stoned and cursed by furious white men who'd tried to lynch their black chauffeurs.

Soon thereafter, Charlie Harris finally gave up on his troubled railroad plan. In 1916, the Interstate Commerce Commission issued a new charter, granting a competing group the right to build "an interurban line . . . from Atlanta, Ga., north to Roswell, thence northeast via Alpharetta to Cumming." This was the same route Harris had been struggling to open since 1908. And just like Harris's Atlanta Northeastern Railroad, it would never be completed.

Instead, the mayor quietly turned his gaze southward, to new opportunities far from the "lawlessness" that had plagued his every effort in Forsyth. The boll weevil had been introduced into Georgia in 1915, and it had quickly devastated the cotton economy of south Georgia. This meant that just as Harris began scouting for some new venture, abandoned farms all over the region were being sold off at bargain prices. In 1919, Harris decided to take the plunge, and he relocated from Cumming to the little town of Cordele, in Crisp County, two hundred miles south of Forsyth. Once there, he formed the South Georgia Land and Auction Company and, with local partners at the Cordele Bank and Trust Company, began buying and selling large parcels of farmland in south Georgia. In Cordele, Charlie Harris would make his fortune in the 1920s, investing all the energy, talent, and drive that had made him a leader in Forsyth.

Harris's departure was in many ways the beginning of the end of resistance to the purge, as moderate figures left one by one or simply learned to hold their peace, as John and Laura Hockenhull had done. The future of Cumming was left in the hands of men like Ansel Strickland, who believed that Forsyth was, and should remain, "a white man's county."

Deputy Mitchell Gay Lummus had made a valiant attempt to stop the lynching of Rob Edwards back in 1912, and twice he tried to unseat Bill Reid as county sheriff. But not long after his second defeat, in 1914, it seems that Lummus, too, had had enough of his troubled home place. If the railways of the new century would not be coming to Forsyth, Lummus decided, he would go to them.

When he filled out his World War I draft card in 1917, Lummus was living in Atlanta and on the payroll of the Georgia Railway and Power Company, where he worked as a motorman on the city's streetcar lines. The former deputy seems to have adapted quickly to life in the city, and he left his second wife and children back in Cumming. He would never again live in Forsyth County.

The room Lummus rented at James Travis's boardinghouse on Piedmont Avenue was so close to the Butler Street railyard that it was a popular address for streetcar drivers and train conductors. But the neighborhood was also teeming with workers and tradespeople of all types, including shoemakers, mechanics, barbers, plasterers, booksellers, upholsterers, and grocers. In the census records of Atlanta's Sixth Ward, where Lummus lived in 1920, one finds blacks and whites living side by side—as well as Christians and Jews, "native-born" Americans and recently arrived immigrants from all over the world. As he walked down Piedmont each morning, heading to the Butler Street yard, Lummus would have passed people chattering in Russian, German, Yiddish, Spanish, Chinese, Turkish, and Italian. And even among his American neighbors, there were people who had come to Atlanta from all over the country. Travis's flophouse may have been only an afternoon's drive south of the "white county" Lummus left behind, but it was, in almost every way, the polar opposite of Forsyth.

Lummus and Harris were once the most visible white allies of the county's black residents, but only a few years after the expulsions, they were gone. And with their exit, the last open opposition to the racial cleansing fell silent. They left behind a place that—unlike other counties that endured episodes of night riding and attempts at racial cleansing—had actually succeeded in closing its borders to African Americans. With no one left to speak out against the bigotry and intimidation, the county went into a kind of Rip Van Winkle sleep, as residents resumed lives that on the surface looked no different from any other rural place in Georgia. White Forsyth's communal crime had been fiery and explosive in 1912, but its erasure would happen slowly, quietly, and one fence post at a time.

15

ERASURE, 1920–1970

I n a detailed survey of land transactions, journalist Elliot Jaspin has shown that while a small minority of Forsyth's black property owners got out early and received something close to fair market value for their land, the vast majority either sold at artificially low prices or simply walked away—knowing that their white neighbors would eventually take over their property. Each transaction is "carefully recorded in oversized books . . . in the basement of the Forsyth County Courthouse," Jaspin writes,

> and each sale tells a tale of black people who struggled to build a life [in Forsyth] and were crushed by the terror. . . . In all, twenty-four African-American landowners and seven churches . . . sold their property [and] the timing of these sales gives a sense of the panic people felt. The worst case was Alex Hunter, who, just three months before the expulsions, bought a farm for $1,500. Faced with death or leaving, he sold it in December 1912 for $550.

Jaspin found that even after selling for a third of his land's value, Alex Hunter was still luckier than many others, who simply walked away and lost everything. "For thirty-four of the black landowners," Jaspin writes,

> there is no record that they ever sold their land. It made no difference. Whites, money in hand, would pay the tax on land they did not own and the clerk would note the transaction . . . simply ignor[ing] the gap in ownership. . . . In the three years after the expulsion, nearly two-thirds of the black-owned farmland that had not been sold was appropriated in this way.

With the racial ban still violently enforced, whites could feel confident that black owners would never appear and try to reclaim the land they had left behind. Even if someone was reckless enough to try, word spread that whites could defend land seizures not just with shotguns and pistols but under a common-law principle known as "adverse possession." If a man went down to the county courthouse, signed an affidavit swearing he had occupied the land "continuously, openly, and notoriously" and had been paying taxes on the lots, then according to state law, the original "adverse possession" would "ripen into title" after seven years, since the owner had taken no steps to repossess his property. In Georgia, this legal right—meant to encourage productive use of abandoned land—included the stipulation that any new claim "must not have originated in fraud [and] must be public, continuous, exclusive, uninterrupted, and peaceable."

Black owners abandoned land in Forsyth for many reasons—from armed invasion, to arson, to dynamite—but everyone in Georgia knew that none of them were remotely "peaceable." Nonetheless, when white residents walked down to the courthouse to register deeds on land they had long ago fenced in as their own, the county clerk rarely even raised an eyebrow. In 1912, the expulsion of Forsyth's black population had made news all over the country, but the thefts that followed were given a legal stamp of approval by the state, and they went unnoticed by anyone but the expelled black property owners themselves. "There was land for the taking," as Jaspin put it, "and in this free-for-all, the [county] tax clerk kept score."

BY THE EARLY 1920s, the elementary schools of Cumming were filled with a generation of white children who had no memory of the black people who once occupied those stolen lots. Most had never seen a black resident of Forsyth, and never would. As the *Macon Telegraph* put it in 1921, "in Forsyth more or less pride is taken that they have run out all the negroes." With the violent raids of 1912 receding into the past, it became possible for civic leaders to boast that while other north Georgia communities continued to suffer episodes of "race trouble," there were no such embarrassments in Forsyth.

The signs that African Americans once lived there had already begun to fade, and the remnants of that old world were visible only to those who knew where to look. A reporter driving north from Atlanta in January of 1921 wrote that "soon after the Chattahoochee has been crossed . . . a lone brick chimney stands amid blackened ruins . . . [and] a mile further on an old stove rises above a pile of stones which once formed the foundations of a little church and school." Many readers must have recalled the year when mobs drove more than a thousand black residents out of Forsyth County, yet the article made no mention of how that abandoned house first turned into "blackened ruins" or who had once occupied that "little church and school" now turning into a pile of mossy stones.

Night riders continued to make headlines in other Georgia counties in the early 1920s, but having once been synonymous with lawlessness, Forsyth found that its "race troubles" were quickly forgotten by many whites, and its reputation was already being rehabilitated. When, in 1923, the *Atlanta Constitution* asked a north Georgia man named Arnold B. Hall to write a profile of the county, he made no mention of the expulsions and called Forsyth "a far-famed county of grand old Georgia where rich lands, rotation of crops and marked advancement in animal industry and horticultural activity are awakening the people with a new purpose, a dynamic zest, and a vigorous vision!"

Forsyth County's white defenders are quick to point out that the racial purge of 1912 was not, as is often believed, absolute. And records confirm that while nearly all of the 1,098 people listed as black or "mulatto" in 1910 were gone from Forsyth by 1920, when a census taker named Vester Buice made his rounds in February of that year, he did eventually come upon a small group of black families living in the Big Creek section, along Forsyth's southern border with Milton County.

The families of Ed and Bertha Moon, Will and Corrie Strickland, and Marvin and Rubie Rocks were all clustered together at the bottom edge of the county, as far as one could get from Oscarville and still be in Forsyth. The most prosperous of the group was Will Strickland, whose father James had been born a slave on the Strickland plantation in 1850. The Strickland farms were so notorious for their harsh treatment of slaves that Hardy, the family patriarch, had become known far and wide as "Devil Hard" Strickland. But James Strickland stayed in Forsyth even after emancipation, and he was among the young, newly freed black men of the county when in 1867 he signed his oath of allegiance at the Cumming courthouse. Just like Joseph Kellogg, he seems to have been both industrious and patient, for by 1900, after decades of sharecropping and saving, he and his wife Rosanna owned the property they worked in Big Creek. By 1910, James's son Will was farming their land and doing well enough, at least, to support a family with ten children.

Apologists for Forsyth have often pointed to the 1920 census roll, and those twenty-three black residents living around Will Strickland's farm, in an attempt to deny that African Americans were forced out. But it seems clear that twenty-three people returning to the county after more than a thousand have been banished does not mean the purge was any less violent or widespread than was reported in the papers. Instead, it suggests that a kind of exemption, or at least protection, was granted to these employees of the white Strickland family, whose power in the county was unmatched.

There is no way to know exactly where the black Strickland, Moon, and Rocks families went during the first waves of violence, but there is strong evidence that they fled along with the rest of the African American community. When Ed Moon filled out a WWI draft card in 1918, he was living forty miles east of Cumming, in Maysville, a town the white Stricklands had helped found in Jackson County in the nineteenth century. Jackson happened to be the birthplace of Forsyth's largest slave owners—Hardy, Tolbert, and Oliver Strickland—and was still home to many of their kin. One likely scenario is that when the mobs of Forsyth threatened black employees like Ed Moon, the white Stricklands simply relocated them to other family farms in Jackson County. And then, at some point after the violence had died down, and prior to the 1920 census, the Stricklands quietly brought some of their black laborers back into Forsyth, where they were isolated but protected as long as they stayed on Strickland property.

Whether it was the lure of wages, the threat of punishment, or a lack of any better option, at some point after 1918, at great risk, those twenty-three people stepped back across the invisible line and were counted as Forsyth residents in 1920. No mention was made in the papers, no mobs assembled at the edge of the Strickland place, and there is no record of their presence other than those few entries that Vester Buice scrawled in his census ledger.

As enraged as locals had been at the sight of the "Seeing Georgia" chauffeurs, they likely knew better than to test the rich and powerful white Strickland clan. That small cluster of black people at the southern edge of the county still numbered sixteen in the census of 1930. Then, at some point after 1930, they were gone. The Moons to Gainesville. Will and Corrie Strickland just nine miles south, to Milton County, near Alpharetta, and Marvin and Rubie Rocks to some new life of which no traces survived.

ACROSS THE CHATTAHOOCHEE, in Hall County, Jane Daniel was just starting to imagine a more ambitious escape—not just from the lynchers and night riders of Forsyth but out of the South altogether. In the census of 1920, we can still find her, age twenty-nine, pinning white people's damp clothes to the line in her backyard, as somewhere in Gainesville Will Butler gripped the wooden handle of a pair of steel pincers and lugged a fifty-pound block of ice through the back door of a white man's mansion. But when the census taker came back to Atlanta Street in 1930, neighbors said that Will and Jane were gone—having boarded a northbound train at the depot in Gainesville and joined so many other young black people of their generation in the Great Migration.

By the early 1930s, Jane Daniel and Will Butler were renting a house at 467 Theodore Street, in the Paradise Valley neighborhood of Detroit. Having grown up in rural Forsyth and then lived in the small railroad city of Gainesville, Jane suddenly found herself at the center of a booming industrial metropolis. Census records show that Jane and Will's neighborhood was filled with others who had been born to sharecroppers and field hands in Georgia, Alabama, South Carolina, Virginia, and Mississippi—but who now worked as cooks, maids, bricklayers, and night watchmen.

And more than anywhere else, the black residents of Detroit worked in the bustling factories of Motor City: Fisher Body, at

*Sign protesting the arrival of black tenants, Sojourner
Truth housing project, Detroit, February 1942*

the corner of Piquette and St. Antoine; Cadillac's Detroit Assembly, on Clark Street; and the Hudson Motors plant, off Jefferson
Avenue. Whereas the backdrop of her youth had been pine forests, cotton fields, and the lazy, deep green waters of the Chattahoochee, the second half of Jane's life would play out amidst
smokestacks and glowing steel ingots, in a city whose pulse in its
heyday one visitor described as "the sound of a hammer against
a steel plate."

One migrant of Jane's generation described the life she left
behind in the Jim Crow South as "like sleeping on a volcano which
may erupt at any moment," and Jane must have felt a similar kind of
relief once she and Will were settled in Detroit—to be out of Georgia, and beyond the reach of the white people who had killed her
first husband, Rob, and celebrated the hanging of her brother Oscar
and her cousin Ernest. Will and Jane never had children, but the
nieces and nephews who knew them in Detroit all understood that
Aunt Janie and Uncle Will had begun their lives far away, among

the crackers and Klansmen down in Georgia. *"Georgia,"* they said years later, "was not a place Aunt Janie ever talked too much about."

BUT IF THE Butlers thought they had escaped white terrorism, they and the rest of Detroit got a rude awakening in the summer of 1943, when the white people of the city decided that they, too, would declare a racially cleansed zone and draw an invisible line that blacks could cross only at risk of their lives.

Racial tensions had been building since the first trainloads of migrants began arriving from the South after World War I. The African American population of the city was just 6,000 in 1910, but by 1929 some 120,000 new black residents had settled in Detroit, and a decade later, in 1940, that number had nearly doubled, to 200,000. During that same span of years, European immigrants were also arriving in unprecedented numbers, and for many of the same reasons: the magnetic draw of high wages and low unemployment, and a chance to escape the violence and deprivation they'd suffered in their homelands.

By the early 1940s, there were simmering tensions between whites and blacks in the city, and they boiled over in the winter of 1942. That was the year the federal government opened the new Sojourner Truth housing project, which was built especially for poor black families but located in a predominantly white area north of Paradise Valley. When the first tenants arrived, on February 28th, neighborhood whites burned a cross in a field near the housing complex, and the next morning a mob of twelve hundred armed white men rallied to keep out black residents—many of whom had already signed leases and paid their first month's rent. Whites formed a picket line in front of the building, and when two cars driven by black men tried to force their way through the line, a melee broke out. The violence ended only when mounted police arrived with shotguns and tear gas.

*White mob dragging an African American man from a
Detroit streetcar, June 21, 1943*

In April of 1942, 168 black families finally moved into the housing complex, under the protection of the Detroit Police Department and sixteen hundred troops of the Michigan National Guard.
Like Jane and Will Butler, the great majority of those families had
migrated to Detroit from the South. As they went to bed on their
first night in Sojourner Truth—with the racist taunts of whites
rising up past the windows of the new high-rise—many must
have wondered if they had simply traded one band of night riders
for another.

The chaos at Sojourner Truth was only a prelude to what Jane and
Will experienced the following summer, when twenty-five thou-

sand workers at Packard walked off the assembly line because black employees had been promoted to jobs that placed them shoulder to shoulder with whites. As one enraged man said outside the plant, "I'd rather see Hitler and Hirohito win than work beside a nigger."

The shoving and shouting outside Packard turned to more serious violence on the night of June 20th, 1943, when two young black men were expelled from Belle Isle Park, in the middle of the Detroit River. On the bridge linking the park to the city, a skirmish broke out between groups of blacks and whites. In the wake of the clash, a rumor quickly spread across the city: that "blacks had raped and murdered a white woman on the Belle Isle Bridge."

Many people surely recognized this as the "old threadbare lie" that had fueled half a century of lynch law in the South. But once infuriated whites believed that a gang of black men had "violated" and killed a white woman and thrown her body into the river, it hardly mattered that the story was untrue. If Jane dared to venture out into the city during the three days that followed, she would have witnessed a familiar scene: black bodies being dragged through the streets by gangs of white men.

Witnesses told of mobs ambushing and beating black passengers as they stepped down off trolley cars; a fifty-eight-year-old black man named Moses Kiska being shot and killed for waiting at a bus stop in the wrong part of town; and an unnamed black man being bludgeoned on Woodward Avenue as four white police officers looked on. Jane and Will's house was just two blocks from Woodward, in the middle of what quickly became a war zone. By the time military troops arrived to stop the rampage, there were thirty-four confirmed killings. Most of the victims had been beaten to death with wooden clubs.

Langston Hughes wrote that at least in the North he had his own "window to shoot from," and in June of 1943, in Detroit, that's exactly what black residents like Jane and Will Butler did: keep watch with loaded rifles, stiff-jawed as they waited for the roving mobs. Many of the attackers had European instead of southern accents, but their faces were contorted with the same hatred Jane had seen so many times in Forsyth. All she could do, as so often in her life, was hope that the future might be different. As it said on the flags flying over Detroit's city hall, *Speramus meliora:* "We hope for better things."

DURING THE SAME decades that Jane and Will struggled to build a new life in the North, Forsyth was deep in its sleep of forgetfulness, as all around it the state of Georgia veered even further in the direction of white supremacy. The 1933 governor's race was won by Eugene Talmadge, a south Georgia farmer who proudly grazed a cow on the lawn of the governor's mansion and courted the votes of poor rural whites by casting himself as the last line of defense against a "Nigra takeover." Talmadge held the governorship for three terms between 1933 and 1943 and was, according to writer Gilbert King, "a racial demagogue who presided over a Klan-ridden regime." In a typical campaign speech in 1942, Talmadge answered a question about school integration by reassuring his segregationist base: "Before God, friend, the niggers will never go to a school which is white while I am Governor."

One of the few glimpses from inside Forsyth during this period comes from a white woman named Helen Matthews Lewis, who moved into the county as a ten-year-old in 1934, when her father was hired as a county mail carrier. Lewis remembered a white community still very much in the grips of its original paranoia and still openly proud of having "run the niggers out" in 1912. "I was told stories [as a child]," Lewis said,

> about how they hung blacks around the courthouse. I knew
> they lynched the guy that they were accusing of [the rape of

Mae Crow]. Stories were told. I could just see bodies hanging all around the courthouse in my mind.

Lewis sometimes caught sight of frightened black delivery-men passing through the county in 1930s: "[Back] then blacks coming in through town on trucks to deliver stuff to the stores were afraid to get out. . . . They would hide in the back." Lewis also remembered that many Forsyth residents were quick to react to even the slightest trespass across the racial border—from the appearance of a black worker on the back of a truck to an old man who strayed into Forsyth while riding a bicycle north toward Hall County. "My father came home from his mail route one day," Lewis said,

> and he said he saw this old black man bicycling through town on his way to Gainesville. My father said "I'm worried he's got to go through Chestatee" . . . [past] the rowdy boys of Ches-tatee. [My father] said "He'll never make it," so he gets in his car and he said "I'm going to go find him," then he goes and picks him up and takes him to Gainesville.

Lewis remembered how another outsider violated the unwritten code in the late 1930s—a woman who moved to the county with her long-serving black maid. "When I was in school" at Forsyth County High, Lewis said,

> this teacher comes to town . . . who had this black woman who was a companion, maid, a person who'd always been in their family. And she taught music and the woman lived with her [until] these boys . . . came with torches and surrounded her house and made her get up in the middle of the night and take the black woman back to Alabama.

When an interviewer in 2010 interjected, "Oh, goodness," Lewis said, "These were my experiences in Forsyth" in the 1930s and '40s. "There was a sense of . . . horror."

Lewis was clearly frightened by tales of lynched men hanging from telephone poles, and by the sight of black workers hiding under tarps when they passed through Cumming. But to her schoolmates, "white Forsyth" seemed like the natural and eternal order of things. By 1941, when Lewis graduated from Forsyth County High, most traces of the black community had long since been burned, dismantled, or silently absorbed into the property of whites.

Of that former time, all that was left were fleeting glimpses, visible only to someone who paid very close attention. Not long before she moved out of the county, Lewis remembered, she was walking up to a friend's front door and noticed faint inscriptions in the stepping-stones that led up to the house. It was only when she knelt down for a closer look that Lewis realized the path she'd been walking on was paved with remnants of black Forsyth. "They [were] gravestones," she said, "from a black cemetery. Someone had dug them up, and took them home, and used them for flagstones."

THE CIVIL RIGHTS clashes of the 1950s and '60s came and went without changing much in the lives of Forsyth's quiet country people, who in the decades after World War II had been busy erecting chicken houses in their old corn and cotton fields, as America's expanding poultry industry brought new prosperity to north Georgia. The county seat may have been just a short drive from Ebenezer Baptist—the home church of Martin Luther King Jr. and one of the epicenters of the American civil rights movement—but with no black residents to segregate from whites, there were no "colored" drinking fountains in the Cumming courthouse, and no "whites only" signs in the windows of Cumming's diners and roadside motels. Instead, as segregationists all over the South faced off against freedom riders, civil rights marches, and lunch-counter sit-ins, Forsyth was a bastion of white supremacy that went almost totally unnoticed.

Even as the nation changed around it, Forsyth's old, unspoken rules remained, and each new generation of enforcers clung to the code their parents and grandparents had handed down. In May of 1968, just a month after King was assassinated, a group of ten black schoolchildren came north from an Atlanta housing project, as part of a church camping trip led by two white Mennonite counselors—who were unaware of Forsyth's racial prohibition. At dusk, as the children pitched their tents in a scenic campground beside Lake Lanier, a gang of white men appeared out of the darkness and forced the group to leave, warning them that "we don't allow niggers in this county after dark." When Atlanta activists returned a week later to protest the intimidation, they had to be protected by the Georgia State Patrol, as whites gathered around the campsite, chanting, "Wait until the night comes!"

Asked about the clash, Roy P. Otwell, president of the Bank of Cumming, assured a reporter that while he was "sorry to read of it ... this sort of thing does not represent Forsyth. ... When we have an incident of this kind it is overplayed and much exaggerated [and] the people of Forsyth County [are] greatly misunderstood."

BY THE EARLY 1970s, many of the lynchers and night riders had begun to die off, taking with them the last living memories of the expulsions. The identities of these men will probably remain a mystery forever now. But the account of Marcus Mashburn, a local doctor, leaves little doubt that many of them were well-known residents who—after waging a months-long campaign of terror against their own neighbors—went back to quiet lives as farmers, storekeepers, tradesmen, and God-fearing, churchgoing Christians.

Mashburn was a country doctor who practiced for decades in

At age seven, I had only the vaguest sense that something "bad" once happened in Forsyth, and no idea at all that it had begun just a few miles from where we lived. My classmates at Cumming Elementary explained to me, the newcomer, why there were "no niggers in Forsyth County," the same way their elders had once explained it to Helen Matthews Lewis in the 1930s. And when my Little League team piled into the back of a pickup truck and joined Cumming's Fourth of July Parade in 1978, I watched a group of Sawnee Klansmen stroll along behind us, all wearing their pointy hoods and white robes, as they waved and lobbed handfuls of Super Bubble to the crowd.

But for all that, Forsyth still seemed normal to me as a kid. It was a quiet, close-knit community, as locals liked to say, where boys played football and baseball and where girls rode horses and took ballet. My friends' fathers spent their weekends fishing and hunting, and on Friday nights you could find almost everyone in the bleachers of the Forsyth County High football stadium. I learned to sit silently when my friends told "nigger jokes" and to keep my family's liberal views to myself. My parents had grown up in the Birmingham of George Wallace and Bull Connor, and the kind of deep-seated bigotry we found in Forsyth was nothing new to them. My father and mother had fought with their own parents over integration, and they had been taunted by racists as they'd marched in civil rights demonstrations in Birmingham and Atlanta. In the same way, they told me, we were going to help change Forsyth County from within.

BUT THEN IN July of 1980, three years after we arrived, something happened that I knew wasn't normal at all. I first heard about it when my mother, who worked as a freelance reporter for the *Gainesville Times*, got a call from her editor, C. B. Hackworth. Hackworth said that the night before there had been a shooting not far from our house, and he asked my mother to drive down to Athens Park Road and try to get the full story.

In those days, it wasn't unusual to hear a shotgun blast echoing across Lake Lanier or filtering through the pines when some good ol' boy was hunting whitetail or flushing out quail. So my mother headed toward Athens Park, expecting to learn about a hunting trip gone wrong, or a domestic violence case, or maybe just some redneck taking a potshot at a stray dog.

But after spending the afternoon stopping at one house after another, she began to sense that something very different had happened on Athens Park Road the day before. No one would talk about the shooting, and more than a few people slammed the door in her face when they realized why she'd come. Over the course of the next few weeks, she learned the truth: that whites in Forsyth had once again attacked a black man for stepping across the county line.

ON THE MORNING of July 26th, 1980, Miguel Marcelli and his girlfriend, Shirley Webb, were invited to a company picnic thrown by Sophisticated Data Research, the Atlanta-based computer firm where Webb worked. The organizers had chosen to hold the gathering on Lake Lanier, which was a popular weekend playground for young professionals, particularly after an extension of Highway 400 made the lake an easy drive from northside Atlanta.

Marcelli, a twenty-eight-year-old Atlanta firefighter, had been born and raised in the U.S. Virgin Islands, and his girlfriend, Shirley Webb, thirty-seven, had moved from her hometown of Chicago to take a job at Sophisticated Data. So as they drove over the two-lane country roads to meet Shirley's co-workers for the company party, Marcelli and Webb knew nothing about Forsyth. When they pulled into the public park where employees and guests were laying out their picnics and setting up a volleyball net, the scene looked idyllic: a shady pavilion set between tall pines and the red-clay banks of the lake.

But soon after they arrived, word started to spread up and down Athens Park Road: there were "a couple of niggers" down at the lake, laughing and frolicking, having a party with a bunch of white friends. As locals at the park watched Marcelli and Webb hit the volleyball back and forth, they were shocked—not just by the appearance of two black faces in Forsyth but by the fact that this man and woman didn't seem to realize where they were, or just how much danger they were in.

MELVIN CROWE'S BRANCH of the family added an *e* at some point, but in Oscarville everybody knew that he was blood kin to Bud, Azzie, and Mae Crow. Melvin's father, Burton, was nine years old in 1912 and had grown up with Obie and Ovie, twin brothers who were among the siblings Mae had been sent to fetch on the day she was attacked. As a son of old Oscarville, born in 1929, Melvin Crowe had learned the story of Mae's death not as a legend but as something his father, uncles, grandparents, and cousins had all witnessed firsthand, and told him about many times.

So when Crowe heard the rumors and drove down to see for himself, he could hardly believe his eyes. There, less than a mile from the spot where Mae had been found with her skull bashed in—where she had sickened and died, and where Ernest Knox had first "confessed his crime"—stood two black people, holding hands and wading knee-deep in the waters of Lake Lanier.

Crowe watched them through somewhat bleary eyes, since, according to his neighbors, he "customarily spent much of Saturday drinking, then driving around the area, sometimes stopping by to see friends." Crowe had been doing exactly that all morning, and after catching sight of Marcelli and Webb, he drove to the house of his friend Bob Davis, and together with a friend of Davis's named Bryine Williams, they started plotting to "do something" about what they'd seen. Before they drove back down Athens Park Road, Davis grabbed a pistol. The idea, Crowe said later, was to scare the black couple away: "We talked about shooting out their tires." For anyone who'd missed his point, he added, "I don't like colored people."

Marcelli got his first inkling of trouble when he heard the crunch of gravel under the tires of a pickup truck, rolling slowly past the grassy picnic area. The vehicle cruised by several times that afternoon, always disappearing up the dirt road leading out of the park only to return a few minutes later. When at one point Marcelli ran over near the truck to get a volleyball, he said he found the driver "looking at me with a mean face." As a black man living in Georgia, Marcelli had seen scowling white men many times before. "I didn't pay much attention," he said. "I just thought maybe he looked like that all the time."

But around six-fifteen p.m., as Marcelli and Webb were shaking the sand out of their towels and packing the trunk of their car, the same truck appeared again, and this time the driver pulled sideways across the road, blocking their exit from the park. A middle-aged white man sat behind the wheel, glaring at them. Without a word, he gunned the engine and drove off.

With the light fading, Marcelli and Webb said good-bye to the rest of Webb's friends and got in their car, eager to put the whole episode behind them and relieved at the thought of getting back to Atlanta. But as they drove up the hill toward the main highway, Webb noticed a huge dust cloud filling the road ahead. At that same moment, inside Melvin Crowe's truck, Bob Davis raised his hand, nodded at Crowe, and said, "Stop and let me out right here."

As Marcelli and Webb drove up the dusty road, struggling to see, Webb suddenly heard a blunt pop, then another, and watched in horror as Marcelli went limp, his body slumping over the steering wheel. "I felt a great weakness come over me," Marcelli recalled later. "Then, I felt a 'wiggling' sensation in my head and neck. I heard Shirley scream and the car seemed to be moving on its own."

When she looked over at Marcelli, Webb said, she "thought he was dead . . . the whole left side of his face was covered in blood." She struggled to grab the steering wheel as the car veered, climbed a bank beside the road, then flipped, the engine revving and smoking as the wheels spun. With Marcelli drenched in blood and unconscious in the front seat, Webb dragged herself out through the shattered rear window. As she staggered away from the overturned car and called out for help, she saw "a group of men . . . standing on a hill above the road," and she headed toward them. But when she got closer, Webb was shocked to find that "they were pointing and laughing." Convinced that these were the same men who had just shot Marcelli, a terrified Webb turned and ran back down the road, screaming for someone to help her.

A local man named Keaton was working in his yard when he heard the sound of gunshots, the squeal of car tires, then shattering glass. He ran to look and found what he described as "an extremely distraught black woman" coming up the road toward him.

"Would you help me? Would you protect me?" Shirley Webb pleaded. "And, please, help him," she said, pointing back toward the wrecked car. Keaton told the woman that he would "instruct his wife to call the police." When she begged him to drive her back to the pavilion so she could find her friends, he repeated that his wife was going to call the police. Leaving Shirley Webb standing in the road—still, for all she knew, in the sights of armed white men—Keaton turned back toward his house, shaking his head and saying, "There's nothing more I can do here."

As Melvin Crowe stood in his driveway, staring in the direction from which the shots had come, Bob Davis came crashing through the woods behind his house. Melvin could see that Davis had taken off his shirt and was wrapping a pistol inside it as he ran deeper into the pines. A few minutes later, Davis walked back empty-handed. Still wild-eyed and gasping for breath, he looked at Crowe and said, "I think I killed the black son of a bitch."

Not even fear of prosecution was enough to quiet Melvin Crowe on the subject, or to dampen his pride when police investigators arrived at his house the day after the shooting. Detective Randy Sims started the investigation at Crowe's front door only because it was the closest house to the spot where glass from a shattered windshield still littered the street. When he and another officer introduced themselves, Crowe blurted out, "I'm not telling [you] anything. . . . Somebody has got to keep the niggers out of Forsyth County. I'm glad it happened."

The exchange convinced investigators that Crowe was not just a run-of-the-mill Georgia racist but saw himself as a defender of the "whites only" rule that had been in effect for nearly seventy years. Having instigated the plot to frighten Marcelli and Webb, and having driven Bob Davis to the scene, Crowe was clearly involved in the crime, and as the officers stood on the lawn listening to what was fast veering toward a confession, they had reason to think that Crowe himself might have been the shooter. But even when Crowe realized that he was a suspect, he didn't tell them about Davis or about how he'd seen his friend hiding a pistol in the woods. Melvin fell silent when asked if he knew who'd pulled the trigger. Having lived in Forsyth all his life, he seemed to fear the consequences of identifying a "person unknown." "I'm not gonna tell who did it," Crowe said to Officer Sims. "I'm not gonna tell . . . because [if I do] I'll get burned out."

The full story of the shooting came to light during the court testimony of Ethel Crowe, an elderly aunt with whom Melvin lived. Born in 1911, Ethel, too, was a child of old Oscarville, and from earliest girlhood she had heard the tale of Mae Crow's rape and murder, with its lesson about the monstrous lust of black men. As a member of the wary, insular community of farmers in Oscarville, she had seen unimaginable changes come to the county since the 1920s. What she hadn't ever seen, even in 1980, was a black person coming toward her on Athens Park Road and stopping right outside her front door.

But that's what happened in the minutes after Bob Davis raced into the woods to hide the gun with which he'd shot Miguel Marcelli. Called to testify about that day, Ethel Crowe described "seeing and hearing a black woman crying in the road." According to news reports, Crowe's "lips began to quiver and she spoke in between quiet sobs" as a courtroom filled with local whites sat in silence. The lawyer for the prosecution asked her what she'd done to help Shirley Webb.

"Nothing," Ethel Crowe told the jury. "Nothing like that ever happened at our house before."

There, in her own driveway, stood a trembling, blood-spattered woman, presenting Melvin Crowe's aunt with a frightening choice: she could either go out and help the woman and her injured boyfriend or she could turn away and pretend that she had never heard the gunshot, the car crash, or the woman's cry for help. Asked what she did when she found Shirley Webb sobbing outside her kitchen window, Ethel Crowe stared into her lap and shook her head.

"Nothing," she said. "Nothing . . . I was scared."

DR. MICHAEL FARNELL, chief surgeon at Grady Hospital in Atlanta, testified that Miguel Marcelli had been shot "behind the left ear with a .38 caliber bullet" and that the entrance wound was close enough to his brain that "Marcelli may suffer neurological problems in addition to injuries already sustained." After emergency surgery, Marcelli recovered, and he was well enough to testify at the trials of Melvin Crowe and Bob Davis and to tell the story of his trip to Forsyth. All-white juries found both men guilty of two counts of aggravated assault.

After almost a century during which black Georgians had been lynched, shot at, beaten, and "burned out" of Forsyth, and during which untold acres of black-owned land had been quietly plundered, two whites had finally been arrested and convicted for stalking and shooting a black man. Rather than acknowledging that Crowe and Davis were the first and only men to face such consequences in the county's long history of white terrorism, the *Gainesville Times* congratulated the juries on dispelling the "myth" of Forsyth's bigotry and intolerance. "Twelve men and women . . . exploded that myth" by convicting Davis and Crowe, the paper said, reiterating the old claim that "the county's unusually white complexion is [not] a preoccupation—it is simply a happenstance."

LOCALS WERE RELIEVED when the convictions brought an end to all the media attention and sent news trucks back down Highway 400 to Atlanta. But the peace and quiet didn't last long. Seven years later, a much larger group of African Americans made the trip north, this time crossing the county line not by chance but by choice. They came to publicly protest seventy-five years of segregation in the county and to demand a new era of "peace and brotherhood in Forsyth."

The whole nation soon learned that there were whites in the county who considered themselves exempt from *Brown v. Board of Education,* from the Civil Rights Act of 1964, and from a host of federal laws against racial discrimination in housing and employment. When a double-file line of black and white civil rights marchers appeared on Bethelview Road on January 17th, 1987, and began walking toward the Cumming courthouse, a raucous army of Forsyth residents was waiting to meet them. Just like their grandparents and great-grandparents, they were convinced that they had a right to live in an "all-white" community. As photographers and news crews set up their cameras, the crowd erupted into a chorus of rebel yells and unfurled a long white banner. "RACIAL PURITY," it said, "IS FORSYTH'S SECURITY."

17

THE BROTHERHOOD
MARCH, 1987

Racial violence was making headlines all over the country in December of 1986 after four black men were beaten by a mob of whites in the Howard Beach section of Queens, in New York City. A twenty-three-year-old African American man named Michael Griffith died after the gang of baseball-bat-wielding white teenagers attacked him for trespassing across an unwritten racial border. Already badly injured and running for his life, Griffith had sprinted across a busy highway, where he was struck by a passing car. In response to the killing, Reverend Al Sharpton led twelve hundred demonstrators through the streets of Howard Beach on December 27th, 1986, as furious local whites screamed racial slurs and demanded that black protesters get out of their neighborhood.

Less than a month after the Howard Beach protests, a man named Chuck Blackburn came up with what he thought was a modest proposal for the people of Forsyth: that all those opposed to "fear and intimidation" gather for a short march along Highway 9, ending at the Blackburn Learning Center, where he taught karate classes and meditation. "Overcoming fear of aggression is a basic theme of martial arts," Blackburn told reporters, and

Cumming, Georgia, January 17th, 1987

with the march he wanted to prove that "racism is on the wane in Forsyth."

Blackburn had moved to Cumming from San Francisco in the early 1980s, and he had been shocked to learn that none of his black friends from Atlanta would set foot across the Forsyth County line. And so in January of 1987, Blackburn announced his plan to protest the situation publicly. He called on like-minded residents to mark the seventy-fifth anniversary of 1912 with what he called a "brotherhood walk," which was timed to coincide with the second annual—and still highly controversial—Martin Luther King Jr. national holiday.

Once local newspapers and radio stations picked up the story, there was widespread opposition to Blackburn's plan. He sent letters to area clergy, in hopes that some of their parishioners might join the walk. But, Blackburn told reporters, "only one minister responded . . . and then he backed down." That minister was Reverend Jim Martin of Shiloh United Methodist, who withdrew his support after his own congregants objected vehemently. "Chuck was talking about there being a silent majority who favor brotherly love and who think race doesn't really matter," Reverend Martin said in the days leading up to the brotherhood walk. "But I don't think he's right. I think he's realized that's not right. It would take changing the hearts of a lot of people."

Blackburn learned just how naive he'd been when the phones at his office started ringing day and night, with men and women, young and old, calling to warn of the consequences if he went ahead with the demonstration. The mildest was a caller who said, "I just don't think it's a good idea for you to try to get the niggers to come up here. . . . That's why we live in Forsyth County—to get away from them." An old woman's voice echoed the sentiment, and added an overt threat: "You can't change it, no matter how bad or how hard you try," she said. "You're going to have to end up leaving this county. Or leave in a box."

Then there were the men, whose voices were laced with such menace that Blackburn and his students armed themselves and posted round-the-clock guards at his storefront school. "I know [someone] whose house was burned," one caller said. "So you'd better watch out." As Blackburn peered out through the blinds and double-checked the door locks, his office phone rang again, and the answering machine clicked to life. Through its little speaker a man whispered, "I got a thirty-aught-six bullet with your name on it."

Fearing for his life, Blackburn canceled the protest on January 9th, telling the *Forsyth County News* that "the threats . . . were much more violent than I thought they would be, and the good folks [in this community] just aren't ready to stand up for it. . . . Forsyth County is just not ready for it yet."

When he announced his decision, the brotherhood walk was taken up by a friend of Blackburn's named Dean Carter. Carter was a white construction worker and fellow martial arts enthusiast who lived in Gainesville, where so many of Forsyth's expelled families had resettled. Carter and his wife, Tammy, also received threats, like one from a caller who told them, "After Saturday . . . you're dead." But they were determined to go ahead, and in the week lead-ing up to the protest, Carter joined forces with the veteran Atlanta activist Hosea Williams, who had been a key member of Martin Luther King Jr.'s inner circle during the civil rights battles of the 1950s and '60s. When Williams agreed to lend his name and expe-rience to the cause, the Brotherhood March—and the shocking story of the Forsyth expulsions—started to gain national media attention.

Faced with so much negative coverage, civic leaders in Cum-ming did what they had always done: rather than acknowledge and confront the county's history, they pointed to racially motivated attacks elsewhere in the state and the country and asked why For-syth, of all places, was suddenly being singled out. "We haven't had any incidents up here as far as race is concerned that I can remem-ber, and I've been here since 1956," said County Commissioner James Harrington—a surprising claim, given that only six years earlier, Atlanta firefighter Miguel Marcelli had been gunned down by Melvin Crowe and Bob Davis. Harrington must have also read newspaper reports about an attack in November of 1986, when "five Mexican construction workers, in the county [to work for] a Cumming man . . . were beaten by four men and a woman who broke into their house." The Mexican men said the whites "threat-ened to kill them unless they left the county."

In the days leading up to the march, the dominant tone of the *For-syth County News* was annoyance, along with an unabashed desire to get the whole thing over with as soon as possible. In a column titled "Let's Get on to Better Things," editor Laura McCullough argued that it was Forsyth residents, not black citizens of Georgia, who were being victimized by the negative attention: "By the time this newspaper is printed, the march for freedom, or brotherhood, or martial arts, or whatever, will be thankfully over. Maybe then we can become Forsyth County again. You remember, the sleepy town north of Atlanta that has its own problems with land rezoning and bulging schools?"

A similar note of irritation came from Cumming–Forsyth County Chamber of Commerce head Roger Crow—another distant relative to Mae Crow. On the Thursday before the march, as tensions rose all over the county, Crow stood on the steps of the courthouse and made a public statement on behalf of the business owners of Forsyth, decrying the violent threats of "outsiders," as well as the march organizers themselves. "We do not condone needless efforts to create havoc," Crow said, "made by those with questionable motives, particularly those from outside the confines of the county." There are those "who would portray Forsyth County as a lawless, racist anachronism," he said, but "this simply is not so. . . . Forsyth County shall not be maligned by inaccurate aspersions cast by a reckless few."

While politicians and businessmen fretted over the damage being done to Forsyth's reputation, others were busy recruiting members for a group they called the Forsyth County Defense League. They responded to the Brotherhood March not with editorials and news conferences but by loading pistols, tying lengths of rope into nooses, and planning a "White Power Rally" for the day of the march. Signs were posted and flyers tucked under windshield wipers all over Cumming, calling on whites to "PROTEST AGAINST THE RACE MIXERS MARCH ON FORSYTH COUNTY!" While Sheriff Wesley Walraven told reporters that the Defense League represented "a small radical element," the wording of the announcement tapped into much broader currents of fear and anxiety in the white community, which had origins in the steady northward growth of Atlanta.

BY THE 1970s, Georgia's interstate highway system had extended the margins of the state capital farther and farther from its old downtown, and put the Atlanta suburbs right on the doorstep of Forsyth. Just as Charlie Harris's ill-fated railroad had promised to bring new ideas, new people, and new commerce into the foothills at the turn of the twentieth century, by the time Chuck Blackburn proposed his brotherhood walk in 1987, droves of Atlanta professionals—like my parents—were moving to "lake houses" inside the county. Along with all that new energy and new capital, the freeway brought with it the possibility that Forsyth might soon see the arrival of large numbers of black residents.

Organizers of the White Power Rally played on whites' fears of the city and presented the gathering not only as a celebration of "white power," but as a defense of the "racial purity" that had defined Forsyth for as long as anyone could remember:

> We are protesting against racemixers . . . like Chuck Blackburn, the Carters, *The Forsyth County News, The Gainesville Times,* and other OUTSIDE AGITATORS AND COMMUNIST RACEMIXERS [who] want to defile our community.

If such a call to arms was meant to mobilize white residents of the county, it worked. Two days before the Brotherhood March, the editors of the *Gainesville Times* predicted that "about 100 members of each group are expected to demonstrate," but just like local law enforcement, they seriously underestimated the crowd. Appalled by the thought of "racemixers" invading Forsyth, on the morning of January 17th, 1987, more than twenty-five hundred whites gathered at the intersection where the Brotherhood March was to begin.

By ten a.m., a gas station on the corner of Bethelview Road and Highway 9 was teeming with pickup trucks and men in white

sheets, camouflage, and hunting gear. Frank Shirley, a county resident and head of the Committee to Keep Forsyth County White,
assured reporters that "most of the demonstrators [are] from Forsyth." As a chartered bus filled with civil rights marchers set out
from the King Center in Atlanta and made its way up Highway
400, Shirley took a turn with the megaphone and whipped up the
crowd, chanting, "Go home, niggers! Go home, niggers!"

Whites milling around the parking lot were treated to the day's
first highlight when a silver-haired man in a suit and trench coat
appeared, waving to the crowd as he leaned on a cane and limped
up Bethelview Road. His name was J. B. Stoner, and for decades
he had been one of the South's most notorious white supremacists. His defense of segregation grew even more legendary in
1977, when he was indicted for the 1958 bombing of Bethel Baptist Church in Birmingham. According to court testimony, Stoner
targeted Reverend Fred Shuttlesworth for the leading role he and
Bethel members had played in civil rights protests in Alabama, and
Stoner had instructed his men to place sixteen sticks of dynamite
outside the church in a burning paint can. Before it could detonate,
the improvised bomb was noticed by a passerby, and men guarding
Reverend Shuttlesworth rushed it into the street. The explosion,
seconds later, rattled windows all over North Birmingham and left
a crater-sized hole in Twenty-eighth Avenue.

After evading prosecution for years, Stoner was finally convicted
in 1980 and sentenced to ten years in prison for ordering the bombing. But after serving six years of his sentence, he was granted early
parole in November of 1986—just two months before the White
Power Rally in Forsyth. Having made headlines as an unrepentant racial terrorist, the newly freed Stoner arrived on Bethelview
Road as a kind of celebrity bigot and was swarmed by young Forsyth men eager to shake his hand and get his autograph. Asked by
a reporter why he'd come to Forsyth, Stoner said, "To aid God in

getting rid of the Jew, part-Jew, and nigger. . . . You bring in the
niggers and you bring in AIDS and drugs. We don't want AIDS
and drugs," he added as the crowd roared its approval, "and we
don't want niggers."

To hundreds of people gathered around him, Stoner embodied
the "never say die" fight against racial integration, even though
by 1987 most segregationists had conceded that battle decades
before. Stoner was a walking anachronism to the millions of people
who would see his face on the evening news that night—a hate-
spewing, church-bombing racist who seemed to have stepped right
out of the 1950s. But in the parking lot of Jim Wallace's gas station,
where the defenders of white Forsyth waited to do battle with the
approaching King Center protesters, J. B. Stoner walked among his
kind and was given a hero's welcome.

Once the excitement of Stoner's entrance died down, the crowd

*J. B. Stoner handing out flyers that read, "Praise God for AIDS . . .
Segregation is necessary because AIDS is a Racial Disease" at the First
Brotherhood March, January 17th, 1987*

was ready for the real action to begin. County Sheriff Wesley Walraven had roped off a section of a nearby pasture, and he ordered the Defense League's supporters to move their rally into the designated area. As they reluctantly made their way toward the field—waving rebel flags and carrying signs that said, "KEEP FORSYTH WHITE!"—Walraven saw just how much larger the counterprotest was than anyone had predicted. Bonnie Pike, an agent of the Georgia Bureau of Investigation (GBI), later admitted that "as the thing began to swell . . . we realized we didn't have enough manpower."

Just before eleven a.m., a roar rose from the crowd, and Sheriff Walraven turned to see a chartered bus rolling up the ramp from Highway 400, then coming to a stop on the shoulder of Bethelview Road. Inside, Hosea Williams stood on the last step of the little stairwell, gripping a megaphone as his field sergeants called out final instructions to the marchers. These were rules Williams had first learned from Dr. King: partner up, walk two by two, stay in line, no yelling, no fighting back, no responding to anything said or done against you, no matter how crude, racist, threatening, or violent.

Such nonengagement resulted from King's deep Christian faith and his study of Gandhi's nonviolent protests, but it also grew out of experience: a strict code of discipline and unwavering nonviolence would help make clear to the cameras of the press and to the eyes of witnesses that the marchers were the victims, not the aggressors. Williams knew—particularly after the carnage of "Bloody Sunday" in Selma—that an image of a white man attacking peaceful protesters could raise more awareness than all the speeches and sermons combined. If a word was said in anger, Williams's team instructed the marchers on the bus, it would not be the protesters who said it. If a fist was raised or a rock thrown, it must not come from within their line.

Sheriff Walraven instructed the bus driver to continue past the counterprotest area and unload his passengers farther up the

*Hosea Williams (front, left) and John Lewis (front, right) leading
marchers across the Edmund Pettus Bridge, March 7th, 1965*

road, in hopes of keeping the two groups as far apart as possible.
When the bus doors opened, march leaders stepped down onto
the asphalt, and out into the gray light of Georgia's famous "white
county." As their eyes adjusted to the glare, it became clear that the
crowd of locals gathered in a nearby field were not spectators but
something much closer to a mob. When they caught sight of Hosea
Williams, hundreds clambered over a barbed-wire fence and ran
toward the marchers.

It was commonly believed, and widely reported, that the peace
marchers themselves were all from outside the county. The *Forsyth
County News* said that "People from Forsyth . . . were conspicuously
absent from the group of [Brotherhood] marchers." But while the
majority of the activists did come from Atlanta, there were excep-
tions. For there on Bethelview Road—having waited in our old red
Buick half the morning, nervously watching a sea of rebel flags

over at the gas station—were my mother, my father, and my eighteen-year-old sister, Rachel.

My father got out of the car and said enough to march leaders to make it clear that while he was white, southern, and a resident of Forsyth, he had come to walk with them and to add his voice to the calls for change. Although they had sat all morning unnoticed by the crowd of counterprotesters, the minute my parents and my sister took their places in line, whites in the crowd started pointing and yelling. "Nigger lovers!" they screamed as my mother and sister stood stone-faced, waiting for the signal to march. "Go back to Atlanta with the rest of them," spat a man a few feet away from my father. "Back to Niggertown, you white niggers!"

AS THE FIRST March for Brotherhood in Forsyth County finally got under way, the counterprotesters gave up all pretense of obeying the

Hosea Williams (center) leading the First Brotherhood March, Forsyth County, January 17th, 1987

sheriff. Walraven admitted to Williams that he had been caught off guard by the large turnout and had only seventy men—including local deputies, state highway patrolmen, and Georgia Bureau of Investigation officers—to try to control several thousand people from the White Power Rally. Given the size and feverish excitement of the crowd, an attack came to seem almost inevitable, and law officers focused their efforts on guarding the line of marchers themselves, leaving too few police to watch the counterprotesters on the margins. Only a few hundred yards into the planned walk, furious whites lined both sides of the road, forming a gauntlet through which the marchers had to pass. Walraven directed the driver to pull his bus up next to Hosea Williams, and it crept along at walking speed, in an attempt to provide at least some cover.

The marchers needed protection, because while most people lining the road stood chanting, "Go home, niggers!" and "Keep Forsyth White," others started hurling anything and everything they could find, pelting the line of marchers with sticks, clods of dirt, bricks, broken beer bottles, and rocks. After Williams was struck on the side of the head, Sheriff Walraven gathered march organizers and warned them that he could no longer guarantee anyone's safety. Williams, however, was determined to continue, and that night on news channels around the world, people watched in shock as the gray-bearded sixty-one-year-old winced and ducked the flying rocks, shook his head in disbelief, and carried on.

BORN IN ATTAPULGUS, Georgia, in 1926, Hosea Williams grew up under Jim Crow, and as a boy of thirteen he nearly suffered the same fate as Ernest Knox and Oscar Daniel when a mob of whites in Decatur County came to his house and accused him of raping a young white girl. By Williams's own account, his grandfather held them off with a shotgun, until "a friendly white neighbor interceded to prevent further violence."

After serving with an all-black army unit in World War II, Williams was awarded the Purple Heart for injuries sustained during a Nazi bombing. When he came home from the war in 1945, still recovering from his wounds, he was nearly beaten to death in a bus station in Americus, Georgia—for having the audacity to wear his army uniform and for trying to take a drink from the "whites only" water fountain. As Williams put it, "I had watched my best buddies tortured, murdered, and bodies blown to pieces. French battlefields had literally been stained with my blood. . . . So at that moment . . . I realized why God, time after time, had taken me to death's door, then spared my life . . . to be a general in the war for human rights."

Williams went on to become a leader of the Southern Christian Leadership Conference (SCLC), and a close confidant of Martin Luther King Jr., who called Hosea "my wild man, my Castro," for his willingness to defy court orders, stare down club-wielding policemen, and march against even the most dangerous white supremacists. Williams was at the Lorraine Motel in Memphis when James Earl Ray assassinated King in 1968, and in the wake of the murder, he vowed to carry on King's work. More than any other member of the SCLC's leadership, he continued to fight at street level, leading marches and protests throughout the 1970s. Along the way, Williams became a prominent and controversial figure in Atlanta politics, ridiculed by many whites after he was arrested on charges of drunk driving and leaving the scene of an accident.

By 1987, nearly twenty years had passed since King's death, and Williams, far from his glory days, was a frequent punch line to racist jokes on the talk-radio stations of Georgia. But as he walked through a hail of rocks and bottles in Forsyth, he also walked back into the arena of his greatest triumphs and returned to the role where his greatest strength—old-fashioned bravery—had always been on display. The more the mob on Bethelview Road screamed and threatened, the more Williams felt in his element. Just as King had taught him, and just as they had done in Birmingham and Savannah, St. Augustine and Selma, Williams met the violence in Forsyth with nonviolence. Walking toward the county courthouse of Georgia's last bastion of segregation, Williams clutched a megaphone and, in his raspy, wavering voice, led the marchers in verse after verse of "We Shall Overcome."

ALL AROUND THEM, officers of the county police and the GBI were making arrests, and when they frisked the handcuffed men, they discovered that many had come to the White Power Rally with loaded guns tucked into their jeans and hidden under their jackets. After Walraven told Williams that he feared a shooting if the demonstration continued, the marchers reluctantly agreed to get back on the bus. As soon as the doors opened and marchers began filing on board, the mob let out a howl of celebration.

As a final act of defiance, the bus drove the last few miles to Cumming, and the marchers made a symbolic gesture of walking across the finish line at Blackburn's school, just outside of town. But as journalist Elliot Jaspin put it, "If the gesture was intended to show that the Brotherhood March had triumphed over racism, it persuaded no one." During the long ride back to the King Center, it was clear to everyone involved that they had been defeated by an army of Confederate flag–waving, rock-throwing whites who weren't about to yield territory their ancestors had been defending since 1912. It was going to take more than one afternoon to end seventy-five years of segregation in Forsyth County.

JOURNALISTS COLLECTED REACTIONS to the day's events and spoke with people on all sides in the conflict: dismayed activists, elated white counterprotesters, and county leaders who claimed that the root of the problem was not Forsyth's history of expulsions and racial violence but the media's unfair portrayal of a peaceful community.

Hosea Williams was typically blunt. "I have never seen such hatred," he told a reporter from the *New York Times*. "I have been in the civil rights movement 30 years, and I'm telling you we've got a South Africa in the backyard of Atlanta. . . . There were youngsters 10 and 12 years old screaming their lungs out, 'Kill the niggers.'" Asked if he planned to return for a second march, Williams said, "I think I have to go back." Reverend R. B. Cotton Raeder, another veteran of the civil rights struggle, echoed Williams's shock. "I've been in many such situations," he said, "but never one that was any worse."

Spokesmen for the chamber of commerce, the city of Cumming, and local churches quickly went into damage-control mode. Roger Crow of the chamber admitted that the violence was "an embarrassment," but he characterized the hundreds of locals who had attacked the marchers as "outsiders." "The vast majority of the citizens [of Forsyth] support the rights of everyone," he said. "They're God-fearing, hard-working, and most of them, law-abiding." B. V. Franklin of the First Baptist Church concurred, saying, "I don't think what we saw was indicative of the people here," and County Commissioner James Harrington assured reporters that "people here don't teach their kids to hate anybody"—even as news stations ran footage of children raising their fists and chanting, "Go home, niggers!"

Roy Otwell Sr., the ninety-two-year-old patriarch of one of the county's most prominent families, summed up the wish of most residents, which was that all those demanding an end to segregation in Forsyth—and a reckoning with the county's past—would simply drop the subject. "If they would let us alone," Otwell said, "it would die down and blacks would be more accepted." Otwell had witnessed the events of 1912 with his own eyes as a seventeen-year-old, and he had lived his entire life in a place that showed no signs of changing. Yet even seven and a half decades after night riders had first terrorized the black residents of Forsyth, Otwell still clung to the idea that the integration of the county was only a matter of time and patience. The march, he believed, had been an unnecessary provocation.

In order to claim that "most people" in Forsyth were innocent bystanders, leaders like Crow and Otwell had to ignore the statements other locals made to reporters. Asked why he had come to the White Power Rally, a thirty-four-year-old Forsyth man named William Griffan said, "I figure they could pick a better place to do it than Cumming. My granddaddy helped run the niggers out of here in 1912. They hanged some." Rayford Grindle, who had lived in the county all his life, told a reporter that "most people here don't want them to move in." His wife, Janice, nodded as they stood outside the Second Baptist Church and added, "This has been our home, and having it all-white is all we know."

Another local man, Ron Seaman, came to the march on horseback, and he made a striking figure at the White Power Rally, galloping back and forth with a rebel flag flowing behind him. Asked what he thought of the protesters, Seaman said, "They ought to have printed up . . . targets and given it to them as they got off the bus."

EVEN AMONG FORSYTH residents who stayed home from the rally, there was plenty of support for the Forsyth County Defense League. Kelly Strickland, who lived only a mile from the scene of the violence, wrote to Governor Joe Frank Harris a few days after the march. "I am tired Governor Harris," she said.

> I just want this to all be over [and] I want everyone to leave us alone. . . . I would, without doubt invite a black person into my home for dinner. I love them and respect them, I just do not prefer to live with them. I am sorry. This is my right.

A Forsyth man named Bill Bolton wrote to the governor to decry not the violence that had greeted the marchers but the suffering whites were enduring as a result:

> We the people of Forsyth County have been used, abused, and criticized without just reason. What ever happened to *our* civil rights? . . . The people in Forsyth County are just trying to carve out a living and build a decent place to raise our families. . . . We have not bothered the rest of the world, so why does the rest of the world want to bother us now?

Others wrote to assure the governor—despite news reports to the contrary—that the "trouble" was the work of outsiders and had nothing to do with Forsyth's history or the majority of residents' feelings toward blacks. As a Mrs. Hartsfield of Cumming put it,

> Most of those arrested were not natives. I knew of no one who even ventured into town that day. . . . Forsyth County is by far the friendliest and safest place we could ever imagine. Everyone waves to everyone on the road. . . . This town has kept a low profile and [we] have been living in peace & harmony. *Until now,* we haven't hurt anyone and certainly don't want the whole country to think badly of us.

The erasure of Forsyth's violent past had been so complete that most residents believed what Mrs. Hartsfield told the governor: that there was no place more peaceful and no place less deserving of the outrage that had followed the attacks on the Brotherhood Marchers. To people who'd spent their whole lives inside the bubble of "racial purity," keeping Forsyth "all white" seemed like the most natural thing in the world.

18

SILENCE IS CONSENT

Television viewers around the country were shocked by scenes from the First Brotherhood March: young white women yelling "Nigger!" in the faces of peaceful protesters; children joining chants of "White Power!" from atop their parents' shoulders; civil rights leaders like Hosea Williams dodging rocks and bottles. Within days, there was talk of a second demonstration, as march organizers regrouped. Dean Carter told the *Gainesville Times* that this second march would go all the way to the county courthouse, and Sheriff Wesley Walraven promised to be ready "even if it takes 300 state troopers and every GBI agent in the state." When forecasters called for snow on the proposed date of the protest, Hosea Williams told reporters, "We're going to march [again] in Forsyth County whether it's cold as ice or hot as it is in hell."

I woke to the sound of helicopters passing over our house on the morning of January 24, 1987, and I realized just how different the second march was going to be when we were stopped at a military checkpoint just outside of Cumming and had to wait as bomb-sniffing dogs checked our car. Forsyth's white supremacists might have dominated the headlines on January 17, but a week later it looked as if the whole county was being dragged, kicking and screaming, into the twentieth century. This time, 1,500 jeering counterprotesters were held in check by 350 state troopers, 185 Georgia Bureau of Investigation agents, and 2,000 soldiers of the Georgia National Guard.

The Second Brotherhood March is the best-known part of Forsyth's story, as it was covered by national and international news outlets, which broadcast images of two hundred chartered buses driving up Highway 400, bringing more than 20,000 peace marchers to Georgia's notorious "white county." Among those who marched were famous veterans of the 1950s and '60s civil rights struggles, including John Lewis, Andrew Young, Julian Bond, Joseph Lowery, and Coretta Scott King, who called the protest "a great coming together of the family, the movement, and the followers of Martin Luther King, Jr." Georgia senators Sam Nunn and Wyche Fowler were near the front of the line, along with NAACP president Benjamin Hooks, U.S. presidential candidate Gary Hart, and dozens of celebrities and media personalities.

Even Miguel Marcelli, the black firefighter shot in Oscarville, made the trip from Atlanta, returning to Forsyth for the first time since he was nearly killed by Melvin Crowe and Bob Davis in 1980. "Seven years ago," he told a reporter, "I could have been dead for no reason and never known what I was killed for. . . . But now I'm going to march for the freedom and the dream of Martin Luther King, Jr." The story of Marcelli's return was typical of the day, which became both a reunion of the American civil rights movement and a repudiation of Forsyth's long history of intolerance. As Reverend Joseph Lowery told locals from the steps of the courthouse, "We did not come to Forsyth County to scare you to death. We came . . . to challenge you to live a life of decency."

When the speeches on the Cumming square were finally over, near dusk, my father, mother, sister, and I walked back to our car and watched dozens of buses, filled with weary peace marchers,

Buses arriving for the Second Brotherhood March, January 24th, 1987

making their way out onto the blue highways of the county and back down the on-ramps toward Atlanta. All around us, national guardsmen were walking toward their operations base in a strip-mall parking lot, where they climbed into troop carriers and left in a long convoy of hulking green trucks. Eventually even the satellite news vans broke down their gear, and the army of journalists disconnected their lapel mikes, closed their notebooks, packed up their cameras, and drove away.

For the second time in a week, we were left alone in Forsyth, and we made the short drive back to our home on Browns Bridge Road just as darkness fell. There, our house on the edge of Lake Lanier, just a few miles west of Oscarville, sat just as it always had: surrounded by pine trees and green pastureland, and ringed with neighbors who came from the old families of Forsyth: Mashburns and Cains, Castleberrys and Stricklands, Whitlows and Bensons and Crows. We knew that these people were, at best, irritated by all the attention and inconvenience the marches had caused and, at worst, infuriated by the thought of thousands of black faces— and white supporters like us—rallying on the Cumming square. Nonetheless, my parents felt elated, just as they had during protest marches in the 1960s. They were certain that we had done something historic: that by speaking out against the racial segregation of the county, we were changing hearts and minds and leading backward Forsyth toward a more just future.

But even at sixteen, I had my doubts. Could a culture of fear as deeply ingrained as Forsyth's really be changed by a peace march— even one attended by twenty thousand people and broadcast all over the world? After seventy-five years of bigotry and one afternoon of imported racial harmony, was it really time to declare that the county had awakened from the long nightmare of "racial purity"? Could we really say, as white observers had been saying since 1912, "All quiet at Cumming. . . . No further trouble expected"?

Brotherhood Marchers walking to the Forsyth County Courthouse

National Guard troops and counterprotesters, January 24th, 1987

LATE ON THE day of the Second Brotherhood March, Roger Crow, head of the county chamber of commerce, shrugged and told a reporter, "When all these people finish their grandstanding, we'll go back to living . . . just like we always have." Another Forsyth resident, writing to the *Gainesville Times,* agreed that once the marchers went home, things would get back to normal in Forsyth: "Whites don't want the blacks [here]," the letter writer said. "We need to put a halt to it and forget about it, and let it go like it's been going for the past 75 years. . . . Drop the subject, because if you don't, there's just going to be trouble." And in an opinion piece for the *Times,* a Forsyth man named Steve Whitmire summed up the feelings of many locals. The Brotherhood March, Whitmire believed, was part of an "anti-Forsyth movement." Despite hours of news footage to the contrary, he assured readers that "not once [have] I ever observed any Forsyth County folks hassle *anyone.*" Whitmire ended with a response to Hosea Williams's call for whites in Forsyth to formally apologize for the expulsions of 1912. "Do you think this is a free ride, Hosea? The world in general, and Forsyth in particular, owes you nothing."

THAT SAME BRAND of defiance was broadcast all over the country when Oprah Winfrey, in only her sixth month as a television talk-show host, arrived in early February of 1987 to film an episode of *The Oprah Winfrey Show* on the Cumming square. The goal, Winfrey said, was "simply to ask *why* Forsyth County has not allowed black people to live here in 75 years." In hopes of getting honest answers, Winfrey and her producers decided to admit only residents of Forsyth into the taping—which meant that besides Oprah and her staff, the televised town-hall meeting was an "all-white" affair.

In a restaurant packed with locals, Winfrey passed a microphone from one white guest to another, asking why they still supported the seventy-five-year-old racial ban. Many in the audience said they regretted the recent violence, but most admitted, even to Winfrey, that they preferred to "Keep Forsyth white."

"You don't believe that people of other races have the right to live here?" Winfrey asked a middle-aged woman. "They have the right to live wherever they want to," she replied. "But we have the right to choose if we want a white community."

Winfrey looked from face to face and asked, "What is it you are afraid black people are going to do?" A tall, bearded man in his mid-twenties stood up and said that more than anything he was afraid "of them coming to Forsyth." "I lived down in Atlanta," the man said, but now "it's nothing but a rat infested slum!" As people around him clapped and nodded their heads in agreement, he said, "They don't care. They just don't care!"

Asked if he meant "the entire black race," the man said no, "just the niggers." When Winfrey raised an eyebrow and asked, "What is the difference to you?" the man offered to help her understand the distinction.

"You have blacks and you have niggers," he said. "Black people? They don't want to come up here. They don't wanna cause any trouble. That's a black person. A nigger wants to come up here and cause trouble all the time. That's the difference." Many in the crowd applauded as Winfrey lowered the mike to her side and simply stared into the camera.

By the time it was over, Winfrey had concluded that "a lot of white people are afraid of other white people in this community," and she told a reporter that as a black woman she was "not very comfortable at all in Forsyth." Her crew made a point of packing up before dark, and when she was asked about the next day's plans, Winfrey said, "I'm leaving."

LESS THAN A week after the second march, and emboldened by its success, Hosea Williams formed the Coalition to End Fear and Intimidation in Forsyth County, with an executive committee that consisted of himself, NAACP president Benjamin Hooks, Coretta Scott King from the King Center, Rabbi Alvin Sugarman of the Temple in Atlanta, and SCLC president Joseph Lowery. Now that the Brotherhood Marches had gotten the whole country's attention, Hosea's coalition hoped to turn a symbolic victory into a real one by negotiating with officials in Forsyth.

On January 30th, 1987, Williams sent a letter addressed to Roger Crow and other civic leaders. It listed the coalition's demands and vowed to organize a third Brotherhood March if they did not receive a reply. "We agree that the majority of the citizens of Forsyth County are loyal, patriotic American citizens," Williams began.

> But there is a sizeable crowd that has been possessed with a violent KKK mentality [and] these lost, un-American sisters and brothers must be redeemed. Yes, we know this is a most difficult job, but if good people like yourself and the other

responsible leaders of Forsyth County will sit around the "Table of Brotherhood" and work with us. . . . all things are possible in the eyesight of God.

After that conciliatory opening, Williams shifted gears and listed the steps county leaders would have to take if they wanted to avoid a repeat of the previous week's march. Williams demanded, first and foremost, that "persons whose land [was] unlawfully seized be fully and completely compensated." He also demanded an investigation into violations of federal laws regarding equal employment opportunity. Third, he demanded an investigation into violations of the 1968 Fair Housing Act and, fourth, that "blacks be employed in local law enforcement in significant numbers." Finally, Williams demanded that "educational exchange programs for teachers, students, ministers, and law enforcement officers . . . be developed between Forsyth and [Atlanta's] Fulton County."

With his list of demands, Williams made it clear that the coalition would not be satisfied with vague promises and smiling reassurances and, instead, wanted specific, concrete action. Twenty-nine years later, Hosea's letter looks like a blueprint for confronting deeply ingrained bigotry and for combating the kind of institutional racism that persists in so many American communities in the twenty-first century—from Ferguson to Charleston, Baltimore to Staten Island. Instead of lip service, the coalition wanted financial reparations; the enforcement of federal laws; an affirmative action program to recruit and retain black police officers; and a comprehensive plan to break down racial barriers through education. Essentially, they believed that Forsyth's "race trouble" in 1987 could be cured with the same methods that had worked in Hall County in 1912: prosecute crimes committed against black victims and stop treating Forsyth whites as if they were somehow exempt from the United States Constitution and the laws of the United States Congress.

The coalition's list of demands was a bold opening, but what happened next was a repudiation of nearly all their goals. Cumming leaders agreed to the formation of the Cumming/Forsyth County Biracial Committee but disagreed on both its composition and its mission. Hosea had proposed that his own coalition make up half of the committee, with the other half drawn from Forsyth groups. But Cumming's white leaders said that the African American half of the biracial committee should be made up of unspecified "leaders of the black community" and that it should work broadly on the issue of race relations and "respond to issues and questions raised in recent weeks."

After a lifetime of fighting for equal treatment—and after being told throughout the 1950s and '60s that white southerners needed patience and time to change—Hosea smelled a rat. His reply was unequivocal:

> Gentlemen, this is almost unbelievable. . . . Please understand [that in order to] change Forsyth County to a just democratic society . . . we will not accept you going out across this State [and] getting some black "Uncle Toms" who are controlled by other white interests.

Hosea also made it clear that he expected the biracial committee to discuss not broad issues of race in America but the coalition's specific, itemized grievances:

> The primary responsibility of the Bi-Racial Community Relations committee is to *solve the demands* that were stated in our communication. If you are not willing to do this then you leave us no other alternative than to launch the same vigorous kind of movement in Forsyth county that we have implemented in Birmingham, Selma, Savannah . . . and other bastions of racism.

After the Brotherhood March's soaring rhetoric about a new day dawning, by early February this is where things stood: a group of local white leaders were unwilling to accept Williams's group as equal partners, even though the coalition included the widow of Martin Luther King Jr., the head of the NAACP, a leading Atlanta rabbi, and the head of the Southern Christian Leadership Conference. Whites in Forsyth were also reluctant to investigate violations of federal employment and housing law or to seriously consider compensating victims of the 1912 expulsions.

Only a week after news cameras recorded shocking scenes of mob violence out on Bethelview Road, the meeting rooms of the Forsyth County Courthouse were also filled with racial strife, as local lawyers and businessmen rebutted the notion that Hosea Williams and the black people he represented deserved anything at all from the county.

GOVERNOR JOE FRANK HARRIS eventually settled the dispute over the makeup of the biracial committee by appointing six members favorable to Cumming whites and six members deemed acceptable by Hosea's coalition. Williams himself was excluded, but his daughter Elisabeth Omilami served instead. This Cumming/Forsyth County Biracial Committee met many times over the next ten months, tasked by the governor with improving race relations in the county.

The most striking thing about the official report the committee submitted to Governor Harris on December 22nd, 1987, is that it contains not one set of findings but two: one position paper written by local white members and another written by the coalition's mostly black, Atlanta-based members. In other words, even after working together for almost a year, the two races were as divided as ever in Forsyth—and above all on the very first issue they discussed: reparations for the victims of 1912.

Not surprisingly, white members of the biracial committee—

many of whom owned large amounts of property in Forsyth—rejected the idea of returning land and paying monetary reparations, and they wrote at length about the fear this demand had stirred up in the local community. Committee co-chairman Phil Bettis, a Cumming title attorney, vehemently denied that land had been stolen in the first place and went on to claim that the exodus of blacks in 1912 could only be "partially attributed" to white violence.

Forsyth members of the biracial committee admitted in their position paper that "racial incidents . . . *allegedly* drove a substantial number of blacks from the confines of Forsyth County," but they claimed that "economics played an instrumental role in the black exodus." They argued that "the advent of the boll weevil, early signs of the depression, and the shifting [of the] black population to Atlanta . . . certainly had an equal impact upon blacks leaving." In their view, most of Forsyth's 1,098 black refugees "voluntarily relocated." It is hard to say whether the authors of the Forsyth position paper knew that the first boll weevil was not introduced into Georgia until 1915. They surely did know, as whites had bragged of it for generations, that the mass exodus of Forsyth's black population was not coincidental with mob violence, but in direct reaction to it.

Despite the denials of men like Phil Bettis and Roger Crow in 1987, when journalist Elliot Jaspin went looking in 2007, he discovered a mountain of evidence that the land of black owners had been plundered—as "abandoned" lots were slowly, quietly absorbed into the property of their former white neighbors. Ironically, the written records of these thefts were housed in the basement of the county courthouse, just below rooms in which the biracial committee met. Nonetheless, the position paper written by Forsyth whites concluded that "the charge of unlawfully taken land . . . is an allegation without sufficient foundation in law or fact."

Today many of those same lots are home not to chicken houses, cow pastures, and hog pens but suburban housing developments, filled with multimillion-dollar homes. What was once stolen with a wink and a nod at the county courthouse has now become some of the most valuable real estate in all of metropolitan Atlanta, in a place that is among the top twenty-five wealthiest counties in America.

AFTER REJECTING HOSEA WILLIAMS'S demands for change, the position paper that white leaders submitted to the governor instead scolded descendants of the expelled families themselves. The report blamed them for "perpetuat[ing] divisive and contrived issues" and for harassing local whites with "an ever-pointing finger of blame" which, the report said, "fosters deep and perhaps volatile resentment."

Having turned the tables and laid the blame on "divisive" African American protesters, the white leaders of Cumming called on blacks to "cast aside confrontational tactics and intimidation." The report ended by declaring that "Forsyth is a thriving, modern suburb of metropolitan Atlanta, with no similarity . . . to 1912. Forsyth County has no apologies to make to anyone. Forsyth County also has no handout, only a welcoming hand for fairness and effort . . . as has built this county for over one hundred and fifty years."

That Bettis and the rest of the white committee members still believed they had "no apologies to make to anyone" suggests the ways in which white Forsyth's denial was not just a product of racism but a primary cause of it. By wiping the crimes of the past out of memory, generations of otherwise decent, law-abiding white citizens could go on believing that each new violent episode was an extraordinary event, for which they bore no real responsibility.

AFRICAN AMERICAN MEMBERS of the biracial committee recognized the role of denial in perpetuating Forsyth's bigotry, and they

said as much in the competing report they sent to Governor Harris. "There seems to be a prevailing philosophy" in Forsyth, wrote
committee member Felker Ward,

> that if the undesirable activity . . . of the hatemongers and
> violence-prone . . . is ignored, it will go away. The fact is, how-
> ever, that . . . seven of the eight people arrested and charged
> after the first march were Forsyth residents. [Such] denial and
> inaction allows for the growth and spread of hate-filled phi-
> losophies and activities. Silence is interpreted as consent.

To combat Cumming leaders' long tradition of remaining silent,
which had indeed been "interpreted as consent" by generations of
violent whites, black committee members recommended that the
governor help Forsyth make an "institutional change that clearly
enforces a democratic atmosphere."

Their position paper called for the creation of a permanent race
relations committee that would "work closely with law enforcement [and] civic, religious and community groups to eliminate
the influence and presence of hate groups and those who operate
through racially motivated violence." Such a committee, the position paper said, "should be empowered to investigate complaints,
hold hearings, gather information . . . provide conflict negotiation,
and monitor human relations progress in the county."

In other words, representatives of the African American community called for the establishment of a permanent watchdog
group in Cumming, legally empowered to investigate racially motivated crimes, to name names when violent incidents did occur, and
to ensure that equal protection under the law was afforded to all
people, even inside the lines of Georgia's notorious "white county."

The creation of such a group must have sounded wildly progressive to Governor Joe Frank Harris when the biracial committee

report reached his desk on December 22nd, 1987. Certainly he never acted on the recommendation. Yet it was a much older idea than many people realized. Had Harris used the power of the governor's office to make it a reality, Forsyth would have finally gotten back to the place where it had last been 120 years earlier, in 1867. That was the year Major William J. Bryan packed up the crates and ledgers of the federal Freedmen's Bureau, locked his office on the Cumming square, and left Forsyth County in the hands of the local sheriff.

GO TO CUMMING today, and you will find that time has wrought many of the changes Hosea Williams's coalition fought so hard, and so unsuccessfully, to achieve in 1987. Back then, the biracial committee's competing reports—one black and one white—were received by the governor not as a solution to Forsyth's ongoing segregation but as evidence of just how intractable the problem was. Governor Harris disbanded the committee without any of Williams's original demands having been answered, without serious discussion of reparations by county leaders, and without the creation of the permanent race relations committee that many saw as vital to the future integration of the county.

Instead, Harris—a pro-business, pro-development Democrat—seemed to echo the leaders of white Forsyth when he told a reporter, "There are other Forsyth counties . . . all around the USA. This is not just a Georgia problem. It's a problem that exists wherever people are." Asked if there was anything he could do to stop the violence and intimidation in Forsyth, Harris downplayed legal remedies and emphasized the role of economic development. "People's attitudes are already changing and have been changing for many years," he said. "The growth and momentum that we're having I think attest to that fact."

Both Hosea and white counterprotesters came out again on the one-year anniversary of the Brotherhood March, in January 1988, but there were fewer demonstrators on both sides this time, and, wary of more negative attention, the people of the county mostly stayed home. Asked if the marches had changed anything in Forsyth, local resident Tom Pruitt shook his head. "It doesn't bother me that they march, but [to some people] it's antagonizing. . . . You can't push yourself on people, they get wild . . . like rattlesnakes."

In 1988, the Southern Poverty Law Center successfully sued Ku Klux Klan organizers for conspiracy to deprive the Brotherhood Marchers of their civil rights, and my mother was a witness at the trial, testifying about her experiences on January 17th, 1987. The class-action civil suit resulted in a judgment that forced Klan leaders to pay nearly a million dollars in damages, and that hobbled both the Invisible Empire and the Southern White Knights.

While it would be nice to think that such victories changed Forsyth overnight, in reality few people of color dared or even wanted to move to the county in the late 1980s and early 1990s, particularly after TV screens all over the country showed crowds of whites chanting "Go home, niggers!" on the Cumming square. For years after the marches, most black Georgians continued to view Forsyth as a place to be avoided at all costs. As Nelson Rivers, the NAACP's regional director, put it, "Forsyth has a negative connotation [for] most African Americans around here. . . . Just like Memphis will forever be the place where Dr. King was assassinated, Cumming will always be known for that march."

IN 1990, CENSUS takers counted a total of fourteen African Americans in Forsyth, out of a total population of more than forty-four thousand. While those fourteen people technically lived within the county's borders, it would be a mistake to conclude that they were part of the cultural or social life of Forsyth or that they felt at home on the streets of Cumming. Instead, these earliest trespasses across the old racial border seem to have occurred as a handful of blacks who lived in northern Atlanta suburbs like Alpharetta, Johns Creek, and Suwanee moved into homes that lay just across the southernmost county line. It is possible that some were among the hundreds of thousands of new arrivals to the state, who came with no knowledge of where exactly the county line was or that moving onto the Forsyth side put them in danger.

Whatever their reasons, those earliest black families took a tentative first step into the old "whites only" zone, and for the first time in living memory, the arrival of African Americans in Forsyth seems to have been met with silence. By 1997, their number had grown to thirty-nine black residents, out of a total population of 75,739. According to the *New York Times,* this still made Forsyth "the whitest of the country's 600 most populous counties . . . with a white population of 99.3 percent." Three years later, at the turn of the new millennium, census workers counted 684 black Georgians who had chosen to live in Forsyth. This still represented only .7 percent of a total population that was nearing 100,000, but ten years later, in 2010, the African American population had increased to 4,510, or 2.6 percent of county residents.

What these numbers show is that in the twenty years after the Brotherhood Marches, time, money, and economic growth slowly but steadily changed Forsyth—into a place that tolerates a small minority of black residents and no longer violently enforces its century-old racial ban. As tens of thousands of Atlanta commuters and new corporate employees moved into the county—increasing its population from 38,000 in 1987 to more than 200,000 in 2015—the old guard of Forsyth and the traditional defenders of "racial purity" were simply outnumbered by newcomers with no history in the county and only the faintest inkling of its racist past. In the early 2000s, Forsyth was among the fastest-growing counties in the entire nation, and once the great tidal wave of Atlanta's suburban sprawl finally broke and washed over Cumming, the place was transformed almost beyond recognition. According to University of Georgia sociologist Doug Bachtel, the old racial ban eventually "died a natural death."

IN 2007, ON the twentieth anniversary of the First Brotherhood March, the *Gainesville Times* noted that at the little crossroads where white supremacists attacked civil rights marchers in 1987, there are now "banks [and] eateries, a supermarket, and that true indicator of suburban life: a Starbucks." Where once there were pine forests and green pastures, there are now acres and acres of subdivisions, with invented names like Sawnee Plantation, Chattahoochee Oaks, and Bethelview Downs.

The people living in those manicured neighborhoods and gated communities are still overwhelmingly white, and many work for the multinational corporations that have established headquarters in the county, including Siemens, Tyson Foods, and Lafarge. But whereas in 1987 non-white residents barely registered in census data, today Forsyth is 10 percent Latino and 8 percent Asian. The African American community still accounts for just 3 percent of the total population, but that number rises every year, as the county's old reputation for bigotry fades into the prosperity and anonymity of the Atlanta suburbs, and as middle-class black Atlantans are drawn north by the same features that have attracted so many white transplants: a short commute to northside Atlanta, deep housing stock, and one of the best public school systems in the state. As Alanda Waller, a new African American resident of Forsyth, told a reporter, "I am the treasurer of the PTA. . . . Come on, that should tell you something. They've come a long way."

A PACK OF WILD DOGS

I f you drive around Cumming today, you will see more than a few black and brown faces among all the white ones—people of color working and shopping in Forsyth County's stores, walking the streets of the town square, and sending their children to the local schools. What you won't find is a single trace of 1912, or any acknowledgment of the racial cleansing that defined the county for most of the twentieth century. Instead, the timeless, placeless veneer of American suburbia has so completely covered over the past that not even the young black men and women working the cash registers of the county seem to realize that Forsyth was "whites only" just a few decades ago, or that the ground under some of its subdivisions, malls, and big-box stores once belonged to earnest, hardworking black farmers.

And how could they know? There is no memorial to the lynching of Rob Edwards. There are no photographs of black leaders like Joseph and Eliza Kellogg, Levi Greenlee, and Byrd Oliver among all the Confederate portraits at the county Historical Society. And no marker anywhere tells new black residents that they are far from the first African Americans to live in Forsyth.

Instead, gazing out over the square is a larger-than-life bronze

statue of Hiram Parks Bell, Confederate Congressman, U.S. Representative, and self-described defender of "white over black domination." Bell is the celebrated native son whose most famous moment
in Washington came when King David Kalākaua of Hawaii was
received as a visiting head of state in November of 1874. As Kalākaua
spoke before Congress, the representative from Georgia was over-
heard joking to a colleague that in the days of southern slavery, the
king "would have brought $1,500 on the block." Bell's caucus of
southern Democrats succeeded, by the end of his second term, in
reversing nearly all the gains African Americans had made under
congressional Reconstruction, and to the end of his days, "Colonel"
Bell was proud of having helped quash what he derided as "this
attempted social revolution, to place the African upon an equality
with the Caucasian."

WALK FROM BELL'S statue to the corner of Main Street and Tribble
Gap Road, and you will find signs of the county's newfound wealth
everywhere: a towering new courthouse, the glass facade of a new
county jail, and gleaming branches of major banks. But nothing
will point you to the spot where the corpse of Rob Edwards hung
from a telephone pole all through the afternoon of September 10th,
1912. Nowhere is there a photograph of those same streets filled
with government troops, sent to stop the mobs of Forsyth and to
quell its recurring "state of insurrection."

Turn west and head out Kelly Mill Road, and you'll come to the
beautifully restored home of Dr. Ansel Strickland, which now
houses the offices of the Cumming–Forsyth County Chamber of
Commerce. Walk inside and you will be greeted by the firm hand-
shake and winning smile of Randall Touissant, vice president
of economic development, a young African American man who
spreads the gospel of Forsyth's pro-business environment around
the globe.

Walk south from Strickland's place, past the public housing project at Social Circle and down a grassy ridge, and you will come to an undeveloped lot, its concrete sidewalks and curb cuts prepared and ready for new construction. Gaze up at the green hills rising on three sides, and you might realize where you stand: at the center of the "natural amphitheater" where carpenters once built and then burned Judge Newt Morris's famous fence. It was to those same hillsides that five thousand people brought their blankets and children and spent the morning of October 25th, 1912, celebrating the double hanging of two black teenagers. Drive out Browns Bridge Road to Pleasant Grove Church in Oscarville, and you will find the only visible reminder of 1912 in the entire county: the headstone of Bud and Azzie Crow's oldest daughter, Mae.

If history is written by the victors, a hundred years after the expulsions the victorious white people of Forsyth have successfully written the racial cleansing completely out of mind. And where anyone familiar with the crimes of 1912 might expect to find signs of reflection, apology, even truth and reconciliation, there is only a deafening silence. Now that they have joined the brave new world of Atlanta, and been rewarded with a level of wealth their dirt-farming, hog-killing, mule-driving ancestors could never have imagined, it's clear that most natives of Forsyth would prefer to leave this whole tale of murder, lynching, theft, and terror scattered in the state's dusty archives or safely hidden in plain sight—in places whose significance is known only to the dwindling handful of people who still remember the stories they once heard at some old timer's feet.

INSTEAD, YOU MIGHT head south to Atlanta, to Martin Luther King Jr.'s birthplace on Auburn Avenue, and wait for someone to buzz you into the King Center archives. Fill out a slip requesting the "Forsyth County Box," and you'll find inside it a stack of dusty old cassette tapes, with names scrawled in pencil on their white labels: "Carl Dickerson," "John Byrd Terry," "Annie Lee Blake."

If you ask to listen to them, a librarian will lead you to a room with a table, a chair, and an old-fashioned tape player. Lean your ear down next to its little silver speaker, and even over the hum of the air-conditioning and the distant drone of a copier, you will hear the faint, frail voices of people who were very old when they were interviewed in the spring of 1987 but only little children in the fall of 1912. Lean down closer, and through the static they will speak of mule carts loaded in the dark, and threadbare quilts thrown over their heads, and the creak of wooden wagon wheels bumping over rocks and muddy ruts, on those dark nights and purple, predawn mornings when their families left Forsyth forever.

KATHLEEN HUTCHINS ANDERSON was eight years old the night her grandmother Catherine Black showed up in Buford, just across the Chattahoochee from Forsyth. A lifetime later, Anderson recalled the shock of seeing her father's mother, always so stoic, suddenly burst into their house in tears.

George and Catherine Black had been born "in slavery times," Anderson remembered, and were almost disbelieving the day in 1911 when their son Alonzo bought them a house and a plot of land out near Sawnee Mountain, not far from their friends Joseph and Eliza Kellogg. There, for the first time in their lives, the Blacks owned a modest cabin, along with thirteen acres of farmland, a horse, and a mule.

This allowed the couple to carve out of the red Georgia clay the kind of quiet, simple life that, according to their granddaughter, was a godsend to two former slaves. Having been the property of white men for much of their lives, they wanted nothing in old age but to be left in peace: to grow the food they ate, pump water from their own well, and do exactly as they pleased. "They were just so

happy to own a house—being enslaved and not having anything
. . . they hadn't even had shoes . . . and then having a home—
they was just tickled to death," Anderson said. "They had four or
five rooms [and] my daddy used to carry us over there on Saturday
nights. We'd spend the night with our grandparents. . . . He would
put us in the wagon and take us over there—and [I'd] sleep at the
foot of their bed."

When an interviewer asked about the night her grandmother
fled the terror in Cumming, Anderson said, "When she came to
our house it was dusk," and

> I just remember her coming in crying, you know. Mama
> hugged her and all. . . . They sent us children into the other
> room, and they sat down and talked. [My grandmother] kept
> saying she was so hurt. They had to run and leave everything
> . . . had to leave their home. They had never owned nothing
> before. I don't think she ever got over what happened . . . I just
> know she cried. It hurt her so bad.

When eight-year-old Kathleen crept in from another room and
climbed into her grandmother's lap, her father tried to shoo her
away, saying Grandma was too tired. But what, Kathleen Anderson
remembered asking, about the dolly she'd left at Grandma's house?

Catherine Black—who had survived slavery, and Jim Crow, and
now a visit from the torch-wielding night riders of Forsyth—turned
her granddaughter to face her and said she was sorry but "a pack
of wild dogs got into the house" and tore that doll up. "I'm going
to buy you a new one," she said, wiping tears from the girl's brown
cheeks. "I'll buy you a new one just as soon as we get back."

AUTHOR'S NOTE

This book would not exist without a kind but determined push from Natasha Trethewey, who challenged me, more than a decade ago, to tell this story. Having grappled with America's racial history so often in her work, Natasha turned to me during a cab ride in New York City and asked why it was that she, a southern woman of color, wrote about "blackness," yet I, a white man from one of the most racist places in the country, never said a word about "whiteness." "Why," Natasha asked, "do you think you're not *involved?*" I am ashamed to recall how I defended my silence. And I am proud to say that her question helped me begin this project.

I knew it would take time to unearth some of my home's buried past, and I had a fundamental problem to overcome: I live in Brooklyn, and everything I wanted to discover, everything I needed to know, was nearly a thousand miles south. To find my way back—and to get closer to the archives, libraries, courthouses, and family stories in which traces of pre-expulsion Forsyth were still preserved—I depended on the generosity of friends old and new. Drew University granted me a sabbatical leave, without which I could never have made vital research trips to Georgia. The Andrew W. Mellon Foundation provided an Arts and the Common Good Grant that helped pay for plane tickets, rental cars, and nights in the hotels of Morrow, Athens, Gainesville, Buford, and Cumming.

As I tried to tame a growing and often overwhelming collection of newspaper articles, letters, military reports, taped interviews, maps, photographs, trial dockets, and census records, I was lucky to have two experienced and generous mentors. Don Fehr, my agent and friend, has been behind this book from the beginning, and I could never have written it without his encouragement and good counsel. Ted Genoways showed me the way forward, as he has so many times—especially through the example of his superb work as a journalist. I am forever grateful for his friendship.

WHEN I STARTED digging in the courthouses, libraries, and archives of Georgia, I realized that there was another problem that had no easy solution. In 1912, Forsyth had its share of educated black preachers, schoolteachers, and property owners—people like Levi Greenlee, Grant Smith, and Joseph Kellogg. But a majority of the county's African American citizens were sharecroppers and field hands, like Buck Daniel and Byrd Oliver, who never owned an acre, signed a deed, or paid a dollar in property tax. This meant that, almost by definition, the victims of Forsyth's racial cleansing were woefully underrepresented in the surviving records, and many left no written trace at all. As the voices of the dead rose all around me, the ones I most desperately wanted to hear were also the faintest and most difficult to make out.

The descendants of the 1912 refugees helped fill in many gaps, and over the past four years I've been fortunate to spend many hours talking and corresponding with the great-grandchildren, grandchildren, and (in a few cases) children of the African American families forced out of Forsyth. I am especially grateful to Deidre Brown-Stewart and Charles Grogan; George and Rudy Rucker; Rojene Bailey; Charles Morrow; Geraldine Cheeks Stephens and

Mabel Lee Sutton; Erma Brooks; Seth Squires; Linda Carruth; and Bonnie Rateree.

More than any other descendant, I spoke with Anthony Neal, who told me about his ancestors Joseph and Eliza Kellogg. Even four generations later, Tony was proud of the monumental effort it had taken for his great-great-grandfather and great-great-grandmother to rise from slavery and become the owners of more than two hundred acres in Forsyth. It was Joseph and Eliza who first established the Kellogg Family Reunion—a gathering that began in 1916 and has continued uninterrupted ever since. It still brings the wide branches of the Kellogg family tree back together once a year, for an event that alternates between Atlanta and Chicago—between those who stayed and those who rode the rails north out of Georgia. The bonds have remained strong even across all that distance, according to Tony, because his ancestors wanted it that way. After losing all they had, he said, family meant everything to Joseph and Eliza Kellogg.

THE GAINESVILLE–HALL COUNTY Black History Society also welcomed me into their annual meeting in 2014. That night, Barbara Borders Brooks became my friend, mentor, and guide to the black community of Gainesville. Together, we drove all over Hall County seeking the scattered diaspora of Forsyth. Most of the descendants Barbara and I visited were too young to have lived through the expulsions themselves, but they did their best to answer my questions, dug fading photographs out of their closets, and put me in contact with wide networks of kin. Sometimes, someone would even lean back, close his or her eyes, and summon up out of the darkness the oldest, most nearly forgotten stories about Forsyth.

In July of 2015, I finally located Oscar Daniel's niece Mattie, who I was amazed to find in a nursing home on the outskirts of Gainesville. After I'd spent a day knocking on doors and chasing one false lead after another, my pulse quickened when I was led

into her room. "I came to ask about your family," I said, approaching Mattie's hospital bed, the manila folder under my arm stuffed
with family trees, newspaper clippings, and long lists of questions.
"Family? I ain't got no family," said Mattie—a dark-skinned, gray-
haired woman of eighty-two. She cut her eyes at me, then turned
back toward a TV, tuned to *Wheel of Fortune*. After half an hour of
my coaxing her toward some memory of Oscar and Ernest, Buck
and Catie, or any of her relatives who'd once lived in Forsyth, Mattie
dismissed me with a wave of her hand.

Only when I went back the next morning—this time carrying, as
a kind of peace offering, a little vase of flowers—did Mattie finally
open up to me, though not about Forsyth, or her father, Cicero, or
the Uncle Oscar who'd died twenty years before she was born, in
1932. Instead, Mattie talked about the one subject that made her
face soften and brighten. When I asked if she knew the name Jane
Daniel, Mattie looked up from the TV. "Aunt *Janie*," she said. "You
talkin' about Janie Butler."

In my research, Jane's trail had gone completely cold after she
was released from the Fulton Tower in October of 1912, and despite
months of searching, I hadn't been able to find her anywhere: not
in Gainesville or Atlanta, not in Memphis or Chicago or New York.
Now, in one sentence, Mattie solved the riddle. "Janie married a
man name of Butler. Will Butler. I took the train to Detroit, stayed
with them one time. Went to school for a year."

As I scribbled and turned the pages of my notebook, I could only
hope that the archives would confirm Mattie's story, which they
did: Jane and her new husband, Will, joined the Great Migration in
the 1920s, and once they were settled, Jane told her brother Cicero
to send his daughter Mattie north. When I asked about that 1945
journey—when Mattie was thirteen and stepped off a train car into
the great churning city of Detroit—she turned and looked straight
at me. "I loved it," she said. "I loved it up there."

MY TRIPS TO Georgia were often dizzying, with a morning spent among African American descendants of the Forsyth refugees followed by an afternoon sitting in Cumming, talking with descendants of white Forsyth. Among the latter group, I am especially grateful to Lorene Veal, who vividly recalled the Oscarville of her girlhood and set me straight on the vast and ever-branching Crow family tree. Henry D. Berry shared stories his mother, Ruth Jordan, had told him about 1912, and he and his daughter Susan Berry Roberts talked with me about George and Mattie Jordan's attempts to help their black neighbors. Jane Stone Hernandez told me all about Isabella Harris; John Salter and Connie Pendley welcomed me into the Historical Society of Forsyth County; and Kathleen Thompson of the *Pickens County Progress* helped me trace refugees who found safety working for the Georgia Marble Company. Above all, thanks to Debbie Vermaat, who answered my endless questions with generosity and grace. As the grandniece of Mae Crow, Debbie has a unique relationship to this story, and I am deeply grateful for her unflinching honesty.

I also owe a debt to several researchers who came before me. Troy Dempsey shared his own work on the expulsions and became a trusted friend; Elliot Jaspin's writing about the seizure of black-owned land was a great help; and Marco Williams's film *Banished* inspired me to reach out to more descendants. More than anyone else, the late Don Shadburn was my guide to "old Forsyth," and he taught me a lot about the white community of the early and mid-twentieth century. Don and I danced a delicate dance, as I probed for documents and information that I was certain he possessed but that he had sometimes discretely, unilaterally decided to keep out of the public eye. Whenever I was in Cumming, we had lunch at Steven's Country Kitchen, and he usually arrived with an armload of maps, photographs, and crumbling old ledgers—some of which looked like they belonged in a museum, not in the trunk of Don's car. He was always collegial and generous, and we formed an unexpected friendship around our shared—and very different— obsessions with the history of home. Don never once let me pick up the check.

My mother and father, Bill and Nan Phillips, deserve special thanks. Raised in the Alabama of Jim Clark, Bull Connor, and George Wallace, they rebelled against segregation in the 1950s and '6os, and they paid a price for that in their own families. Their bravery has been an inspiration all my life.

Thanks are due to many other friends who listened at one point or another. Some of them may not remember how much they helped, but I do: Mary Anne Andrei, Joelle Biele, Will Cox, Matt Donovan, Jesse Dukes, Merrell Feitell, Serge Filanovsky, David Gessner, Jennifer Grotz, Renee Morris Hand, Rachel and Jeff Hayden, Chester Johnson, Neil Levi, Joe Murphy, Tom Platoni, James and Paula Phillips, Hirsh Sawhney, Delphine Schrank, Tom Sleigh, and Patrick and Lisa Whelchel. Deep gratitude to Tiphanie Yanique and Moses Djeli for their generosity and invaluable insights.

Alane Salierno Mason is a brilliant editor, and it has been a joy and an education to be one of her writers. To paraphrase Wallace Stegner: Oh, how beautiful a thing it is to work with those who know their job! I am grateful to all of her colleagues at Norton, and especially to Marie Pantojan for her tireless help. Thanks also to Bonnie Thompson, my wonderful copy-editor, for improving this book in so many ways.

This project began with my awe and wonder at a photograph of the Forsyth prisoners, and my spirits lifted each time I found a new image. I wish there were more pictures of the African American community of Forsyth, but just as most field laborers left no more than an X beside their names, the poor people of the county rarely found themselves in front of a camera. In my search for whatever scraps of imagery remain, I was lucky to correspond with many photographers and collectors, and I am deeply grateful to Joe Tomasovsky, Molly Read Woo, James Michael, Bob Ramsak, Jeff Slate, Ben Chapnick on behalf of Charles Moore, and Spider Martin. Thanks to Gary Doster for his vintage postcards of Cumming, and to Melissa Montero at the Associated Press.

I didn't know John Witherspoon back when we both lived in Georgia, but he also stumbled into that Ku Klux Klan celebration in January of 1987—when I was a junior in high school and he was a young Atlantan with a VHS recorder. It was surreal to watch his footage together thirty years later, and to realize that we might have been standing shoulder to shoulder when Frank Shirley picked up a microphone and screamed out over the Cumming square, "White Power!" Thanks to John and his videos for confirming so many of my memories of that day.

My research would not have been possible without the help of the expert archivists and librarians who so quietly and nobly preserve the past for all of us. Thanks especially to Stephen Engerrand and Allison Hudgins at the Georgia Archives; Nathan Jordan at the National Archives in Morrow; Cynthia Lewis at the King Center Archives; Jada Harris at the Atlanta History Center; Chuck Barber of the Hargrett Rare Book and Manuscript Library; the Georgia Newspaper Project at the University of Georgia; the University of North Georgia Library; the New York Public Library; the Rose Library at Drew University; the Pratt Institute Library; and New York University's Bobst Library. Thanks to John Guillory and Ernest Gilman of the NYU English Department for teaching me what to do once those fading relics were placed in my hands.

Finally, Ellen Brazier, Sid Phillips, and Cam Phillips gave more hope, encouragement, and patience to this project than anyone. To the three who matter most: *love, love, love.* Love beyond words.

NOTES

INTRODUCTION: LAW OF THE LAND

xii *"all hell broke loose"*: Ruth Mae Jordan Berry, handwritten account, November 1980, courtesy of Henry Dan Berry.

xvi *"We white people won"*: "White Protestors Disrupt 'Walk for Brotherhood' in Georgia Town," *New York Times,* January 18, 1987.

xx "Girl Murdered by Negro at Cumming," *Augusta Chronicle,* September 10, 1912; "Confessed His Deed," *Atlanta Constitution,* October 4, 1912.

xxii *sustained campaign of terror*: For an overview of racial cleansing in twentieth-century America, see James W. Loewens's *Sundown Towns: A Hidden Dimension of American Racism* (New York: New Press, 2013).

CHAPTER 1: THE SCREAM

1 *"at once sounded an alarm"*: "Two Companies of Militia Prevent a Serious Race Riot," *Macon Telegraph,* September 8, 1912.

1 *"a negro man in her bed"*: "Troops Rushed to Cumming in Autos to Check Race Riot," *Atlanta Journal,* September 7, 1912.

2 *"SAWNEE KLAVERN"*: Don Shadburn, *The Cottonpatch Chronicles* (Cumming, GA: Pioneer-Cherokee Heritage Series, 2003), Appendix H, 478–79.

2 *The farm in Vickery's Creek*: 1880 U. S. Census, Vickerys Creek, Forsyth, Georgia; roll 147; p. 402C; Enumeration District 075; image 0085; FHL microfilm 1254147.

3 *died of meningitis*: Forsyth County Heritage Book Committee, *Forsyth County, Georgia Heritage, 1832–2011* (Waynesville, NC: County Heritage, Inc., 2011), 222.

3   *Lillie, eleven, Jewell, eight*: 1910 U. S. Census, Settendown, Forsyth, Geor-
     gia; roll T624_188; p. 10B; Enumeration District 0043; FHL microfilm
     1374201.

3   *declared his candidacy*: "County Candidates," *Macon Telegraph*, June 21, 1912.

4   *men held as accomplices*: "More Trouble at Cumming," *Augusta Chronicle*,
     September 12, 1912.

4   *Morgan and Harriet Strickland*: 1910 U. S. Census, Big Creek, Forsyth,
     Georgia; roll T624_188; p. 18A; Enumeration District 0036; FHL micro-
     film 1374201; Forsyth County Return for Colored Taxpayers, 1912, Big
     Creek District, Georgia Archives, Morrow, GA.

4   *"rounded up suspects"*: "Two Companies of Militia Prevent a Serious Race
     Riot," *Macon Telegraph*, September 8, 1912.

4   *black men and white women*: Roberto Franzosi, Gianluca De Fazio, and
     Stefania Vicari, "Ways of Measuring Agency: An Application of Quantita-
     tive Narrative Analysis to Lynchings in Georgia (1875–1930)," *Sociological
     Methodology* 42 (2012), 1–42.

5   *"will probably be the victim"*: "Threatened Lynching at Cumming Averted,"
     Atlanta Georgian, September 7, 1912, home edition.

5   *"no excitement prevailed"*: Ibid.

6   *"a determined spirit"*: "Threatened Lynching at Cumming," *Atlanta Geor-
     gian*, September 7, 1912, final edition.

6   *one of the first "white primary" systems*: C. Vann Woodward, *The Strange
     Career of Jim Crow* (New York: Oxford University Press, 2002), 85.

6   *the chaotic war year of 1863*: 1880 U. S. Census, Little River, Cherokee,
     Georgia; roll 140; FHL microfilm 1254140; p. 254B; Enumeration District
     026; image 0089.

7   *educated black man*: 1910 U. S. Census, Big Creek, Forsyth, Georgia;
     roll T624_188; p. 16B; Enumeration District 0036; FHL microfilm 1374201.

7   *"a sorry white woman"*: "Two Companies of Militia Prevent a Serious Race
     Riot," *Macon Telegraph*, September 8, 1912.

7   *"the infuriated mob was upon him"*: "State Troopers Rescue Negroes at
     Cumming, Ga.," *Atlanta Constitution*, September 8, 1912.

8   *burn Grant Smith alive*: "Troops Rushed to Cumming in Autos to Check
     Race Riot," *Atlanta Journal*, September 7, 1912.

8   *to treat and dress his wounds*: "Militia Prevents Clash of Races at Cum-
     ming," *Columbus Enquirer-Sun*, September 8, 1912.

9   *North Georgia Agricultural College*: "Alumni Personals," *Delta of Sigma
     Nu Fraternity*, 26.3 (1909), 988.

9   *at the University of Georgia*: *Register of the University of Georgia* (Athens, 1906), 112.

9   *"stupendous results"*: "Railroad Meeting at Cumming, Georgia," *Atlanta Constitution*, March 11, 1871.

9   *"build a road through the county"*: *Carroll County Times*, January 12, 1872.

9   *"the sum of $20,000"*: "They Want a Railroad," *Atlanta Constitution*, August 29, 1891.

10   *Plans for the Atlanta Northeastern*: "Petition for Charter," *Marietta Journal*, July 9, 1908.

10   *"The line which is to be built"*: "Trolley for North Georgia," *Atlanta Constitution*, January 9, 1910.

10   *To many of the county's wary hill people*: For more on the anxiety of change in the new century, see Steven Hahn, *The Roots of Southern Populism* (New York: Oxford University Press, 2006), 37.

12   *largest black-owned property in the county*: Forsyth County Return for Colored Taxpayers, 1912, Big Creek District, Georgia Archives, Morrow, GA.

12   *Cumming city limits*: "Sheriff Sales," *Baptist Leader*, January 19, 1893.

12   *first and only black member*: Garland C. Bagley, *History of Forsyth County*, vol. 2 (Milledgeville, GA: Boyd Publishing, 1990), 691.

13   *"25 cent pieces"*: Ibid., 812.

14   *"women and children"*: "Trouble at Cumming Prevented by Militia," *Atlanta Journal*, September 8, 1912.

14   *"armed for war"*: Ibid.

14   *"pitched battle between the races"*: "Race Riot, Sheriff Shot," *Macon Telegraph*, July 28, 1912.

14   *"a plot to burn the town"*: "Race Riot Ends, Order Reigns in Plainville," *Macon Telegraph*, July 29, 1912.

15   *armed black men*: "Race War: Whites Clash with Negroes Near Calhoun," *Atlanta Constitution*, July 28, 1912.

15   *"the battle was maintained"*: "Plainville Quiet After Two Days of Excitement," *Macon Telegraph*, July 30, 1912.

15   *"a band of negroes"*: "Shot in Race Riot," *New York Times*, July 29, 1912.

CHAPTER 2: RIOT, ROUT, TUMULT

17   *[But] "while we were sitting there"*: Isabella D. Harris, letter to Max Gilstrap, January 28, 1987, postscript p. 5–6. Courtesy of Hargrett Rare Book and Manuscript Library / University of Georgia Libraries, ms2687(m).

18   *"fully 500 white men"*: "Threatened Lynching at Cumming Averted,"
       Atlanta Georgian, September 7, 1912, final edition.

18   *"many arms and munitions"*: "Troops Rushed to Cumming in Autos to
       Check Race Riot," *Atlanta Journal*, September 7, 1912.

18   *"old rifles, shotguns ancient and modern"*: "Terror in Cumming, Race Riot
       Feared," *Atlanta Georgian*, September 11, 1912, home edition.

19   *"A hundred or more white men"*: "Threatened Lynching at Cumming
       Averted," *Atlanta Georgian*, September 7, 1912, final edition.

19   *"They accepted the warning"*: *Columbus Enquirer*, September 8, 1912.

19   *"We wants nigger for dinner!"*: Isabella D. Harris, letter to Max Gilstrap,
       January 18, 1987, postscript p. 1.

21   *"Night Riders are said to have killed"*: "Riders Burn 4 Churches," *Washington Post*, February 1, 1910, 4.

21   *"Terror exists"*: "Terror Reign in Georgia," *Washington Post*, December 16,
       1910.

21   *"Owing to the posting of anonymous placards"*: *Chicago Defender*, January
       28, 1911.

22   *"to apprehend the outbreak"*: *The Code of the State of Georgia, Adopted
       August 15th, 1910* (Atlanta: Foot & Davies), 1912, article 2, §6480. §141–42;
       Acts of 1912.

22   *"repealing the powers"*: "Hitch in the Law," *Augusta Chronicle*, September
       14, 1912, 2.

22   *safeguard the supply of cheap black labor*: For more on the exploitation and
       reenslavement of African American workers in the twentieth century, see
       Douglas Blackmon, *Slavery By Another Name* (New York: Anchor, 2009).

22   *"a number of the more rabid"*: "Threatened Lynching at Cumming Averted,"
       Atlanta Georgian, September 7, 1912, final edition.

23   *Fifty-two soldiers of the Candler Horse Guards*: "Troops Rushed to Cumming in Autos," *Atlanta Journal*, September 7, 1912.

23   *"When soldiers are called upon"*: "Soldiers Who Shot Augustans Acquitted," *News Herald* (Lawrenceville, GA), September 24, 1912.

24   *"The suppression of anarchy"*: *Railway Age and Railway Review* 55.2 (1913),
       52.

24   *"hollow square"*: *Report of the Adjutant General of the State of Georgia, 1911–1912* (Atlanta: Charles P. Byrd), 1912, appendix 2, 12.

25   *"the soldiers formed a double column"*: "Trouble at Cumming Prevented by
       Militia," *Atlanta Journal*, September 8, 1912.

25 *"Serious Race Riot Averted"*: "State Troops Rescue Negroes at Cumming," *Atlanta Constitution,* September 8, 1912.

26 *"There are many white women in the South"*: Ida B. Wells-Barnett, *Southern Horrors* (pamphlet, 1892), reprinted in Ida B. Wells-Barnett, *On Lynchings* (Amherst, NY: Humanity Books, 2002), 31.

26 *"has not been made public"*: "Threatened Lynching at Cumming Averted," *Atlanta Georgian,* September 7, 1912, final edition.

27 *"The town is perfectly quiet"*: "Cumming Girl, Throat Cut, Found in Woods," *Atlanta Georgian,* September 9, 1912.

27 *Azzie had gone to church that morning*: Note dated December 5, 2000, written by Esta Gay Crow Wetherford, sister of Mae Crow, on the reverse side of Mae's portrait. Courtesy of Debbie Vermaat.

27 *The two girls had stood chatting*: Ruth Mae Jordan Berry, handwritten account, November 1980, courtesy of Henry Dan Berry.

28 *"several of the searchers"*: "Girl, 18, Throat Cut, Found Unconscious in Woods Near Cumming," *Atlanta Georgian,* September 9, 1912, home edition.

28 *"she had evidently been there"*: Ibid.

29 *"seething with bitterness"*: "Cumming Negro Caught by Posse," *Atlanta Georgian,* September 10, 1912, home edition.

29 *"the inflamed state"*: "Two Negroes to Hang October 25th," *Atlanta Georgian,* October 4, 1912.

CHAPTER 3: THE MISSING GIRL

30 *Like most farmers' children*: Shadburn, *Cottonpatch Chronicles,* 247, n. 1.

31 *"one of the most prominent planters"*: "Cumming Ga. Girl, Throat Cut, Found in Woods," *Atlanta Georgian,* September 9, 1912, final edition.

31 *when Mae's grandfather Isaac walked to Dawsonville*: Muster Roll of Company L, 38th Regiment, CSA (ancestry.com); 1860 U. S. Census, Population Schedule. NARA microfilm publication M653, 1,438 rolls. Washington, DC: National Archives and Records. See especially Forsyth County, Georgia, roll M653_121; p. 491; Selected U.S. Federal Census Non-Population Schedules, 1850–1880, Census Year: 1870; Chestatee, Forsyth County, Georgia.

31 *property-owning yeoman farmer*: 1880 U. S. Census, Chestatee, Forsyth, Georgia; roll 147; FHL microfilm 1254147; p. 444B; Enumeration Dis-

trict 078; image 0170. 1900 U. S. Census, Chestatee, Forsyth, Georgia; roll 197; p. 1A; Enumeration District 0033; FHL microfilm 1240197.

31 *"no property to dispose"*: Indigent Pension Application, Isaac Crow, For-syth County, 1904, Confederate Pension Applications, RG 58-1-1, Georgia Archives, Morrow, GA.

32 *"It is said that 36 percent"*: "The Mortgaging of Farm Lands," *Atlanta Con-stitution*, December 9, 1888, 18.

32 *The combined effect of all these forces*: For more on the downward spiral of property owners like the Crows, see William F. Holmes, "The South-ern Farmer's Alliance: The Georgia Experience," *Georgia Historical Quarterly* 72.4 (1988), 628; and C. Van Woodward, *Origins of the New South, 1877–1933* (Baton Rouge: Louisiana State University Press, 1951), 175–204.

33 *sixty-three people*: Alan Candler and Clement Evans, eds., *Georgia: Sketches, Counties, Towns, Events, Institutions & People*, vol. 2 (Atlanta: State Historical Association, 1906), 47.

34 *$100 in personal property*: *Georgia Tax Digests* [1875], Forsyth County, Georgia Archives, Morrow, GA.

34 *a "total estate" of five dollars*: *Georgia Tax Digests* [1890], Forsyth County, Georgia Archives, Morrow, GA.

34 *Buck and Catie had taken in four relatives*: 1900 U. S. Census, Wil-sons, Hall, Georgia; roll 202; p. 13B; Enumeration District 0077; FHL microfilm 1240202.

35 *common-law wife*: Ruth Mae Jordan Berry, handwritten account, Novem-ber 1980.

35 *"I remember passing these children"*: Ibid.

36 *"hired man"*: 1910 U. S. Census, Chattahoochee, Forsyth, Georgia; roll T624_188; p. 7A; Enumeration District 0041; FHL microfilm 1374201.

37 *"I [went] to schoole that morning,"* Ruth Mae Jordan Berry, handwritten account, November 1980.

37 *whites from both sides of the river*: "Cumming, Ga., Girl, Throat Cut, Found in the Woods," *Atlanta Georgian*, September 9, 1912, final edition.

38 "Mr. Shackelford identified it": "Negro Is Rushed in Fast Machine to Ful-ton Tower," *Atlanta Constitution*, September 10, 1912.

38 *"The man ask Ern"*: Ruth Mae Jordan Berry, handwritten account, Novem-ber 1980.

39 *"Mock Lynching"*: "Mock Lynching Extorts Truth," *News Tribune* (Duluth, MN), October 1, 1912, 12.

40 *"barefooted, fiendish-looking"*: "Troops on Guard," *Atlanta Constitution*, October 4, 1912.

40 *"eager to unearth a clue"*: "Cumming Ga. Girl, Throat Cut, Found in Woods," *Atlanta Georgian*, September 9, 1912, final edition.

40 *"Mr. Marvin Bell"*: "Rapist Brought Here," *Gainesville News*, September 11, 1912.

41 *most revered statesman*: In 1998, the Georgia General Assembly passed a law creating the new Bell-Forsyth Judicial Circuit, named for Hiram Parks Bell, and in 2004 the Historical Society of Forsyth christened its new home the Hiram Parks Bell Research Center.

41 *"Colonel Bell"*: *Biographical Directory of the United States Congress, 1774–2005*, House Document 108-222.

41 *"white over black domination"*: Hiram Parks Bell, *Men and Things* (Atlanta: Foote and Davies, 1907), 135–36.

42 *"If the prisoner had not been spirited away"*: "Negro Is Rushed in Fast Machine to Fulton Tower," *Atlanta Constitution*, September 10, 1912.

42 *"On account of the intense feeling"*: "Rapist Brought Here," *Gainesville News*, September 11, 1912.

43 *"wild rumors of lynching"*: Ibid.

43 *"rumor was passing freely"*: "Negro Is Rushed in Fast Machine to Fulton Tower," *Atlanta Constitution*, September 10, 1912.

43 *"the distance from Gainesville to Atlanta"*: Ibid.

44 *"more race trouble is feared"*: Ibid.

CHAPTER 4: AND THE MOB CAME ON

45 *"Those men had raped [Mae] many times"*: Ruth Mae Jordan Berry, hand-written account, November 1980.

46 *"went immediately"*: "Mob Batters Down Jail Door at Cumming," *Atlanta Georgian*, September 10, 1912, final edition.

46 *"The country roads"*: Ibid.

46 *"mob spirit"*: "Cumming Jail Stormed," *Atlanta Journal*, September 10, 1912.

46 *a mob of more than two thousand men*: "Mob Lynches Negro," *Watchman and Southron*, September 14, 1912.

47 *the sheriff "left the jail"*: "Mob Batters Down Jail Door at Cumming," *Atlanta Georgian*, September 10, 1912, final edition.

47 *a future Klansman himself*: Shadburn, *Cottonpatch Chronicles*, Appendix H, 478.

48 *"no excitement among the people"*: *Daily Constitutionalist*, June 11, 1862, 3.

48 *"summarily hung"*: "Outrages in Georgia," *Chicago Tribune*, July 8, 1870, 3.

49 *"a jet black, greasy negro"*: "Wanted to Lynch Him," *Atlanta Constitution*, August 28, 1886, 8.

49 *"Gober gave him the limit allowed by law"*: "Twenty Year Term," *Macon Telegraph*, December 25, 1897.

50 *"locked the doors of the jail"*: "Mob Batters Down Jail Door at Cumming," *Atlanta Georgian*, September 10, 1912, final edition.

50 *"the mob came on"*: Ibid.

50 *"farmers known to all the countryside"*: "Mob Batters Down Door at Cumming," *Atlanta Georgian*, September 10, 1912, final edition, one star.

51 *"but these were soon drowned"*: "Mob Batters Down Door at Cumming," *Atlanta Georgian*, September 10, 1912, final edition, two stars.

51 *"Pistols and rifles cracked"*: Ibid.

51 *"as soon as the guns"*: "Negro Lynched by Mob at Cumming," *Marietta Journal*, September 13, 1912.

53 *"the mountaineers were threatening"*: "Negroes Is Rushed in Fast Machine to Fulton Tower," *Atlanta Constitution*, September 11, 1912.

53 *"hurrying from the town"*: "Mob Batters Down Door at Cumming," *Atlanta Georgian*, September 10, 1912, final edition, two stars.

53 *"it was not touched"*: "Dr. Ansel Strickland Scores Daily Papers," *North Georgian*, November 22, 1912.

53 *"farmers known to all the countryside"*: "Mob Batters Down Door at Cumming," *Atlanta Georgian*, September 10, 1912 final edition, two stars.

54 *"parties unknown"*: Shadburn, *Cottonpatch Chronicles*, 209.

54 *"The provocation of the people"*: "Editorial," *Cherokee Advance*, October 4, 1912.

54 *"no further trouble"*: "Cumming Jail Stormed," *Atlanta Journal*, September 11, 1912.

54 *"remarkable self-restraint"*: "Editorial," *Gainesville Times*, September 11, 1912.

CHAPTER 5: A STRAW IN THE WHIRLWIND

55 *"the clouds of race war"*: "Bloodhounds on Trail of Cumming Firebug," *Atlanta Georgian*, September 11, 1912, extra edition.

55 *"Rumors that the negroes"*: "Terror in Cumming," *Atlanta Georgian*, September 11, 1912.

56 *when Laura Nelson confronted the white men*: "Mother and Son Lynched," *Clinton Mirror* (Clinton, IA), May 27, 1911.

57 *"stomped to death"*: Philip Dray, *At the Hands of Persons Unknown* (New York: Modern Library, 2003), 246.

58 *"Another lynching at Cumming"*: "Sheriff Saves Three Negroes," *Atlanta Constitution*, September 12, 1912.

58 *"The people of Cumming"*: "Quiet Reigns in Cumming," *Atlanta Georgian*, September 12, 1912, home edition.

59 *"lock the doors of the jail"*: "Mob Batters Down Jail Door at Cumming," *Atlanta Georgian*, September 10, 1912, final edition, one star.

60 *"I realized it was too late"*: "Quiet Reigns in Cumming," *Atlanta Georgian*, September 12, 1912, home edition.

61 *"when darkness came"*: "Trouble Over at Cumming," *Atlanta Georgian*, September 12, 1912, extra edition.

61 *"No disorder of any kind"*: "Sheriff Saves Three Negroes," *Atlanta Constitution*, September 12, 1912.

63 *"the police system of the South"*: W. E. B. Du Bois, *The Souls of Black Folk* (Oxford: Oxford University Press, 2007), 178.

63 *"lawlessness" after dark*: "Forsyth People Ask for Troops," *Augusta Chronicle*, October 19, 1912.

63 *"Negroes Flee from Forsyth"*: *Atlanta Constitution*, October 13, 1912; "Enraged White People Are Driving Blacks from County," *New York Times*, December 26, 1912

64 *"a score or more of homes"*: "Forsyth People Ask for Troops," *Augusta Chronicle*, October 19, 1912.

64 *"Take a typical church"*: Du Bois, *Souls of Black Folk*, 92.

65 *Faint traces of other black churches*: Garland Bagley, *History of Forsyth County*, vol. 2, 845; Sheltonville Historical Society, "A Report of the Records/Committee on the History of Sheltonville and the Sheltonville Community," April 20, 1962.

65 *"the negro's victim"*: "Girl Murdered by Negro at Cumming," *Augusta Chronicle*, September 9, 1912.

65 *"beat her into unconsciousness"*: "Second Outrage Shocks Cumming," *Macon Telegraph*, September 10, 1912.

66 *"although every effort was made"*: "Negro Is Rushed in Fast Machine to Fulton Tower," *Atlanta Constitution*, September 10, 1912.

66 *"the death of two white women"*: "Martial Law in Cumming," *Atlanta Georgian*, October 2, 1912.

66 *"she will likely recover"*: *Gainesville News*, September 9, 1912.

66 *"those fiends of hell, negroes"*: "Letter from Mr. and Mrs. L. A. Crow," *North*

Georgian, October 1914, quoted in Shadburn, *Cottonpatch Chronicles,* 235–36.

67   *"all hell broke loose":* Ruth Mae Jordan Berry, handwritten account, November 1980.

67   *"shooting at any black":* Interview with Susan Berry Roberts, granddaughter of Ruth Jordan, January 6, 2016.

67   *twenty-seven acres:* Forsyth County, *Return of Colored Taxpayers, 1912,* New Bridge District, Georgia Archives, Morrow, GA.

67   *"to get news of the goings on":* Interview with Susan Berry Roberts, January 6, 2016.

68   *"Pa told this man":* Ibid. Records confirm that on October 11, 1912, Garrett Cook sold to a white man named George Olivet for $200. Deed Book 2, p. 101, Forsyth County Courthouse.

68   *"until no colored was left":* Ruth Mae Jordan Berry, handwritten account, November 1980.

68   *"the subject was never again brought up":* Interview with Henry Dan Berry, son of Ruth Jordan, January 8, 2016.

68   *"They looked ahead of them":* Isabella Harris, letter to Max Gilstrap, January 24, 1987.

69   *"Certain men":* Quoted in Shadburn, *Cottonpatch Chronicles,* 230.

CHAPTER 6: THE DEVIL'S OWN HORSES

70   *"but very few residents":* "Cumming Blacks to Waive Trial," *Atlanta Constitution,* September 9, 1912.

70   *"the members of the mob":* "Six Blacks Threatened with Lynching," *Atlanta Constitution,* September 8, 1912.

70   *"The real thing that upsets me":* "Leaders in Georgia County Say Outsiders to Blame for Violence," *Wilmington Morning Star,* January 19, 1987, p. 10A

71   *the original KKK all but defunct:* David M. Chalmers, *Hooded Americanism: The History of the Ku Klux Klan* (Durham, NC: Duke University Press, 1981), 18–19.

71   *fellow clansmen to battle:* Sir Walter Scott, *The Lady of the Lake,* "Canto III: The Gathering," lines 1–18.

72   *screened at the White House:* London Melvin Stokes, *D. W. Griffith's "The Birth of a Nation"* (Cambridge: Cambridge University Press, 2007), 111.

72   *"See! My people fill the streets":* D. W. Griffith, *The Birth of a Nation,* 1915, at 2:48:48.

72   *"people of the county"*: Ruth Mae Jordan Berry, handwritten account, November 1980.

72   *"with their horrible faces"*: Isabella Harris, letter to Max Gilstrap, January 24, 1987.

73   *treaty after another was broken*: Francis Paul Prucha, *The Great Father: The United States Government and the American Indian* (Lincoln: University of Nebraska Press, 1995), 235–42.

74   *integrated frontier community*: For more on Cherokee families in Forsyth prior to the Indian Removal Act, see Don Shadburn, *Unhallowed Intrusion: A History of Cherokee Families in Forsyth County, Georgia* (Cumming, GA: Pioneer-Cherokee Heritage Series, 1993).

74   *"there was such excitement"*: "A Georgia Jaunt," *Atlanta Constitution*, July 15, 1894, 2.

74   *"Our [white] neighbors"*: "New Echota," *Cherokee Phoenix*, May 27, 1829, 2

75   *"an industrious Indian"*: "Atrocious Injustice," *Cherokee Phoenix*, May 18, 1833, 3.

76   *Two of the largest Cherokee removal forts*: Shadburn, *Cottonpatch Chronicles*, 5.

76   *"search out"*: David A. Harris, *Stories My Grandmother Told Me* (Unpublished manuscript in the collection of the Historical Society of Forsyth County, 1964), 14.

76   *"the execution of the most brutal order"*: Diary of John G. Burnett, quoted in James C. Cobb, *Georgia Odyssey* (Athens: University of Georgia Press, 1997), 5.

77   *sixteen thousand native people*: Prucha, *The Great Father,* 235–42.

77   *"were worked exclusive of slave labor"*: Shadburn, *Cottonpatch Chronicles*, 192 (emphasis added).

78   *The largest slaveholders*: Selected U.S. Federal Census Non-Population Schedules, 1850–1880, Census Years: 1850 and 1860; District 31, Forsyth, Georgia [database online]. Provo, UT: Ancestry.com, 2010.

78   *15 percent of all households*: Stephen A. West, *From Yeoman to Redneck in the South Carolina Upcountry, 1850–1915* (Charlottesville: University of Virginia, 2008), 204.

78   *Most prominent among them*: 1840, 1850, and 1860 U. S. Census—Slave Schedules [database online]. Provo, UT: Ancestry.com, 2004.

79   *fathered by their white owners*: Interview with Deidre Brown-Stewart and Leroy Brown, October 25, 2014.

79   *"git me mo' slaves"*: "Ex-Slave Interview: Aunt Carrie Mason, Milledgeville, Georgia," in *The American Slave: A Composite Biography*, ed. George Rawick (Greenwood, 1972), vol. 13, 112.

79 *"made an honest living"*: Hiram Parks Bell, *Men and Things* (Atlanta: Foote and Davies, 1907), 51.

80 *Resentful of their rich white neighbors*: Gladys-Marie Fry, *Night Riders in Black Folk History* (Knoxville: University of Tennessee Press, 1975), 82–109.

80 *"the slave's arms were bound"*: Rawick, *The American Slave*, 328.

81 *Eliza made repeated attempts to escape*: Interview with Anthony Neal, April 2, 2014.

CHAPTER 7: THE MAJESTY OF THE LAW

83 *The U.S. Supreme Court: Norris v. Alabama*, 294 U.S. 587 (1935).

84 *"a state of insurrection"*: "Martial Law Will Be Declared in Forsyth," *Atlanta Constitution*, September 28, 1912.

84 *"each one offered an excuse"*: "Lawyers Appointed to Defend Negroes," *Atlanta Georgian*, October 1, 1912, 2.

84 *a partner in the Atlanta Northeastern*: *Railway Review*, 48 (1908), 733.

84 *the defense team*: "Cumming Is Quiet on Eve of Trial," *Atlanta Constitution*, October 3, 1912.

86 *"the barefooted, fiendish-looking type"*: "Troops on Guard," *Atlanta Constitution*, October 4, 1912.

87 *"a personal guard"*: "Cumming Is Quiet on Eve of Trial," *Atlanta Constitution*, October 3, 1912.

87 *stop for lunch*: A. M. Light later submitted a reimbursement request for "wagon transportation furnished [to] troops en-route to Cumming"; Alice Mashburn received $28.75 for "meals furnished troops on duty"; and the proprietors of the Merchant's Hotel at Buford requested compensation for meals totaling $65.50. Correspondence Files of the Adjutant General's Office, October 1912, Georgia Archives, Morrow, GA.

87 *a camp perimeter*: "Cumming Is Quiet on Eve of Trial," *Atlanta Constitution*, October 3, 1912.

87 *"the mountaineers of north Georgia"*: "Troops Off to Cumming with Six Negroes," *Atlanta Georgian*, October 2, 1912, extra edition.

88 *"came to the camp"*: "Cumming Is Quiet on Eve of Trial," *Atlanta Constitution*, October 3, 1912.

89 *"a fourteen-karat son of a bitch"*: Steve Oney, *And the Dead Shall Rise* (New York: Vintage, 2004), 522.

89 *"the will of the people"*: "Letter to the Editor" by Ansel Strickland, *North Georgian*, November 22, 1912.

89   *"Little time will be required"*: "Trials at Cumming," *Gainesville Times*, October 2, 1912.

91   *"turned State's evidence"*: Royal Freeman Nash, "The Cherokee Fires," *The Crisis* 11.1 (1915), 266.

91   *"crowded as never before"*: "Bayonets Guard Blacks as Trial at Cumming Begins," *Atlanta Journal*, October 3, 1912.

91   *"mountaineers [who had] been gathering weapons"*: "Martial Law in Cumming as Blacks Are Tried," *Atlanta Georgian*, October 2, 1912, extra edition.

91   *"ordered to discard"*: "Martial Law in Cumming as Blacks Are Tried," *Atlanta Georgian*, October 2, 1912.

92   *"any disorder"*: "Troops Uphold Law," *Atlanta Constitution*, October 2, 1912.

92   *"their minds were not clearly unbiased"*: "Troops Guard Negroes' Trial at Cumming," *Atlanta Georgian*, October 3, 1912, home edition, 5.

92   *"a watchman"*: Ibid.

92   *E. S. Garrett and William Hammond*: Shadburn, *Cottonpatch Chronicles*, 478–79.

92   *"expedite the trial"*: "Troops Guard Negroes' Trial at Cumming," *Atlanta Georgian*, October 3, 1912, home edition, 5.

93   *"was compelled to repeat the pathetic story"*: "Troops on Guard as Two Rapists Are Convicted," *Atlanta Constitution*, October 4, 1912.

94   *"they borrowed a lantern"*: "Troops Guard Negroes' Trial at Cumming," *Atlanta Georgian*, October 3, 1912, home edition, 5.

96   *"one of the most revolting rape cases"*: "Troops on Guard as Two Rapists Are Convicted," *Atlanta Constitution*, October 4, 1912.

CHAPTER 8: FASTENING THE NOOSE

97   *"should it be en-route"*: "Troops Guard Negroes' Trial at Cumming," *Atlanta Georgian*, October 3, 1912, home edition, 5.

98   *"enough determined men"*: Ibid.

98   *"at a safe distance"*: "Troops on Guard," *Atlanta Constitution*, October 4, 1912.

98   *"Major Catron has 24 men"*: "Troops Guard Negroes' Trial at Cumming," *Atlanta Georgian*, October 3, 1912, home edition, 5.

98   *"a few prominent citizens"*: Ibid.

99   *$1.2 million*: "Contracts to Let," *Steam Shovel and Dredge*, 12 (1908), 764.

100 *"If any one of the six"*: "Bayonets Guard Blacks as Trial at Cumming Begin," *Atlanta Journal*, October 3, 1912.

100 *The subpoena list*: Shadburn, *Cottonpatch Chronicles*, Appendix K, 489.

100 *"Jane Daniel was a complete surprise"*: "Troops on Guard as Rapists Are Convicted," *Atlanta Constitution*, October 4, 1912.

101 *"she was left for dead"*: Ibid.

102 *"the negroes satisfied"*: Ibid.

102 *"from Cumming to hell"*: "Letter to the Editor" by Ansel Strickland, *North Georgian*, November 22, 1912.

103 *"We the jury"*: Shadburn, *Cottonpatch Chronicles*, 217.

103 *"the choice tenors of the regiment"*: "Troops on Guard," *Atlanta Constitution*, October 4, 1912.

104 *"a shade more human-looking"*: Ibid.

104 *"We the jury"*: Don Shadburn, *Cottonpatch Chronicles*, 217.

105 *"All things changed at midnight"*: "Troops on Guard," *Atlanta Constitution*, October 4, 1914.

106 *"It speaks well for the citizens"*: "Governor Is Pleased with Militia," *Atlanta Constitution*, October 6, 1912.

106 *"I want to thank both officers and men"*: "Troops on Guard," *Atlanta Constitution*, October 4, 1914.

106 *"worn and bedraggled"*: "Troops Return from Forsyth," *Atlanta Constitution*, October 5, 1912.

106 *"make a run for it"*: Ibid.

107 *"the absence of witnesses"*: "Two Negroes to Hang Oct. 25," *Atlanta Georgian*, October 4, 1912.

CHAPTER 9: WE CONDEMN THIS CONDUCT

108 "The anti-negro movement": "Georgia in Terror of Night Riders," *New York Times*, December 25, 1912.

109 *"Every so often"*: "Tears Flowed Years After Forced Exodus," *Gainesville Times*, January 22, 1987.

110 *"turn back to look for them"*: Ibid.

111 *"Recently warnings have been sent"*: "Georgia in Terror of Night Riders," *New York Times*, December 25, 1912.

111 *"Three wagon loads"*: "Cumming Negroes to Hang Oct. 25th," *Cherokee Advance*, October 11, 1912.

111 *"anonymous letters"*: "Gainesville Invaded by Negroes," *Savannah Tribune*, October 19, 1912.

112 *"My Dear Gov"*: A. J. Julian to Joseph Mackey Brown, February 22, 1913. Joseph Mackey Brown Papers, MSS41, box 4, folder 3, Atlanta History Center.

113 *"deplore[d] the action"*: Joseph Mackey Brown to A. J. Julian, February 25, 1913. Joseph Mackey Brown Papers, MSS41, box 4, folder 3, Atlanta History Center.

114 *"They drove out a cook"*: Royal Freeman Nash, "The Cherokee Fires," *The Crisis* 11.1 (1915), 268.

115 *"effort on the part of some unknown persons"*: "Resolution Adopted by Mass Meeting of the Citizens of the Town of Cumming at Court House of Forsyth County, Wednesday, October 16, 1912." Correspondence of Governor Joseph Mackey Brown, Georgia Archives, Morrow, GA.

115 *"Quite a number of black churches"*: "To His Excellency, Joseph M. Brown, Governor," letter from Charles L. Harris, October 17, 1912. Correspondence of Governor Joseph Mackey Brown, Georgia Archives, Morrow, GA.

115 *"We condemn this conduct"*: "Resolution Adopted by Mass Meeting of the Citizens of the Town of Cumming at Court House of Forsyth County, Wednesday, October 16, 1912." Correspondence of Governor Joseph Mackey Brown, Georgia Archives, Morrow, GA.

116 *"We pledge ourselves"*: Ibid..

116 *"investigate these depredations"*: "Ask Aid to End Crime in Forsyth," *Atlanta Constitution*, October 18, 1912.

116 *"I am in receipt of your letter"*: "Mssrs. C. L. Harris & J. F. Echols," October 21, 1912, Correspondence of Governor Joseph Mackey Brown, Georgia Archives, Morrow, GA.

117 one of the earliest Prohibition laws: David M. Fahey, "Temperance Movement," *New Georgia Encyclopedia;* http://www.georgiaencyclopedia.org /articles/history-archaeology/temperance-movement, accessed October 1, 2015.

117 *Judge Newman's Northern District court*: Minute Book of the United States Court, Northern District, Judge William T. Newman, 1912–1913. National Archives, Morrow, GA.

119 *"Old Man Roper"*: Royal Freeman Nash, "The Cherokee Fires," *The Crisis* 11.1 (1915), 266.

119 *"A gentleman of Forsyth County"*: *Dahlonega Nugget*, October 18, 1912.

CHAPTER 10: CRUSH THE THING IN ITS INFANCY

120 *"the influx of negoes"*: "Trouble Brewing in Hill Country," *Atlanta Constitution*, October 14, 1912.

120 *"a crowd variously estimated"*: "Drove Negroes Off Gaines Building," *Gainesville Times*, October 16, 1912.

121 *"a mob of whites appeared"*: "Trouble Brewing in Hill Country," *Atlanta Constitution*, October 14, 1912.

121 *"Not only has the entire section"*: Ibid.

122 *"Cursing the negro"*: Ibid.

123 *"The men alleged"*: "Nightriders Arrested That Shot Up House Near Flowery Branch," *Gainesville News*, October 16, 1912.

123 *"Bud Martin"*: Ibid.

124 *"We don't need any military"*: "Arrest Is Made in Race Trouble," *Atlanta Constitution*, January 31, 1921, 9.

124 *"Horace Smith"*: "Five Men Arrested for Running Negroes Off Gaines Building Last Thursday," *Gainesville Times*, October 16, 1912.

124 *"If we could have gotten"*: Royal Freeman Nash, "The Cherokee Fires," *Crisis* 11.1 (1915), 267.

125 *"When the crackers in Hall County"*: Ibid., 268.

CHAPTER 11: THE SCAFFOLD

126 *"Now what is the law?"*: "Letter to the Editor" by Ansel Strickland, *North Georgian*, November 22, 1912.

126 *"within one mile"*: Minute Book of the Forsyth County Superior Court, October 4, 1912. Forsyth County Courthouse.

126 a *"temptation to mob violence"*: "Reform in Legal Hangings," *Atlanta Constitution*, October 26, 1912.

127 *When Morris learned*: "Thousands Cheer at Hanging," *Keowee Courier*, October 30, 1912.

129 *"The weather was ideal"*: *Report of the Adjutant General of the State of Georgia, 1911–1912* (Atlanta: Charles P. Byrd, 1912), Appendix 2, 22.

129 *"a heap of charred embers"*: "Thousands Cheer at Hanging," *Keowee Courier*, October 30, 1912.

130 *the sound of a hammer*: Interview with Don Shadburn, February 24, 2014.

131 *"the side of the mob"*: *Report of the Adjutant General*, Appendix 2, 20.

131 *"The ground selected"*: Ibid., Appendix 2, 23.

131 *"a few relatives of the Sheriff"*: Ibid., Appendix 2, 21.

132 *"He was boisterous"*: Ibid., Appendix 2, 20–22.

132 *"took up their position"*: "Knox and Daniel Hung Last Friday," *Forsyth County News*, October 31, 1912.

132 *"Most of these people"*: *Report of the Adjutant General,* Appendix 2, 21.

133 *"shortly before his death"*: "Knox and Daniel Hung Last Friday," *Forsyth County News,* October 31, 1912.

133 *"neither negro had a word to say"*: "Fence Was Burned to See a Hanging," *Augusta Chronicle,* October 26, 1912.

133 *a story passed down in the Crow family*: Interview with Debbie Vermaat, January 20, 2015.

135 *"The heavy rope"*: "Murderer Snell Dies on Gallows," *Atlanta Constitution,* June 30, 1900.

136 *"table of drops"*: The English system of calculating drops ("divide the weight of the patient in pounds into 2240, and the quotient will give the length of the long drop in feet") was widely adopted in the United States. See Hugo Adam Bedau, ed., *The Death Penalty in America* (New York: Oxford University Press, 1982).

136 *"the noose about their necks"*: "Knox and Daniel Hung Last Friday," *Forsyth County News,* October 31, 1912.

137 *"cut the rope trigger with a hatchet"*: Ibid.

138 *"The trap was sprung"*: *Report of the Adjutant General,* Appendix 2, 23.

138 *eleven minutes*: For more on the procedures of early-twentieth-century hangings, see http://capitalpunishment.uk.org/hangings (accessed December 1, 2015).

138 *"ringside seats"*: Ruth Mae Jordan Berry, handwritten account, November 1980.

139 *piece of old hemp rope*: Interview with Don Shadburn, February 24, 2014.

139 *"they would be burned"*: *Report of the Adjutant General,* Appendix 2, 20–21.

139 *"called Dr. Selman"*: Ibid., Appendix 2, 23.

CHAPTER 12: WHEN THEY WERE SLAVES

142 *a white merchant named George Kellogg*: Interview with Anthony Neal, April 2, 2014.

142 *By 1870*: Selected U.S. Federal Census Non-Population Schedules, 1850–1880, Census Year: 1870; District 31, Forsyth, Georgia [database online]. Provo, UT: Ancestry.com, 2010.

143 *"Qualified Voters"*: Georgia, Office of the Governor. *Returns of Qualified Voters Under the Reconstruction Act, 1867.* Georgia Archives, Morrow, GA.

143 *ratified the Fourteenth Amendment*: Christopher C. Meyers, ed., *The Empire State of the South: Georgia History in Documents and Essays* (Macon, GA: Mercer University Press, 2008), 172.

144 *the day of Joseph and Eliza's wedding*: Records of Marriages, Book D, 1868–1877, 154. Forsyth County Courthouse.

144 *the bill Lincoln signed into law*: H.R. Exec. Doc. 11, 39th Congress, 1st Session, 1865, 45 (Serial 1255); reprint Circular No. 5, May 30, 1865.

145 *"power delegated to these resident white appointees"*: H.R. Exec. Doc. 1, 40th Cong., 2nd sess., 1867, 673–74 (Serial 1324).

145 *Major William J. Bryan*: Order of Col. Caleb Sibley; W. J. Bryan, letter to O. O. Howard, Washington, DC. *Records of the Field Offices for the State of Georgia, Bureau of Refugees, Freedmen, and Abandoned Lands, 1865–1872*, Cumming Office section, National Archives at Washington, DC, M1903, roll 45.

147 *"All this in Forsyth County"*: W. J. Bryan, report to Col. Caleb Sibley, May 1968. *Records of the Field Offices for the State of Georgia, Bureau of Refugees, Freedmen, and Abandoned Lands, 1865–1872*, Marietta Office section, National Archives at Washington, DC, M1903, roll 58.

147 *John A. Armstrong*: Records of Binding Cases, Probate Court Records of the Forsyth County Courthouse, box 40, "Colored."

147 *"ideas inherited from slavery"*: Eric Foner, *A Short History of Reconstruction* (New York: Harper, 2014), 59.

148 *"Thomas . . . binds himself"*: "Binding Agreement: H. W. Strickland and Thomas Strickland, Free Boy of Color," March 1866, Records of Binding Cases, Probate Court Records of the Forsyth County Courthouse, box 40, "Colored."

148 *"now holds without consent"*: Records of the Field Offices for the State of Georgia, Bureau of Refugees, Freedmen, and Abandoned Lands, 1865–1872, Cumming Office section, National Archives at Washington, DC, M1903, roll 45.

148 *Thomas Riley*: Quoted in Jonathan Dean Sarris, *A Separate Civil War* (Charlottesville: University of Virginia Press, 2012), 148.

148 *"I am fully satisfied"*: Records of the Field Offices for the State of Georgia, Bureau of Refugees, Freedmen, and Abandoned Lands, 1865–1872, Cumming Office section, National Archives at Washington, DC, M1903, roll 45, 112.

149 *"affairs are in a worse condition"*: Letter from W. J. Bryan to Major Mosebach, October 31, 1868. Marietta Office section, National Archives at Washington, DC, M1903, roll 58.

149 *"Until the freedmen are protected"*: Letter from W. J. Bryan to Major Mosebach, August 27, 1868. Marietta Office section, National Archives at Washington, DC, M1903, roll 58.

150 *ceased all operations*: For authoritative studies of the Freedmen's Bureau

in Georgia, see Paul A. Cimbala, *Under the Guardianship of the Nation: The Freedmen's Bureau and the Reconstruction of Georgia, 1865–1870* (Athens: University of Georgia Press, 1997), and Sara Rappaport, "The Freedmen's Bureau as a Legal Agent for Black Men and Women in Georgia," *Georgia Historical Quarterly* 73.1 (1989), 26–53.

150 *"terrorized [Forsyth] just after the War"*: George Harris Bell recollections, originally in the *Gainesville News*, September 26, 1906. Excerpt reprinted in "Days of Long Ago," *Gainesville Times*, May 16, 1976.

150 *"a number of citizens"*: Ibid.

151 *"Atlanta Compromise" speech*: Booker T. Washington, Speech before the Cotton States and International Exposition in Atlanta, September 18, 1895. From a version of the speech recorded in 1906, Columbia Gramophone Company, G. Robert Vincent Voice Library, Michigan State University, DB 191.

151 *"the Negro . . . should make himself"*: Booker T. Washington, *Up from Slavery* (New York: Doubleday, 1901), 202.

152 *Joseph Kellogg had inherited*: Selected U.S. Federal Census Non-Population Schedules, 1850–1880, Census Years: 1880; District 879, Forsyth, Georgia [database online]. Provo, UT: Ancestry.com, 2010.

152 *an additional fifty acres*: *Georgia, Property Tax Digests, 1793–1892*, Militia District 879, Post Office: Cumming, Year: 1890 [database online]. Provo, UT: Ancestry.com, 2011.

152 *"the Kelloggs were themselves landlords"*: 1900 U. S. Census, Cumming, Forsyth, Georgia; roll 197; p. 2B; Enumeration District 0036; FHL microfilm 1240197.

152 *in April of 1910*: 1910 U. S. Census, Cumming, Forsyth, Georgia; roll T624_188; p. 6A; Enumeration District 0039; FHL microfilm 1374201.

CHAPTER 13: DRIVEN TO THE COOK STOVES

153 *"After going all the way"*: "Obear Censures Public Hanging," *Atlanta Constitution*, October 16, 1912.

154 *"An official may compromise"*: "A Disgrace to Georgia," editorial, *Atlanta Constitution*, November 7, 1912.

154 *"a wealthy farmer of Forsyth county"*: "Assassins Wound Forsyth Farmer," *Atlanta Constitution*, October 30, 1912, dateline October 29, 1912.

155 *"Deputy Sheriff Lummus"*: Ibid.

156 *People of color*: Ann Short Chirhart, "'Gardens of Education': Beulah Rucker and African-American Culture in the Twentieth-Century Georgia Upcountry," *Georgia Historical Quarterly*, Winter 1998, 834.

156 *"Gainesville is being invaded"*: "Trouble Brewing in Hill Country," *Atlanta Constitution* October 14, 1912.

156 *electric streetlamps*: William L. Norton, Jr., *Historic Gainesville and Hall County: An Illustrated History* (San Antonio, TX: Historic Publishing Network, 2001), 29–30.

157 *State Industrial and High School*: For more on Byrd Oliver and Beulah Rucker Oliver, see Beulah Rucker Oliver, *The Rugged Pathway* (n.p.: 1953), and Ann Short Chirhart, "'Gardens of Education': Beulah Rucker and African-American Culture in the Twentieth-Century Georgia Upcountry," *Georgia Historical Quarterly*, Winter 1998.

158 *the two were married*: Marriage license of William Butler and Jane Daniel, February 5, 1914, Hall County, in *Georgia, Marriage Records from Select Counties, 1828–1978* (ancestry.com); 1920 U. S. Census, Gainesville Ward 2, Hall, Georgia; roll T625_261; p. 5B.

158 *George Collins*: Kathleen Thompson, "Racial Violence in North Georgia, 1900–1930," *Pickens County Progress*, October 13, 2011.

158 *the two hundred acres*: Forsyth County Return for Colored Tax Payers, 1912, Cumming District, Georgia Archives, Morrow, GA. For more on Joseph Kellogg's land transactions, see Elliot Jaspin, *Buried in the Bitter Waters* (New York: Basic Books, 2007), 135.

160 *"exchange for negro property"*: "A Bargain" (classified advertisement), *Atlanta Constitution*, March 22, 1914, A10.

160 *"If something is not done"*: "Georgia Negroes in Terror," *Keowee Courier*, December 25, 1912.

161 *"I am reliably informed"*: *Journal of the Senate of the State of Georgia*, Regular Session, June 15, 1913, 21.

161 *"show an excess of negro"*: "White Man Predominates in Culture of Cotton," *Atlanta Constitution*, December 8, 1914.

162 *"The extraordinary Heats here"*: Thomas Stephens, *The Hard Case of the Distressed People* (London: 1742), quoted in Jeffrey Robert Young, ed., *Pro Slavery and Sectional Thought in the Early South, 1740–1829* (Columbia: University of South Carolina Press, 2006), 63.

163 *"the black labor of the past"*: "White Man Predominates in Culture of Cotton," *Atlanta Constitution*, December 8, 1914.

164 *"a day of pleasure to the ladies"*: "Dr. A. Strickland on the Wash Tub," undated letter to the editor, *North Georgian,* reproduced in Garland C. Bagley, *History of Forsyth County,* vol. 2 (Milledgeville, GA: Boyd), 1990, 622.

164 *twenty-one million horses*: Emily R. Kilby, "The Demographics of the U.S. Equine Population," in *The State of the Animals IV* (Washington, DC: Humane Society Press, 2007), 176.

165 *the Model T of the agricultural world*: William White, "Economic History of Tractors in the United States," Economic History Association, March 26, 2008; https://eh.net/encyclopedia/economic-history-of-tractors-in-the-united-states, accessed October 1, 2015.

166 *"altogether inadvisable"*: "At Princeton, Woodrow Wilson, a Heralded Alum, Is Recast as an Intolerant One," *New York Times,* November 22, 2015.

166 *"absolute fair dealing"*: Quoted in Cleveland M. Green, "Prejudices and Empty Promises: Woodrow Wilson's Betrayal of the Negro, 1910–1919," *The Crisis* 87.9 (November 1980), 380.

167 *"Your inauguration"*: "An Open Letter to Woodrow Wilson," *The Crisis* 5.5 (March 1913), 236–37.

168 *"Your manner offends me"*: "Mr. Trotter and Mr. Wilson," *The Crisis* 9.3 (January 1915), 119–20.

168 *Department of the Treasury and the U.S. Postal Service*: Ibid.

168 *"the votes of ignorant negroes"*: Woodrow Wilson, *A History of the American People,* vol. 9 (Harper & Brothers, 1918), 58.

168 *"A Negro's place is in the cornfield"*: Quoted in Cleveland M. Green, "Prejudices and Empty Promises: Woodrow Wilson's Betrayal of the Negro, 1910–1919," *The Crisis* 87.9 (November 1980), 383.

169 *Ophelia Blake*: Don Shadburn, *Pioneer History of Forsyth County, Georgia* (Milledgeville, GA: Boyd), 1981, 287; 1910 U. S. Census, Cumming, Forsyth, Georgia; roll T624_188; p. 1A; Enumeration District 0039; FHL microfilm 1374201.

170 *"aroused practically the entire town"*: "Dynamite Exploded Under Negro Houses in Cumming," *Atlanta Constitution,* March 20, 1913.

170 *"Dr. John"*: "Dr. John H. Hockenhull," *Forsyth County News,* November 23, 1922.

171 *Will Phillips*: "Negro Who Is Charged with Robbing Stores in Cumming Is Arrested," *Atlanta Constitution,* April 9, 1914.

172 *forty years on the Georgia chain gang*: *Georgia's Central Register of Convicts,* 1817–1976, Series 21/3/27. Georgia State Archives, Morrow, Georgia.

172 *"Sheriff W. W. Reid"*: "Governor Harris Asks Return of Negro Now in Florida," *Atlanta Constitution*, October 19, 1915, 7.

CHAPTER 14: EXILE, 1915–1920

173 *"Every family was run out"*: "A County Without a Negro in It," *Daily Times-Enterprise* (Thomasville, GA), October 7, 1915, 4.

174 *"rushed them out of the county"*: "County Bars Colored Men," *Appeal* (St. Paul, MN), September 14, 1915.

174 *The list of participants*: "Stoddard to Lead Tourists," *Atlanta Constitution*, September 3, 1915.

176 *"The good farmers of Hall county"*: "Ms. Martin Insists Trouble Was Serious," *Macon Telegraph*, October 9, 1915.

176 *"Mr. McCullough and his guests"*: "State Tourists Come To-night to Atlanta," *Atlanta Georgian*, October 5, 1915.

177 *"rocks hurled at the cars"*: "Georgia Tourists Are Greeted with 'Irish Confetti,'" *Atlanta Constitution*, October 5, 1915.

177 *"most cordial"*: Ibid.

178 *"was quite pale"*: "Ms. Martin Insists Trouble Was Serious," *Macon Telegraph*, October 9, 1915.

178 *"A sense of duty"*: "Seeing Georgia Tourists Stoned," *Macon Telegraph*, October 5, 1915.

179 *"bury its fangs in the body politic"*: Ibid.

179 *"the wonders of this section"*: "Tourists Find Motoring in Georgia Like a Trip in Enchanted Land," *Atlanta Constitution*, October 4, 1915.

180 *"Georgia Crackers"*: "Georgia Crackers Rock Negro Chauffeurs," *New York Age*, October 14, 1915; "Negro Chauffeurs Are Stoned by Georgia Mob," *Huntingdon Press* (IN), October 5, 1915.

180 *"an interurban line"*: *Railway Age Gazette*, 60 (1916), 377.

180 *In 1919, Harris decided to take the plunge*: "Among Cordele Leaders Who Plan Section's Growth," *Macon Telegraph*, September 23, 1920.

181 *He would never again live in Forsyth County*: *Forsyth County, Georgia Heritage 1832–2011* (Waynesville, NC: County Heritage, Inc., 2011), 222. According to his granddaughter, one day Lummus went to Atlanta "and never came home . . . he was never seen again" in Forsyth.

181 *The room Lummus rented*: 1920 U. S. Census, Atlanta Ward 6, Fulton, Georgia; roll T625_252; p. 3B; Enumeration District 114; image 1101.

CHAPTER 15: ERASURE, 1920-1970

183 *"and each sale tells a tale"*: Elliot Jaspin, *Buried in the Bitter Waters* (New York: Basic Books, 2007), 136.

184 *"there is no record"*: Ibid.

184 *"continuously, openly, and notoriously"*: "Adverse Possession," Legal Information Institute, Cornell Law School, https://www.law.cornell.edu/wex, accessed August 6, 2015.

184 *"must not have orginated in fraud"*: *Park's Annotated Code of the State of Georgia, 1914, Embracing the Code of 1910* (Atlanta: Harrison Company, 1915), §4164 "Adverse Possession," 2341.

185 *"There was land for the taking"*: Jaspin, *Buried*, 136.

185 *"run out all the negroes"*: "Let's Stop Advertising," *Macon Telegraph*, January 28, 1921.

185 *"a little church and school"*: "Serious Race Trouble in North Georgia," *Norfolk Journal and Guide*, January 22, 1921.

186 *"a far-famed county"*: "Forsyth Makes Advances," *Atlanta Constitution*, October 28, 1923.

186 *records confirm*: 1920 U. S. Census, Big Creek, Forsyth, Georgia; Roll: T625_257; Page: 16B; Enumeration District: 49; Image: 592.

186 *James had been born a slave*: 1880 U. S. Census; Big Creek, Forsyth, Georgia; Roll: 147; FHL 1254147; Page: 408D; Enumeration District: 076; Image: 0098.

186 *signed his oath of allegiance*: Georgia, Office of the Governor. Returns of qualified voters under the Reconstruction Act, 1867. Georgia Archives, Morrow, GA.

186 *But James Strickland stayed in Forsyth*: 1900 U. S. Census; Big Creek, Forsyth, Georgia; Roll: 197; Page: 11A; Enumeration District: 0030; FHL microfilm: 1240197.

186 *By 1910*: 1910 U. S. Census; Big Creek, Forsyth, Georgia; Roll: T624_188; Page: 16B; Enumeration District: 0036; FHL microfilm: 1374201. James Strickland's 80 acre farm was on land lots 2-1-990 and 2-1-1000. Forsyth County Returns for Colored Taxpayers, 1912, Georgia Archives, Morrow, GA. According to Forsyth genealogist Donna Parrish the Will Strickland property was sold by his heirs on February 5th, 1943. http://www.donnaparrish.com/forsyth/1912/strickland_james.html, accessed 8/14/2011.

187   *Ed Moon filled out a WWI draft card*: World War I Draft Registration Cards, 1917–1918 [database online]. Provo, UT, USA: Ancestry.com, 2005. Registration State: Georgia; Registration County: Jackson; Roll: 1557077.

188   *sixteen in the census of 1930*: 1930 U. S. Census, Big Creek, Forsyth, Georgia; Roll: 357; Enumeration District: 0001; FHL microfilm: 2340092.

188   *Great Migration*: For more on the history of northern migration, see Isabel Wilkerson's *The Warmth of Other Suns: The Epic Story of America's Great Migration* (New York: Vintage, 2011).

188   *By the early 1930s*: Interview with Mattie Daniel, February 23, 2014; Directory of the City of Detroit, 1930, *U.S. City Directories, 1821–1989*, Ancestry .com, accessed November 13, 2015; 1940 U. S. Census, Detroit, Wayne, Michigan; roll T627_1839; p. 9B; Enumeration District 84-25.

189   *"the sound of a hammer"*: Kenneth Stahl, "The Great Rebellion: A Socioeconomic Analysis of the 1967 Detroit Riot," http://www.detroits -greatrebellion.com/The-Road-to-67-.html, accessed October 1, 2015.

189   *"like sleeping on a volcano"*: Laura Arnold, as quoted in Glenda Elizabeth Gilmore, *Gender and Jim Crow: Women and the Politics of White Supremacy in North Carolina, 1896–1920* (Chapel Hill: University of North Carolina Press, 1996), 132.

190   *"ever talked too much about"*: Interview with Mattie Daniel, February 23, 2014.

190   *The African American population of the city*: Campbell Gibson, *Population of the 100 Largest Cities and Other Urban Places in the United States: 1790 to 1990* (Washington: U.S. Bureau of the Census, Population Division, Working Paper 27, 1998).

191   *168 black families*: "The 1943 Detroit Race Riots," *Detroit News* online, February 10, 1999, http://blogs.detroitnews.com/history/1999/02/10/the -1943-detroit-race-riots/; accessed February 27, 2015.

192   *"I'd rather see Hitler"*: Ibid.

192   *"the Belle Isle Bridge"*: Ibid.

192   *thirty-four confirmed killings*: Ibid.

193   *"We hope for better things"*: Ibid.

193   *"Klan-ridden regime"*: Gilbert King, *Devil in the Grove* (Harper, 2013), 262.

193   *"Before God, friend"*: Rome News-Tribune (GA), August 2, 1942.

193   *"I was told stories"*: Interview with Helen Matthews Lewis by Jessie Wilkerson, May 28 2010 (U-0490). Southern Oral History Program Collection 4007, Southern Historical Collection, Wilson Library, University of North Carolina at Chapel Hill.

194 *"My father came home"*: Ibid.

194 *"When I was in school"*: Ibid.

195 *"used them for flagstones"*: Ibid.

196 *"we don't allow niggers"*: "Cumming Deplores Racial Harassment," *Atlanta Constitution*, May 8, 1968, 3.

196 *"Wait until the night comes!"*: Stephen Tuck, *Beyond Atlanta: The Struggle for Racial Equality in Georgia* (Athens: University of Georgia, 2003), 242.

196 *"sorry to read of it"*: "Cumming Deplores Racial Harassment," *Atlanta Constitution*, May 8, 1968, 3.

197 *"in traveling over the county"*: Garland C. Bagley, *History of Forsyth County*, vol. 2 (Milledgeville, GA: Boyd Publishing, 1990), 614.

197 *"people of the county"*: Ruth Mae Jordan Berry, handwritten account, November 1980.

197 *"As they grew older"*: Bagley, *History*, 614.

CHAPTER 16: THE ATTEMPTED MURDER OF MIGUEL MARCELLI

198 *since they were children*: Interview with Deidre Brown-Stewart, October 25, 2014.

200 *Sophisticated Data Research*: "Gunshot Victim Returns for March," *Gainesville Times*, January 23, 1987, 10A.

201 *"spent much of Saturday drinking"*: "Trial Hears 2nd Witness in Forsyth," *Gainesville Times*, November 18, 1980, 12A.

202 *"We talked about shooting"*: "Forsyth Jury Convicts Crowe in Shooting Here," *Forsyth County News*, November 25, 1980.

202 *"looking at me with a mean face"*: "Forsyth Shooting Trial in Third Day," *Gainesville Times*, November 19, 1980, 14A.

203 *"I felt a great weakness"*: Ibid.

203 *"a group of men"*: "Gunshot Victim Returns for March," *Gainesville Times*, January 23, 1987, 10A.

203 *"an extremely distraught black woman"*: "Trial Hears 2nd Witness in Forsyth," *Gainesville Times*, November 18, 1980, 12A.

203 *"Would you help me?"*: Ibid.

203 *"There's nothing more I can do here"*: "Forsyth Shooting Trial in Third Day," *Gainesville Times*, November 19, 1980, 14A.

204 *"I think I killed the black son of a bitch"*: Ibid.

204 *"I'm not telling"*: Ibid.

204 *"I'll get burned out"*: Ibid.

205 *"I was scared"*: "Forsyth Jury Finds Man Guilty of Assaulting Black," *Gainesville Times,* November 20, 1980.

205 *"a .38 caliber bullet"*: "Trial Hears 2nd Witness in Forsyth," *Gainesville Times,* November 18, 1980, 12A.

206 *"Twelve men and women"*: "A Myth Exploded in Forsyth County," *Gaines-ville Times,* November 21, 1980, 4A.

206 *"it is simply a happenstance"*: "Lily-White Forsyth Looks Ahead—Racial Change Is Blowing in the Wind," *Atlanta Journal,* November 8, 1977.

CHAPTER 17: THE BROTHERHOOD MARCH, 1987

207 *A twenty-three-year-old African American man*: "A Racial Attack That, Years Later, Is Still Being Felt," *New York Times,* December 18, 2011.

207 *"Overcoming fear"*: "March," *Gainesville Times,* January 15, 1987, 10A.

208 *"only one minister"*: "Proposed 'Walk for Brotherhood' Is Cancelled," *Forsyth County News,* January 11, 1987.

209 *"Chuck was talking about"*: "Couple Hopes to Revive March," *Forsyth County News,* January 14, 1987.

209 *"I got a thirty-aught-six bullet"*: "Racist Threats Fail to Break Efforts for a Freedom March," *New York Times,* January 11, 1987.

209 *"the threats . . . were much more violent"*: "Proposed 'Walk for Brotherhood' Is Cancelled," *Forsyth County News,* January 11, 1987.

210 *"After Saturday . . . you're dead"*: "Racist Threats Fail to Break Efforts for a Freedom March," *New York Times,* January 11, 1987.

210 *"five Mexican construction workers"*: "Racists Rout Brotherhood March," *Bangor News,* January 19, 1987, 11.

210 *"By the time this newspaper is printed"*: "Let's Get on to Better Things," *Forsyth County News,* January 18, 1987.

211 *"We do not condone needless efforts"*: "The Right to Demonstrate," *Gaines-ville Times,* January 16, 1987.

212 *"We are protesting against racemixers"*: Plaintiff's Exhibit 61, *Hosea Williams v. Southern White Nights of the Ku Klux Klan,* District Court of the Northern Division of Georgia, March 24, 1987.

212 *more than twenty-five hundred whites gathered*: "Mob of 2,500 Racists Attacks 75 Marchers," *Gainesville Times,* January 18, 1987.

213 *"most of the demonstrators"*: "Klan Supporters Hold Own 'March.'" *Forsyth County News,* January 18, 1987, 3

213 *"Go home, niggers!"*: "White Protestors Disrupt 'Walk for Brotherhood' in Georgia Town," *New York Times*, January 18, 1987, 24.

213 *the 1958 bombing of Bethel Baptist Church*: Diane McWhorter, *Carry Me Home: Birmingham, Alabama; The Climactic Battle of the Civil Rights Revolution* (New York: Simon & Schuster, 2001), 133–35.

214 *"we don't want niggers"*: "Klan Supporters Hold Own 'March,'" *Forsyth County News*, January 18, 1987.

214 *the parking lot of Jim Wallace's gas station*: "Klan Supporters Hold Own 'March,'" *Forsyth County News*, January 18, 1987.

215 *"as the thing began to swell"*: "Terror in Forsyth," *Gainesville Times*, January 18, 1987, 2B.

216 *"People from Forsyth"*: "Walk," *Forsyth County News*, January 18, 1987, 3A.

218 *had only seventy men*: *Hosea Williams v. Southern White Nights of the Ku Klux Klan*, District Court of the Northern Division of Georgia, March 24, 1987, Civil Action C87-565A.

218 *Only a few hundred yards*: "Police Admit We Lost Control," *Gainesville Times*, January 18, 1987, 2B.

218 *"a friendly white neighbor"*: Peter Levy, ed., *The Civil Rights Movement in America* (Santa Barbara: Greenwood / ABL-CLIO, 2015), 338.

219 *"I had watched my best buddies tortured"*: Christopher M. Richardson and Ralph E. Luker, *Historical Dictionary of the Civil Rights Movement*, 495.

219 *"my wild man, my Castro"*: Taylor Branch, *Pillar of Fire: America in the King Years, 1963–65* (New York: Simon & Schuster, 1998), 124.

219 *charges of drunk driving*: "Civil Rights Veteran Hosea Williams Faces Battle to Keep His Credibility," *Los Angeles Times*, September 1, 1991.

220 *"it persuaded no one"*: Elliot Jaspin, *Buried in the Bitter Waters* (New York: Basic Books, 2007), 142.

221 *"I think I have to go back"*: "Walk," *Forsyth County News*, January 18, 1987, 3A.

221 *"I've been in many such situations"*: "White Protestors Disrupt 'Walk for Brotherhood' in Georgia Town," *New York Times*, January 18, 1987, 24.

221 *"The vast majority of the citizens"*: "Second 'Freedom March' Set for Saturday," *Forsyth County News*, January 21, 2012.

221 *"I don't think what we saw was indicative"*: "County Leaders Denounce Violence," *Forsyth County News*, January 18, 1987, 2A.

221 *"If they would let us alone"*: "Georgia County Haunted by 1912 Incident," *Gainesville Sun*, January 23, 1987.

222 *"I figure they could pick a better place"*: "Police Admit: 'We Lost Control,' "
       Gainesville Times, January 18, 1987, 2B.

222 *"most people here don't want them"*: "Rights Groups May Pursue Effort in
       White County," *New York Times,* January 19, 1987, A15.

222 *"They ought to have printed up . . . targets"*: "Police Admit: 'We Lost Con-
       trol,' " *Gainesville Times,* January 18, 1987, 2B.

222 *"I am tired Governor Harris"*: Correspondence of Governor Joe Frank Har-
       ris, Forsyth County Folder, March 5, 1987. Georgia Archives, Morrow, GA.

223 *"We the people of Forsyth County have been used"*: Ibid., January 28, 1987.

223 *"Most of those arrested were not natives"*: Ibid., January 29, 1987.

CHAPTER 18: SILENCE IS CONSENT

224 *"even if it takes 300 state troopers"*: "Carter Vows Return to Forsyth,"
       Gainesville Times, January 19, 1987.

224 *"We're going to march"*: "Williams: March Birth of a New Struggle,"
       Gainesville Times, January 23, 1987, 9A.

225 *350 State Troopers*: John McKay, *It Happened in Atlanta* (Globe Pequot,
       2011), 151.

225 *"a great coming together"*: "Forsyth at a Glance," *Gainesville Times,* January
       22, 1987, 7A.

225 *"Seven years ago"*: "Black Man Shot in Forsyth Plans to Return," Associ-
       ated Press, January 24, 1987.

225 *"to live a life of decency"*: Tyler Bridges, *The Rise of David Duke* (Jackson:
       University Press of Mississippi, 1994), 128.

228 *"When all these people finish"*: "Calm and Quiet Returns to Cumming,"
       Gainesville Times, February 1, 1987, 11A.

228 *"Whites don't want the blacks"*: "Leave Forsyth Like It Is Now," *Gainesville
       Times,* January 18, 1987, 4A.

229 *"Do you think this is a free ride?"*: "Forsyth Has Too Much Class," *Gaines-
       ville Times,* February 1, 1987, 2F.

229 an *"all-white" affair*: Hosea Williams and other march leaders picketed
       the broadcast for barring blacks from the audience and were arrested by
       Forsyth sheriff Wesley Walraven for "unlawful assembly." Oprah told
       reporters she was "very, very sorry" about the arrest and said, "I have
       nothing but respect for Hosea Williams." "Talk Show Pickets Busted in
       Georgia," *Hour* (Norwalk, CT), February 10, 1987, 2

230 *"a lot of white people are afraid"*: "Talk Show Pickets Busted in Georgia," *Hour* (Norwalk, CT), February 10, 1987, 2.

230 *"We agree that the majority of the citizens"*: Hosea Williams to Roger Crow, January 30, 1987. Historical Society of Forsyth County, Cumming, GA.

231 *"persons whose land [was] unlawfully seized"*: Ibid.

232 *"leaders of the black community"*: Cumming Mayor H. Ford Gravitt, et al., to Hosea Williams, February 2, 1987. Historical Society of Forsyth County, Cumming, GA.

232 *"The primary responsibility"*: Hosea Williams to Roger Crow, February 4, 1987. Historical Society of Forsyth County, Cumming, GA.

234 *"racial incidents . . . allegedly drove"*: *Report of the Cumming/Forsyth County Biracial Committee,* December 22, 1987, 2.5–2.6. Hargrett Rare Book and Manuscript Library, University of Georgia.

234 *the first boll weevil*: P. B. Haney, W. J. Lewis, and W. R. Lambert, "Cotton Production and the Boll Weevil in Georgia: History, Cost of Control, and Benefits of Eradication," *Georgia Agricultural Experiment Stations Research Bulletin,* March 2009, 2.

234 *quietly absorbed into the property of their former white neighbors*: Elliot Jaspin, *Buried in the Bitter Waters* (New York: Basic Books, 2007), 135–36.

234 *"the charge of unlawfully taken land"*: *Report of the Cumming/Forsyth County Biracial Committee,* December 22, 1987, Hargrett Rare Book and Manuscript Library, University of Georgia, 2.8.

235 *top twenty-five wealthiest counties*: American Community Survey, U.S. Census Bureau; http://www.census.gov/programs-surveys/acs/data/summary -file.html, accessed August 5, 2015.

235 *"an ever-pointing finger of blame"*: *Report of the Cumming/Forsyth County Biracial Committee,* December 22, 1987, Hargrett Rare Book and Manuscript Library, University of Georgia, 2.9; 2.23; 2.1.

235 *"cast aside confrontational tactics"*: Ibid., 2.23.

236 *"There seems to be a prevailing philosophy"*: Ibid., 3.17.

236 *"work closely with law enforcement"*: Ibid., 3.21.

237 *"People's attitudes are already changing"*: "Georgia, It's a Diverse State," *USA Today,* August 31, 1987, 11A.

238 *"It doesn't bother me"*: "Anniversary March Peaceful in Forsyth," *Item* (Sumter, SC), January 17, 1988, 6A.

238 *a million dollars in damages*: *McKinney v. Southern White Knights, et al.,*

United States District Court for the Northern District, Civil Action Number 1:87-cv-565-CAM, October 25, 1988.

238 *"Forsyth has a negative connotation"*: "Many See Their Future in County with a Past," *New York Times*, April 8, 1999, A18.

239 *"the whitest of the country's 600 most populous counties"*: Ibid.

239 *"684 black Georgians"*: U.S. Census Bureau. Population data for Forsyth County, Georgia. Prepared by Social Explorer (accessed February 20, 2014).

240 *"died a natural death"*: "Forsyth County Overcomes Racist Reputation with Population Boom," *Savannah Morning News*, March 14, 1999, 11A.

240 *"banks [and] eateries"*: "Painful Past, Prosperous Future," *Gainesville Times*, January 17, 2007.

240 *"I am the treasurer of the PTA"*: "Georgia County Draws Minorities," Bloomberg Business, March 18, 2011.

EPILOGUE: A PACK OF WILD DOGS

242 *"this attempted social revolution"*: Hiram Parks Bell, *Men and Things* (Atlanta: Foote and Davies, 1907), 135–36.

244 *thirteen acres of farmland*: Forsyth County Return for Colored Tax Payers, 1912, Cumming District, Georgia Archives, Morrow, GA.

244 *"They were just so happy"*: Kathleen Anderson, taped interview, 1987. Forsyth County Box, King Center Archives, Atlanta, GA.

245 *"I just remember her coming in crying"*: Ibid.

245 *"a pack of wild dogs"*: Ibid.

CREDITS

24 *The Marietta Rifles, "Riot Duty Company,"* c. 1908. Photo published by Alfred Selidge Postcard Co., St. Louis, Missouri.

30 *Mae Crow, circa 1912.* Photo courtesy of Debbie Vermaat.

31 *Crow household in the census of 1910.* 1910 U. S. Census, New Bridge, Forsyth, Georgia; roll T624_188; page 11B; Enumeration District: 0041; FHL microfilm: 1374201.

36 *Ernest Knox, October 2, 1912.* From "Troops on Guard as Two Rapists Are Convicted," *Atlanta Constitution,* October 4, 1912.

42 *U.S. Representative Hiram Parks Bell.* Library of Congress Prints and Photographs Division. Brady-Handy Photograph Collection: LC-BH832- 158.

52 *Charlie Hale, Lawrenceville, Georgia, 1911.* Photo courtesy of the Georgia Archives, COB831-82.

54 *West Canton Street, Cumming, c. 1912.* Postcard published by the Cumming Drugstore, courtesy of Gary Doster.

57 *The lynching of Laura Nelson, 1911.* Postcard published by G. H. Farnum, 1911.

86 *Jane Daniel, Oscar Daniel, and Toney Howell being led toward the Atlanta train terminal, October 2, 1912.* From the *Atlanta Georgian,* October 2, 1912.

88 *The Forsyth prisoners at Buford, Georgia, October 2nd, 1912.* From the *Atlanta Constitution,* October 4, 1912.

90 *The lynching of Leo Frank outside Marietta, Georgia, 1915.* Photo courtesy of the Atlanta History Center, Kenneth G. Rogers Collection.

93 *The Cumming Courthouse, c. 1912.* Postcard published by the Cumming Drugstore, courtesy of Gary Doster.

95 *Ed Collins, October 1912.* From the *Atlanta Georgian,* October 2, 1912.

109 *Byrd Oliver, date unknown.* Photo courtesy of the Beulah Rucker Museum, Gainesville, Georgia.

114 *The children of Jeremiah and Nancy Brown, who were expelled from Forsyth in 1912.* Photo Courtesy of Charles Grogan. Nancy (Greenlee) Brown was the granddaughter of Reverend Levi Greenlee Sr.

129 *The Fifth Regiment en route from the Fulton Tower to Terminal Station, Atlanta.* From "Soldiers Guard Gallows—Sheriff Springs Trap," *Atlanta Georgian,* October 25, 1912.

134 *Azzie Crow, mother of Mae, c. 1950.* Photo courtesy of Debbie Vermaat.

141 *A crowd near the gallows where Knox and Daniel were hung, with Sawnee Mountain in the distance, October 25, 1912.* Photo courtesy of Jimmy Anderson.

142 *Three witnesses to the Knox and Daniel hangings, October 25, 1912.* Photo courtesy of Jimmy Anderson.

175 *The "Seeing Georgia" tourists en route to Forsyth, October 3, 1915.* From the *Atlanta Constitution,* October 10, 1915, 6.

189 *Sign protesting the arrival of black tenants, Sojourner Truth housing project, Detroit, February 1942.* Arthur S. Siegel, *White Sign Racial Hatred.* Library of Congress, Prints and Photographs Division, FSA/OWI Collection, LC-USW3-016549-C.

191 *White mob dragging an African American man from a Detroit streetcar, June 21, 1943.* Associated Press.

208 *Cumming, Georgia, January 17, 1987.* Steve Deal/AP.

214 *J. B. Stoner handing out flyers at the First Brotherhood March, January 17, 1987.* Photo courtesy of Southline Press, Kenan Research Center at the Atlanta History Center.

216 *Hosea Williams and John Lewis leading marchers across the Edmund Pettus Bridge, March 7, 1965.* Black Star/Charles Moore.

217 *Hosea Williams leading the First Brotherhood March, Forsyth County, January 17, 1987.* AP Photo/Gene Blythe.

226 *Buses arriving for the Second Brotherhood March, January 24, 1987.* Photo courtesy of Joe Tomasovsky.

227 *Brotherhood Marchers walking to the Forsyth County Courthouse.* Photo courtesy of Joe Tomasovsky.

228 *National Guard troops and counterprotesters, January 24, 1987.* Photo courtesy of Joe Tomasovsky.

INDEX

Page numbers in *italics* refer to figures and illustrations.